CHINESE VILLAGE POLITICS IN THE MALAYSIAN STATE

Harvard East Asian Series 95

The Council on East Asian Studies at Harvard University, through the Fairbank Center for East Asian Research, administers research projects designed to further scholarly understanding of China, Japan, Korea, Vietnam, Inner Asia, and adjacent areas.

CHINESE VILLAGE POLITICS IN THE MALAYSIAN STATE

Judith Strauch

Harvard University Press
Cambridge, Massachusetts
and London, England
1981

Library of Congress Cataloging in Publication Data

Strauch, Judith, 1942-
   Chinese village politics in the Malaysian state.

   (Harvard East Asian series; 95)
   Bibliography: p.
   Includes index.
   1.   Chinese in Malaysia — Politics and government.
2.   Malaysia — Politics and government.   3.   Local
government — Malaysia.   4.   Villages — Malaysia.
I.   Title.   II.   Series.
DS595.2.C5S77   305.8'951'0595   80-20519
ISBN 0-674-12570-3

For my mother

Preface

During the Malayan communist insurgency of the 1950s, euphemistically termed the "Emergency," more than half a million dispersed squatters and small landholders, most of whom were Chinese and were thus suspected of giving aid to the predominantly Chinese guerrillas, were brought together forcibly by British and Malayan security officials into some five hundred fenced and curfewed resettlement camps. Most of these "new villages," as they were called (the name has stuck, though they are of course no longer new), have persisted as viable social units long after the fences were opened in 1958. This book is a study of the social and political life of one of these Chinese villages two decades later, as it is played out today in the context of a Malay-dominated bureaucratic state. In the town I call Sanchun, the preexisting market center and the attached new village together now house some five hundred families, over four-fifths of them Chinese — shopkeepers, wage laborers, and rubber smallholders. The local Malays and Indians are allied socially and politically with the surrounding Malay *kampong*s (villages), nearby rubber estates, and the district capital with its population of Malay civil servants, rather than with the town of Sanchun, which is essentially a Chinese community.

Most of the generalizations made about overseas Chinese throughout Southeast Asia are based on urban data, in part because in most countries Chinese are primarily urban, and in part because that is the body of data that was collected in the 1950s and 1960s. In Malaysia, however, the rural and semirural Chinese merit closer attention as an important segment of the community, both numerically and politically. Concern over governmental neglect of new villages has been a critical issue since the communal riots of 1969. In 1971 a new federal ministry with full cabinet status was established to deal with issues relating specifically to new villages, though the focus of this ministry is today less exclusive. In the Second and Third Malaysia Plans (1971-1975 and 1976-1980) the new villages are treated as a separate category in government economic planning and analysis. But until now little scholarly attention has been given the new villages. The few studies that exist have relied chiefly on survey data, and none has treated a single village in depth or placed such a village firmly in the broader context of Malaysian society, as this book does.

My study is based on a total of twenty-two months of fieldwork in Malaysia, beginning with an eighteen-month stay in 1971-1972. I first spent four months familiarizing myself with the new villages, visiting a number of them up and down the country and studying relevant historical and statistical material available in Kuala Lumpur, the capital. No single new village, of course, can represent the full range of diversity that these communities display. Size ranges from a few hundred people up to a highly atypical twenty-seven thousand (Jinjang, just outside Kuala Lumpur), and the location of a village in relation to larger towns, labor markets, and agricultural land resources is crucial in determining the character of each as well. The small market town of about three thousand people in southern Perak where I finally chose to focus my research is reasonably representative of the sort of new village that is numerically most common, however. I lived in Sanchun for the next fourteen months, and I later returned for visits of two months each in 1976 and 1978.

My field methodology included lengthy socioeconomic family surveys, the use of national census data to compare with and corroborate my own, and reference to the limited range of local records and documents that were available. But the most valuable data come from participant observation of community life and activities and from long and frequent discussions and interviews with friends, neighbors, and key informants. I attended scores of committee meetings, banquets, and informal late-evening gatherings in the coffee shops, as well as a number of weddings and funerals and the annual graveyard visitations and temple festivals. Mandarin is widely spoken among Chinese in Malaysia as a school language. Among men, except the elderly, it is almost universal. My own spoken Mandarin is quite adequate for daily interaction, and I worked alone for most of the research period. I was joined by a multilingual assistant for the family interviews, many of which had to be conducted in other Chinese languages, and for a series of in-depth interviews with key informants.

A grassroots political party mobilization, begun in late 1971, proved to be of focal interest for my study. I made contact with state and national leaders who came down to visit the villages, including Sanchun, and it was possible for me then to interview and observe party workings at the state level. These higher-level contacts proved particularly useful in my later visits, when I was able to interview those who have remained in power throughout some major political upheavals, as well as some who have dropped out of politics in disillusionment. Thus, although my field data are gathered primarily at the village level, the larger perspective into which I place the overall study does not rest on secondary sources alone.

For the reader interested in Chinese or in overseas Chinese (*huaqiao*) society in general (rather than or in addition to political processes), some comments about the peculiar nature of the Chinese community in Malaysia may be helpful.

The experience of Chinese in West Malaysia differs significantly from that of ethnic Chinese elsewhere in Southeast Asia and the rest of the world in a number of respects. Most notable is the unusual demographic balance. Malaysian Chinese are nationally an extremely large minority; their proportion of the peninsular population (35.4 percent) contrasts sharply with that in Thailand (10.0 percent), Indonesia (2.6 percent), and the Philippines (1.4 percent), for example. Only Singapore, a very special case, has a higher percentage of ethnic Chinese (74.5 percent) (Heidhues 1974: 3). In five of the eleven peninsular states of Malaysia, all along the relatively densely settled west coast, ethnic Chinese are approximately 40 percent of the population, and in one state, Penang, they make up 56 percent. As elsewhere in Southeast Asia, Chinese are overrepresented in the urban areas, but in Malaysia they are found in large numbers in small towns and rural farming areas as well. The 1970 Malaysian census shows that of the roughly 3.1 million Chinese in West Malaysia, 47 percent, not quite one and a half million, live in urban centers with populations over ten thousand, 23 percent in towns with one to ten thousand, and 30 percent in population concentrations of under one thousand people. There is a clear tendency for Chinese in Malaysia, as elsewhere, to specialize in commercial occupations. Again, however, Malaysia differs from the stereotypical case: according to the Third Malaysia Plan's breakdown of the occupational data collected in the 1970 census, only 19.8 percent of the Chinese-Malaysian work force are in the "sales" category, and another 32 percent are classified under "professional and technical workers," "administrative and managerial workers," "clerical workers," and "services and others." Fully 42.8 percent are categorized as "agricultural workers" or "production workers" (mostly in manufacturing and construction) (Malaysia 1976b: 78-82).

All proper names relevant to levels below those of federal and state divisions, both of persons and places, are fictitious. Spellings of proper names are not standardized but follow common Malaysian usage, thus sometimes giving a hint as to the speech-group membership of the bearer (for example, the surname pronounced *Chen* in Mandarin would be spelled Chan, Tan, and Ding by Malaysian Cantonese, Hokkiens, and Hokchius, respectively). Proper nouns aside, Chinese and Malay terms are rendered in Pinyin and in the official orthography, respectively. For the reader's convenience I include both a Chinese character list (appendix A) and a list of the Sanchun leaders referred to frequently throughout the text (appendix B).

The present Federation of Malaysia is comprised of the former Federation of Malaya on the Malayan peninsula and two Borneo states, Sabah and Sarawak. In colonial times Singapore was an integral part of British territory in the area as well. The terms *Malaya* and *Malayan* will generally be used to indicate the entire sphere of British influence on the peninsula, including Singapore and the two other Straits Colonies, Malacca and Penang, which joined with the Federated Malay States to form the Federation of Malaya. It will be clear from the context when the political unit is referred to specifically. To avoid repetition, *Malaysia* and *Malaysian* will generally be used even when the actual unit of reference is West Malaysia rather than the entire federation. The *Malay* people, or the *Malays*, are those of the Malay ethnic group; *Malayans* and *Malaysians* are members of all ethnic groups who were or are citizens of the Federation of Malaya or the Federation of Malaysia, respectively. Monetary amounts are given throughout in Malaysian dollars (*ringgit*). In 1972 US$1.00 was equal to about M$2.90; by 1978 that figure had fallen to about M$2.40.

The field research on which this book is based has been generously supported by a number of different institutions over the years. The original fieldwork in 1971-1972 was undertaken under grants from the National Science Foundation and the National Institute of Mental Health; funds for the 1976 research were provided by the Department of Anthropology, the East Asian Research Center, and the Clark Fund, all of Harvard University; research in 1978 was supported by a grant from the Joint Committee on Contemporary China of the American Council of Learned Societies and the Social Science Research Council. I acknowledge this support with gratitude.

I am also grateful to many individuals in a number of government offices in Malaysia who at various times provided assistance — in particular, in the Ministry of National Unity, the Ministry of Technology, Research, and Local Government, the Department of Statistics, and the local district office. Numerous Malaysian political figures have been very generous with their time, providing in their answers to my questions both needed information and valuable perspectives on the issues that interested me. A number of scholars at the University of Malaya have provided both logistical assistance and congenial intellectual exchange. Dr. Chai Hon Chan, Dr. Lee Kam Hing, Mr. Michael Ong, Dr. Lee Poh Ping, and Ms. Loh Wei Leng have all been good critics as well as good friends; they do not necessarily fully agree with my analyses of their country. Without the aid of my field assistants, Mr. Yap Yew Fong and Ms. Ng Kwai Hing, much of this data might not have been gathered; I would like to thank them both for their very capable work.

The development of the perspectives on politics, ethnicity, and anthropology that are embodied in this book has come about as a process of continuing intellectual interchange with numerous colleagues and friends over the years. Those who have read and commented on parts or all of this manuscript, offering both criticisms and encouragement, include Ezra Vogel, John Pelzel, Arthur Wolf, Harumi Befu, James L. Watson, Rubie Watson, and Heng Pek Koon. Cynthia Enloe has been particularly helpful, both in her attention to detail and in her concern with the more general questions that must be raised. From G. W. Skinner I have learned a great deal about both the art and the craft of exemplary scholarship. To all these people I am extremely grateful.

My greatest debt of gratitude, of course, is to the people of Sanchun. Their warmth and hospitality in accepting me and my inquisitiveness and strange ways into their community, and their cooperation and helpfulness in providing me with needed information and understanding, made the study possible and the experience pleasant and memorable. I write about them in such detail with concern as well as pleasure; it is my sincere hope that I will cause neither embarrassment nor inconvenience to the people who have been such good friends to me. Because of the nature of the analysis I offer of the community and its political life, I must be true to the facts as they appeared to me. Personalities are the stuff of politics, and it has unfortunately not been possible to disguise individuals fully, though all names have been changed. In a very few instances, where I was convinced that an important point could be made clearly and accurately with a careful composite description of characters and events, I have indulged in minor poetic license. I hope that my portrayal of Sanchun will be read as a sympathetic one, for it is meant to be. I am very grateful to the people of Sanchun for making this book possible, and more, for teaching me a great deal about the quality of life.

Contents

Tables

Figure

Map

Abbreviations

ADO   assistant district officer
ARO   assistant resettlement officer
BN   Barisan Nasional
CAO   Chinese-affairs officer
DAP   Democratic Action Party
DO   district officer
MCA   Malaysian Chinese Association (before 1963, Malayan)
MCP   Malayan Communist Party
MIC   Malaysian Indian Congress (before 1963, Malayan)
MPAJA   Malayan People's Anti-Japanese Army
NOC   National Operations Council
PAP   People's Action Party
PAS   Parti Islam se-Malaysia
PI   Parti Islam
PMIP   Pan-Malayan Islam Party
PPP   People's Progressive Party
TOL   temporary occupation license
UMNO   United Malays National Organization

1

Issues and Settings

Local politics cannot be understood in isolation, for the local community is but a part of a larger social and political system. As new states caught up in the process that has been termed "nation building" seek tighter control over political action within their domains, power has become increasingly centralized, and local systems on the political periphery today find their political and sociocultural autonomy on the wane. Studies of the mechanisms of centralization in both industrialized and Third World countries abound. This book, by contrast, is concerned not with the sprawling bureaucracies and involuting financial and legal structures of capital cities, but with the concrete impact of centralization on local systems far removed from the centers of power. The vast majority of the world's people pass their lives in such communities. For them it is not the means but the impact of centralization that is of most immediate concern. This perspective—the view from the bottom, so to speak—merits closer attention than it usually receives. It must be presented to complement the more familiar view from the top, for both are crucial to an understanding of the world we are creating today.

This book examines the centralizing political and administrative structures of a single new nation, Malaysia, and the ways in which their operations define the parameters of political and to some extent social life in a single small community within this nation, Sanchun. Malaysia is a multiethnic nation dominated politically by a single ethnic group, the Malays. Sanchun is a rural market town made up primarily of Chinese. Though its origins as a trading center go back nearly a hundred years, the most important event in Sanchun's history was the formation of a "new village" adjacent to the shops in 1951. This was a forced relocation center established to house Chinese squatters and smallholders who were seen by the British and

Malayan military authorities then waging war against a guerrilla insurgency to be potential supporters of the guerrillas, who were also primarily Chinese. With the appending of the new village Sanchun's population tripled in size and its character changed noticeably, as rubber farmers, tappers, loggers, and other wage laborers came to outnumber the shopkeepers who had founded the community a generation or two before. Sanchun no doubt felt the direct hand of central power most sharply during the years of the military Emergency, but political and administrative structures operating since that time have continued to play a crucial role in shaping the community and its life and character. Moreover, as Chinese in a Malay-dominated state, the people of Sanchun feel themselves to be encapsulated, held in an uncertain limbo in which their interests are subordinated to those of the state, by structures informed by dimensions not only of politics and power but of ethnicity as well.

Like most small-scale, face-to-face communities of the type that tend to attract anthropologists, Sanchun is a town in which personal histories, kinship links, economic activities, and expressions of social concern through participation in local rituals and organizations all figure prominently as factors that influence local politics and contribute to the configurations of local leadership. But increasingly, as the modern state makes greater demands on its members, penetrating ever deeper into everyday life, it is the pervasive domination by an expansive state system that is the determining element shaping the internal political life of the local community. Political actors draw on externally based resources to establish themselves locally; at the same time they become subject to constraints imposed by the structures of the state. Center-periphery power relations set parameters for local action that cannot be denied. However freely Sanchun's game of local politics appears to be played, however fascinating and seemingly endless are the variations invented by individual personalities manipulating internally based social and cultural rules and resources, it is the broader political environment that effectively lays down the limits of variation. The complexities of local rivalries and competitions for support and legitimacy are more readily comprehensible if the condition of encapsulation is acknowledged.

Sanchun is a specific case, but it is not a special case. This rural market town offers lessons that can be applied to understanding similar situations of ethnic pluralism and political encapsulation elsewhere. The particular configuration of historical events and the resulting ethnic and power constellations that obtain today in Malaysia are roughly paralleled in many Third World countries, though differing in detail. Small towns and villages throughout Asia, Africa, and South America have found themselves forced to adapt to radical changes in encapsulating power structures as foreign colonial and military governments of various sorts have given way to independent rule. Moreover, ethnic minority communities are found not in the Third World alone, but throughout Europe and North America as well; all face special problems in coming to terms with centralized power structures that show varying degrees of sensitivity to their inclinations to preserve ethnic distinctiveness.

Focus on a single community such as Sanchun permits a close understanding of the complex weave of human relations played out within a face-to-face village society where kinship, friendship, and deep-seated personal enmity are factors constantly to be reckoned with. State expansion and bureaucratization do not obliterate these face-to-face dynamics, but they do alter the patterns and their implications. My primary aim is to elucidate internal political relationships — the distribution, uses, and abuses of local power, authority, and influence — among Sanchun's leadership elite. But many of the crucial factors determining that distribution and manipulation of power within Sanchun in fact originate in the external political structures of Malaysia's bureaucracy and party system. Some of the external influences that affect communities like Sanchun are quite deliberately injected by outside authorities as part of a conscious center-periphery policy. At other junctures, the impact felt in such communities is but a side effect of higher-level confrontation and conflict between competing interests, parties, or individuals. Both kinds of factors are at work in Sanchun — those that represent concerted efforts at control and those that simply spin off from power struggles occurring elsewhere. The end effect is the same, as jointly such influences combine to shape decisively the social and political world of the encapsulated community.

Anthropology and the Study of Politics

One of the first tasks of anthropologists whose interests turned to the study of politics was to establish that "politics" had meaning outside of formalized state structures of the sort that form the province of political scientists. It was shown that in tribal and island groups, small-scale societies studied by anthropologists, processes that were political in nature — that is, concerned with power and with public goals — were generally intermeshed with kinship and ritual behavior rather than organized separately in easily recognizable, rationalized bureaucratic institutions; but they were nonetheless there. The classic *African Political Systems* (Fortes and Evans-Pritchard 1940) set forth a typological framework for the comparative analysis of a range of political systems that included bands and segmentary lineage societies as well as centralized states; it was followed by an abundance of work analyzing diverse political forms. The intellectual contribution of such work was considerable. In Balandier's view, "political anthropology . . .

has universalized thought—extending it to Pygmy and Amerindian groups that have a minimum of central power—and broken the spell that the state has long exerted on political theorists" (1970: 187).

Nonetheless, anthropologists, too, were fascinated by the state or, where the state was lacking, its approximate functional equivalent. The unit of analysis was the "society," whether it was an egalitarian hunting group, a higher-order lineage integrated through its segments, or a chiefdom or traditional kingdom. Two biases of thought followed naturally. First, since analysis of the political organization of internally integrated and coherent autonomous systems was the object, certain assumptions, often unwarranted, had to be made about the fields of study supplying the empirical data—assumptions that certified the relevance of the data to the theoretical question at hand. Despite the glaringly obvious presence of colonial administrations, most of these analyses treated encapsulated societies *as if* they represented a continuation of a mythical pristine condition; the political processes and structures observed were taken to be operating as a natural and uninterrupted outgrowth of autochthonous development. A trenchant critique of anthropological work of this type focuses on the implications of the anthropologist's unacknowledged political and cultural membership in the dominant imperialist society (see, for instance, Asad 1973). One need not refer to ideology, however, to see a more basic intellectual problem at hand. Evans-Pritchard tells us that "the social anthropologist studies societies as wholes—he studies their ecologies, their economics, their legal and political institutions, their family and kinship organizations, their religions, their technologies, their arts, etc., as parts of general social systems" (1951: 11). In fact, of course, the societies in question too often were simply special cases of local-level systems, influenced not merely by contact with contiguous but equally "autonomous" groups, as the theory would have it, but by encapsulation and domination by superior political powers that ruled by force. No such society is a "whole," but rather a part, no matter how loosely incorporated or indirectly ruled, and its internal processes must be seen in that light.

A second intellectual bias grows out of the first. Theoretical concepts derived from the analysis of largely autonomous political systems have for the most part been applied with slight if any modification to the study of local-level communities existing within larger encapsulating systems. Precise definitions of concepts such as power, legitimacy, and authority are sought, for example, in Weberian terms, and applied in that form in anthropological analyses (Balandier 1970: 39-40). Friedrich, however, calls our attention to a relevant quality of political theory and suggests the problem that ensues:

> Theories of legitimacy and similar phenomena share one feature: they are largely or entirely limited to a special and rare kind of leader—the

one who is "on top," who is relatively or completely sovereign and whose legitimacy is consequently a matter of relations downwards to followers, subjects, and other inferiors within the body politic . . . Kings, state dictators, and presidents continue to enjoy a perhaps undue priority in the thinking of sociologists and philosophers with an interest in the purely theoretical aspects of politics and government. (1968: 266)

Such a priority in thinking is particularly inappropriate to anthropologists, who almost by definition draw data virtually exclusively from situations in which the leadership under study is by no means completely sovereign nor the system autonomous.

Most societies empirically observable in the world today comprise several political levels. Usually the highest level, the center of power, wields considerable dominance over the lower levels, on the conceptual periphery of power. Studies based on anthropological methodology usually examine lower-level units that are subordinate, directly or indirectly, to the higher or central power. Recent political anthropology is beginning to reflect this reality, a trend that derives in part, no doubt, from the proportional growth in literature treating peasant rather than tribal societies. Peasant communities have long been seen to be "part societies," tied to urban centers that provide the "great tradition" to their "little traditions," dominating them culturally as well as economically and politically. Thus it is not surprising that in the work of Bailey and Nicholas on India, Gallin on Taiwan, and Friedrich on Mexico there is clear recognition of the role played by the political center in influencing the politics of social groups on the periphery. Orientations developed in these works provide a useful point of departure for analyzing the Sanchun material. A careful study of Sanchun and its relationship to higher powers over time will permit a refinement of conceptual approaches to aid in understanding the complex interrelationships of the many parts making up the larger state system.

Local-Level Politics and Encapsulation

Local-level politics has been defined by Swartz as politics occurring within communities small enough to be characterized by relationships of a diffuse rather than specialized nature ("multiplex" rather than "simplex") and in which "politics is incomplete in the sense that actors and groups outside the range of the local, multiplex relationships are vitally and directly involved in the political process of the local group." He carefully draws the semantic distinction between "local-level" and "local" politics, the latter being "not incomplete as local-level politics is," but then grants that the ideal type represented by isolated, autonomous, but multiplex politics may not exist (Swartz 1968: 1). If "local politics" exists anywhere, it certainly is not within the sort of political system I am concerned with here; Sanchun politics, as my study will demonstrate, cannot be understood in isolation from Malaysian politics. Thus for the sake of convenience I use the term *local* and *local-level* interchangeably to refer to what are in fact local-level politics and processes.

The conceptual distinction is important nonetheless, for a surprising number of studies persist in treating what is actually local-level politics, strictly defined, almost as if it were local politics; that is, they make little more than passing reference to the external actors, groups, or political systems that are acknowledged to have a strong influence on the small community and its multiplex relationships. Swartz and his collaborators have tried to solve this problem through definition and delineation of political "fields," "arenas," and "boundaries" (Swartz, Turner, and Tuden 1966: 27-28; Swartz 1968: 6-15). For Swartz, a political field is defined for a particular event or related events (process or processes) and encompasses "the individuals and groups, together with their repertories of resources, values, and rules directly involved in the process or processes centering on [public] goals" (1968: 15). Arenas encompass fields but also include individuals and groups (and their repertories) directly involved with constituents of the field, but not with the particular processes concerned. Boundaries of both fields and arenas fluctuate, expanding or contracting depending on the processes being studied; they are permeable, and they are empirically determined in each instance. Thus influences external to the system being studied are seen to wax and wane, depending on the episode under consideration.

Units so narrowly conceived, in my view, are overly limited. The notion that the unit of analysis exists in reference only to a single event or a series of related events (processes) (Swartz et al., 1966: 12-13) tends to obscure the broader reality of power relationships that in fact exist over time, as ongoing relationships between units at different conceptual levels of an integrated system, one of which has power over the other and sets parameters delineating possible action. The heuristic use of a limited field as a unit of analysis too often leads to neglect of the factors excluded at the edges of that field, or even hidden within it, simply because in a given sequence of events they do not appear to be moving, so to speak, and thus do not catch the eye. We are enticed by the comparative ease with which *actual* action may be analyzed, and thus miss the wider range of *possible* action. However, only when we are aware of what might have or could have happened (and by extension, what could not have happened) can we understand the significance of what did or did not in fact occur. Actual political events in Sanchun and communities like it tell us only part of the story of local politics. Future events and relationships will be affected by the degree to which present actions have approached or stretched the limits of possible action. Consequently, a more inclusive framework is needed, which will extend the boundaries of what is to be considered relevant in systemic relationships beyond what can be observed in a single event.

This delineation of units of analysis lies at the heart of what Vincent, in a recent review of the state of the field, highlights as the central tension within "action theory" in political anthropology. Action theory "differs from evolutionary and structural anthropology by virtue of its attention to processes, to political formations other than categories and corporate groups, and . . . by its underpinnings in a particular mode of fieldwork that resulted in a distinctive form of finely grained political ethnography" (Vincent 1978: 175). Though many political anthropologists of this bent share an interest in major themes such as political leadership, factionalism, and power brokerage, however, there is serious divergence of opinion between those who "consider the multi-stranded political relations of the locality to form a viable closed system for analysis" (Vincent 1978: 177) and those who stress the need for placing such analysis firmly within the context of the wider political economy encompassing the locality.[1] Worsley expresses the latter view: "This is not to say that we cannot describe a flower without, every time, having to recite or construct a philosophy of Nature or a theory of biology. It is not to say that we must always study the total macro-structure of a society (a disease that affects Latin American Marxists, for instance). But it is to say that the analysis of situations has always to be informed by an awareness of the world within which situations and encounters are located, and more than that, requires an explicit conceptualization of what that world looks like" (1974: 10).

The notion of encapsulation, consciously and explicitly incorporated in any analysis of localities, can facilitate such a conceptualization. We should consistently think of local-level systems and local-level politics as *encapsulated* — that is, surrounded, encompassed, enclosed. With this conception firmly implanted, we can no longer contemplate the political processes in Sanchun and similar communities without at the same time holding an active consciousness of the implications inherent in the strict contrast between *local-level* and *local*, so lucidly set forth in Swartz's definitions. These implications are crucial in the daily lives of people in Sanchun and similar encapsulated local systems everywhere.

Bailey offers an elaboration of the concept that differentiates small encapsulated systems (Structures A) from larger encapsulating entities (Struc-

---

1. The logical extension of this view ultimately places the analysis of encapsulated politics within a framework of dependency relations encompassed by a global economic system, as Vincent points out (1978: 177). Though I will not carry the argument systematically to such lengths in this book, it is clear that an important feature of the world political environment within which Malay politics encapsulates Chinese-Malaysian politics is the existence of China and the importance of Chinese economic networks throughout East and Southeast Asia.

tures B; mnemonic, *B* stands for *big*) in terms of size, control of political resources, degrees of differentiation and specialization of political roles, and value systems or world views ("traditional" versus "modern"). The form and impact of actual encapsulation, of course, vary, both between and within state systems. Bailey posits a continuum of "severity" (from the perspective of Structure A) of encapsulating relationships, ranging from nominal encapsulation through indirect rule and culminating in purposive integration or absorption within Structure B. "Encapsulation proper" is equivalent to the indirect rule that was prevalent under certain forms of colonialism, in which the local middleman mediated all contact between the two structures such that Structure A was effectively sealed off from Structure B (Bailey 1969: 144-155, 175).

Nonetheless, variations on this theme can still properly be termed encapsulation. Most common today, in a world system of nation-states, is the situation in which Structure B, the state, decides that all politically or culturally peripheral groups or local systems within its boundaries must join in full and equal participation in the processes of "modernization," "development," and "nation building." Thus *encapsulation* of local systems moves purposefully toward the goal of *integration*, a structural assimilation that if successful ultimately implies the end of Structures A as such. Fully integrated local systems would cease to be distinctive units operating with a meaningful degree of autonomy, constituting separate political "arenas" for their members. As Bailey notes, a policy of total integration "is adopted by virtually all the developing nations: they seek, with varying degrees of determination and success, to put an end to casteism or communalism or tribalism or regionalism and to make a united nation" (1969: 151).

In Malaysia and in many other plural nations, however, contradictions exist between such policies of integration and constitutional guarantees of cultural and religious freedom. In Malaysia, local systems tend to be ethnically or communally distinct; Chinese live in rural market centers, villages, or urban neighborhoods that are likely to be both structurally and socially separate from similar Malay communities. Thus the units that lie at the periphery of power are unlike entities, and as such they find themselves in greatly contrasting situations of encapsulation. The boundaries between the central powers and the differentiated units on the periphery differ in permeability, and the importance of the local middleman as cultural broker varies. The "severity" of the situation must be measured not simply along the continuum from indirect rule to integration, but in terms of an ethnic dimension as well. Ethnic commonalities or contrasts, as we will see in the Malaysian case, are crucial in shaping the relationships between the state and its various constituent local communities. Ethnic diversity can exacerbate structural contradictions and power imbalances, persistently complicating the processes of integration.

Bureaucratic Encapsulation in Plural Societies

Political centers of power employ a variety of means to exercise hegemony of differing strengths over their respective peripheries. In some cases military coercion is the primary vehicle for encapsulation; domination, rather than functional or structural integration, results. Total integration of the sort that most new states are aiming for today is more likely, however, to be sought through processes that can be collectively characterized as "bureaucratic" encapsulation, in which organizational patterns and structures are extended downward to encompass and integrate lower-level units into a coherent state system. While the state probably controls a considerable military and police force, of which the public is no doubt well aware, it is intended to be the encapsulating vehicle of last resort, on call for use only if the bureaucratic penetration should be resisted or frustrated.

Center-periphery relations and the means by which the center integrates or attempts to integrate the periphery have been the focus of a considerable body of literature in political science. Tarrow summarizes and evaluates three current formulations, which he terms the diffusion-isolation model, the dependency-marginality model, and the bureaucratic-integration model, drawn from functionalism, Marxism and economic anthropology, and organization theory, respectively. The first draws attention to the "moral hegemony" of the elites, the second to the attempts of the elites to construct a "coherent ruling coalition," and the third to the "institutional and interpersonal linkages" between center and periphery. Tarrow's synthesis argues that empirical combinations of variations on these central elements determine the ultimate impact of elite-oriented policies on the periphery, shaped particularly by the interaction of "elite coalitional strategies" and "institutional linkages" (1978: 32, 42).

All of these approaches share a common concern with a similarly conceived fundamental division between center and periphery, a "horizontal" cleavage between higher level and lower level, or modern urban culture and traditional rural culture, or state power and oppressed masses. While this horizontal cleavage is unquestionably significant, undue preoccupation with it can obscure the equally critical vertical fissures that complicate center-periphery relations in most political systems. The power center, united by the common interests of power, tends to appear relatively homogeneous, so the view from the center tends to offer only limited recognition of the diversity that may and usually does exist on the periphery.

One principle of vertical cleavage that is prominent in the many plural societies of the world today is ethnicity, a phenomenon that has a variety of meanings and manifestations. In most of the multiethnic states of the Western world, a few notable exceptions aside, the ascendancy of one group over others and the long process of historical adaptation have led to

9

patterns of mutual accommodation that, although possibly not yet final, have at least achieved a certain stability. Ethnic pluralism and its ramifications tend to be seen as just one issue among many, and less pressing than most others (the economy, international relations, and so on), despite the periodic resurgence of ethnic salience. In the new plural states of the Third World, however, "modern" history is telescoped into a few short decades. Ethnic tensions that are centuries-old, once muted or at least obfuscated by the same colonial presence that created or exacerbated them, now take center stage in the modern process of nation building.

In relatively homogeneous industrialized states, or in those where a single majority ethnic group has long dominated the state apparatus, horizontal solidarities and corresponding horizontal cleavages are comparatively consistent. In such systems, ruling and elite coalitions of the sort that interest Tarrow bring together groups whose critical internal oppositions are of vested private interest more often than of fundamental communal values, ideologies, and conceptions of "we" versus "they."

The plural postcolonial state in the process of modernizing a traditionally oriented and historically divided society faces quite a different set of institutional problems. Although central government elites are likely to share a Westernized education and life-style as well as common development goals for their country, they also represent competing ethnic groups of asymmetrical strengths and considerable cultural diversity. Interests and loyalties are multiple and often mutually contradictory, and solidarities and cleavages occur both horizontally and vertically. Leaders are dependent for their status on a delicate and tenuous blend of grassroots support from their own community, on the one hand, and acceptability to and recognition from elites of other communities, possibly more powerful than their own, on the other. The leaders of subordinate ethnic groups try simultaneously to satisfy two contending constituencies—the masses of their own community, and the dominant elites of the more powerful group. Ruling coalitions here are built on the shaky foundations of underlying ethnic opposition.

The basic issues, compromises, and resolutions in such a plural state take on a new light when seen from the periphery rather than from the center. The view from the center is focused through the lens of its own plans and goals for national development. But that lens blurs the clarity of the conceptions that Sanchun and similar communities hold of their own identities and interests. The web of organizational strands, both bureaucratic and political, that constrains local movement and autonomy is more clearly visible when seen through Sanchun eyes. Linkages throughout the system may be vertical, lateral, or diagonally oblique; they may be based on ethnicity, on structural hierarchy of either bureaucracy or party, or simply on pragmatic recognition of the loci of power and influence. The conceptual unraveling of the web presents a fascinating challenge.

The Malaysian Political Context

The Malaysian ethnic mosaic is extremely complex, and a certain amount of simplification is necessary to permit the basic analysis to proceed. In West Malaysia, Malays make up 53.2 percent of the population; Chinese, 35.4 percent; and Indians, 10.6 percent.[2] Although there has been some cultural exchange across these boundaries, each group has for the most part retained its own cultural and political identity, despite cohabitation of the peninsula for over a century. From the beginning of political party activity in the postwar years, communal divisions have been explicitly acknowledged in political organization. The first independent government was formed by an intercommunal Alliance Party, each component party drawing membership from one of the three main ethnic groups. This formula remained unchanged until 1974, when an expanded Barisan Nasional (National Front) became the ruling coalition. The Barisan incorporated a number of prominent opposition parties, some of which are multiethnic in makeup, but the locus of real power within the government has remained the same—the United Malays National Organization (UMNO).

Through the UMNO and through overrepresentation in the various state as well as federal bureaucracies, Malays dominate government and politics in Malaysia. Non-Malays, the structurally opposite category commonly referred to in Malaysia today, must in fact be subdivided into component subgroups—Chinese, Indians, and so on—to be understood, for the groups differ significantly in size, class structure, and political power vis-à-vis Malays. By virtue of their numbers and their prominent role in the national economy, the Chinese constitute the functionally opposite number of the Malays; it is between the Chinese and the Malays that a *modus vivendi* must be achieved and maintained if the nation is to prosper and avoid the ever-threatened explosion of the ethnic time bomb. This study focuses explicitly on Malay-Chinese relations and on the encapsulation of local-level Chinese politics by the Malay-dominated state, as it wields its power, on the one hand, through bureaucratic channels staffed largely by

---

2. Specific demographic and historical conditions in East Malaysia (the Borneo states of Sabah and Sarawak) are sufficiently different from those in West Malaysia to necessitate their exclusion from consideration in this study, although the potent forces of encapsulation are felt in local politics there as well. When for simplicity's sake I refer to Malaysia, I mean, in fact, West Malaysia, or peninsular Malaysia.

Malays and, on the other, through the UMNO's effective hegemony over virtually all party politics, Malay and non-Malay alike.

The sets of ongoing political relations that must undergird the day-to-day stability and the long-range development of Malaysia involve connections of various sorts and strengths across both horizontal and vertical cleavages. First, simple vertical linkages are important. Both Malay and Chinese national elites, in the communal formula established before independence and still holding rather firmly, are responsible to the masses of their own ethnic communities—responsible to them and, perhaps more important, responsible for their support of the ruling government. These are ideally straightforward relationships of elite-mass ethnic solidarity, bridging horizontal cleavages, but at the same time creating vertical ones, as ethnic communities maintain separate leadership and separate political identities.

Second, in a roughly horizontal linkage, Malay and Chinese elites must work together in the ruling councils; in practice this is an unequal relationship, with most of the real power in the hands of the Malays. Again, the relationship is ideally straightforward: elites unite in horizontal solidarity, governing in the manner they believe best serves national interests. The contradiction lies, of course, in the fact that other interests, both perceived communal interests and more immediate personal interests, may conflict with perceived national interests. Elites are then caught in a conundrum, forced to choose between horizontal and vertical solidarity.

Third, and most complex, is the question of crosscutting relationships: what roles do Malay and Chinese elites play relative to the common folk of the other ethnic community? For Chinese elites, the short answer is easy: virtually none. Individual Chinese do hold positions such as ministerial appointments in which their decisions and actions affect Malays as well as Chinese. But in the overall constellation of power, Malay interests are well protected, and a member of the Chinese elite would be unable to act independently vis-à-vis those interests. Nonetheless, actions of Chinese elites as leaders of their own community are of indirect importance to Malays, because Chinese leaders are charged with maintaining general Chinese support for the government, or, failing that, acquiescence in its actions.

The Chinese population at large, by contrast, is more directly concerned with and at least implicitly connected to members of the Malay elite. The same individuals who are Malay leaders are also national leaders—the prime minister, heads of major ministries such as home affairs, finance, education, trade and industry, and defense, the sultans and chief ministers of most states, and the king. Malays in these posts must ideally serve as responsible officials accountable equally to and concerned equally for all communities, and they must project an image of national identity and solidarity that embraces all citizens. Within the government bureaucracy, a large proportion of civil servants and state and federal employees in all branches and at all levels are Malays. The administrative policies that order daily life in the small town are products of Malay-dominated ruling circles, and the people who carry out those policies at intermediate levels are largely Malay.

Although all Chinese are constantly aware of the Malay role in the power structure, the Chinese villager tends to try when possible to minimize direct contact with Malay authorities. Rather than bridge the vertical cleavage of ethnicity directly, the villager is likely to look upward within the ethnic group and ask a fellow Chinese higher on the prestige ladder to make the horizontal connection crossing ethnic lines. Moreover, the Chinese local leader often does the same thing: to accomplish local bureaucratic ends, he looks upward within his (communal) party structure, asking a state party leader to mediate for him with the (Malay) district-level bureaucracy. Thus a tendency toward "encapsulation proper" persists, as Chinese political leaders at all levels serve as specialized middlemen linking their fellow Chinese further down the scale into the Malay-dominated political system. Rather than integration per se, an attenuated encapsulation prevails; political life in Sanchun demonstrates this critical reality.

In this setting, linkages, alliances, and coalitions at all levels of society combine what appears on the surface to be situational flexibility and fluidity with a certain degree of underlying rigidity based on the givens of ethnicity and power. Center-periphery relations ideally incorporate not only elements of dominance, demanding compliance and submission, but also elements of solidarity, promising consonance and unity of interests as a basis for legitimacy and trust. Such solidarity must be founded in common ethnicity or level of power, however. The Malay-dominated center shares bonds of common ethnicity with the Malay periphery, and bonds of common material interest with the Chinese elites who share some power at the center, but in relation to the Chinese periphery an operational commonality is lacking. The Malay center dominates the Chinese periphery, but it is able to offer little direct inducement to or assurance of solidarity; instead it seeks merely to minimize alienation and fall back on acceptable neutrality. It is left to the subordinate Chinese element of the center, from its ambiguous position of uncertain proximity to real power, to act as mediator and convey an aura of solidarity and inclusion embracing the Chinese periphery. It is a task that is not always easily accomplished.

Dimensions of Encapsulation

Though the power differential is certainly a crucial element in the relations between center and periphery, as is clear in the Malaysian case, equally important is a complex cultural dimension that may provide either bonds or barriers between the political center and its subordinate systems. Bailey is particularly concerned with cultural incongruities that fit loosely under headings of "traditional" and "modern" world views (1969: 147-148; 1971). I will term such views *orientations*: they are by nature malleable, subject to influence, pressure, persuasion, and ultimate transformation. The Malaysian case highlights a second strand in the cultural dimension, however, that is less amenable to reorientation or redefinition and thus of greater potential strength and persistence as either bond or barrier — *ethnicity*.

A traditional orientation embodied in village values might manifest itself, for example, in the persistence of village perceptions of higher authorities in terms more appropriate to an earlier feudal or patrimonial system than to a contemporary democratic capitalist state. Villagers might resist "universalistic" values, rejecting local officials appointed because of skills rather than kinship links; or they might grow impatient with the notion of delayed gratification that is necessary to the long-term success of many development programs. Central power holders would understandably seek to change such orientations to facilitate the integration of the village into their national development plans.

But ethnicity, as it manifests itself in a plural society, is not merely an attitude or orientation readily amenable to redefinition in response to persuasion or exhortation from above. Rather, it is a state of being, a fundamental conceptual pitting of "we" against "they." This opposition may vary in intensity according to situation, and in response to decisions taken by policy makers and powerholders to make much or little of its importance. Nonetheless, the basic ethnic distinctions persist; while they can often be de-emphasized, they can seldom be eliminated entirely.

Moreover, though the notion of a traditional-modern continuum is inherently oversimplistic, it may still be loosely applicable as a measure of center-periphery incongruity in developing nations. But in Malaysia, as in most multiethnic societies, ethnic distinctions do not correlate neatly with membership in Structure B or Structures A. Rather, these "we" and "they" conceptions serve effectively to create vertical links between *some* Structures A and *some members* of Structure B, and corresponding vertical cleavages separating others.

In the Malaysian case, the comparison of the two main ethnic groups reveals an intriguing reversal of center-periphery proximity along "orientation" and "ethnic" strands of the broadly cultural dimension of encapsulation. Malay local systems are, of course, much more similar to the Malay central power holders in terms of the sentiments and solidarities that constitute ethnic identity than are Chinese local systems, whose ethnic solidarity links them only to the second echelon of power. But it is the Chinese who participate more fully in the "modern" sector of the economy — in petty commerce and as both urban and rural proletariat as well as in the higher ranks of the capitalist elites, while Malays remain tied dispropor-tionately to traditional agriculture. Local systems of both communities, then, are subject to a bifurcated encapsulation situation. A given Structure A may conform in terms of either ethnicity or orientation to the model deemed desirable by central policy makers concerned with both national unity and development. But seldom does a single local system satisfy the demands of the center in both respects. Center-periphery policies, I will argue in the next chapter, are consequently compartmentalized vis-à-vis the different sectors of the periphery.

Within a plural society dominated by one ethnic group sharing lesser amounts of power with other ethnic groups, bureaucratic encapsulation takes on a somewhat more rigid cast than in a society lacking sharp and salient ethnic divisions. The local system on the political periphery of the multiethnic society will find its power relationship with the center shaped not only by the degree to which it shares a common orientation toward val-ues underlying state goals for modernization and development, but, more importantly, by the actual position of the national leaders of its own ethnic community in relation to real power at the center—that is, by ethnicity. The political actors in the less powerful ethnic group's local systems, far from operating autonomously, find themselves sharply constrained by ele-ments of the larger political scene. On the one hand, they are manipulated as much as served by their own leaders, who are striving for greater na-tional power, in part, perhaps naively, through enhanced grassroots sup-port. On the other hand, they are hamstrung by national leaders of the dominant group, who are determined to maintain the status quo in their own favor.

Ethnicity and Class in Malaysia

Sanchun is a Chinese community in a Malay-dominated state, and the sali-ence of the ethnic factor in its particular situation of encapsulation must be acknowledged, as the analysis to follow will show. But class divisions are also important in the structuring of super- and subordination in Malaysian society at large.

The rich ethnic mosaic that meets the observer's eye in any town or city in Malaysia has tended to focus both scholarly and journalistic attention on ethnic issues. Now, however, there is a growing call, appropriately, for rec-ognition of internal differentiation based not in cultural and racial cate-gories but in antagonistic class interests. State power is seen to support the interests of the elites of all ethnic groups, but particularly the Malay elites who hold that power, against those of the peasants and workers. British administration and labor policies in the colonial era contributed to the ethnic patterning of occupations that is observable today; those policies were not accidental, but served the political and economic interests of the foreign rulers (see, for example, Stenson 1976, Hamilton 1978). Similarly, the contemporary political economy of Malaysia can be understood only when continuing foreign interests, which represent over half of the share capital investment in the country, are kept in mind (see, for example, Mann 1977, Lim 1979, Snodgrass n.d.). Moreover, Malay political elites are among those realizing rapid increases in personal wealth while inequities in income distribution nationally are seen to be growing (see, for example, Hirschman 1974, Grace 1976). The radical analysis now current is summed up by one writer as follows: "While the origins of ethnic conflict can be traced to the colonial past, its continued presence today must be attributed to the post-colonial state and the manipulation of ethnic issues by Malay bureaucrat capitalists in their drive for more and more economic power" (*Southeast Asia Chronicle*, April 1980: 23).

There is indeed considerable evidence to support a rather cynical view of the current government's positions on ethnic issues, evidence that should not be dismissed lightly. But the argument only loses force when implicit in it is the assumption that what Nagata terms "subjective pluralism" — the continuing perception by most Malaysians, particularly those educated in the vernacular schools, of their society in ethnic terms (1975, 1980) — is merely an epiphenomenon of ruling-class policies. Mullard and Brennan, for example, argue that the notion of pluralism is no longer strictly applicable to Malaysian society, for it is increasingly "shaped by the forces of urbanization and modern economic development" (1978: 351). They maintain that an increase in the urban proportion of the population (from 15.9 percent in 1947 to 28.7 percent in 1970) "suggests that a gradual erosion of racial and ethnic allegiances is beginning to take place" (1978: 350). Although they call for more critical empiricism to replace the "ideologized liberal" model of pluralism based on Furnivall, however, they offer no empirical evidence for the putative relationship between increasing urbanization and alleged decreasing ethnic salience. Thus they themselves fall into implicit reliance on the equally ideologized models of modernization and of the "melting pot," models that are empirically refuted in Malaysia as well as in numerous other cases throughout the world. They are moved by their obvious attachment to the persuasive argument that "social control in Malaysia is inescapably related to the nature of the prevailing economic system" (1978: 351) to seek an explanation that denies what Nagata, for example, with others, sees as an empirical reality: "As yet there is a very underdeveloped sense of class consciousness in Malaysian society, either within its component ethnic segments or for the country as a whole. What sense of class there is tends to be more frequently verbalized among those with higher or English medium education, and projected on to other ethnic groups" (1975: 134).

Skepticism regarding the authenticity of ethnic identification informs much of the current critical political analysis of nations like Malaysia. But ethnicity is nonetheless a genuine force that lends itself successfully to political manipulation precisely because it is authentically felt at some level, a level that varies with the individual as well as the situation. Enloe (1980: x) rejects the view that a choice must be made between class and ethnicity as the "real basis of social organization," and argues convincingly that "it is the particular *pattern* of relationships among class, ethnicity, and sex that determines how power and authority are used and maintained." She notes that "state elites exploit ethnic divisions at the same time as they publicly deplore them," a position that most other critical analysts could readily agree with, but unlike most she goes on to offer a third element in the apparent paradox: she argues that "central power-wielders also fear genuine ethnic attachments that rival the artificial state." Rather than opting for a satisfying but simplistic analysis based on either class or ethnicity, she addresses the full complexity of social and political reality with such questions as: "Why do state elites find ethnicity of *special* value in structuring and utilizing coercive power? How do state elites combine class, sex and ethnic cleavages to ensure state-supportive divisions of labor?" Some would argue that ethnicity in Malaysia today is most appropriately seen as little more than a tool employed by the ruling class to obfuscate objective relations of production, a true understanding of which would necessarily enable the working masses of all races to unite and successfully oppose the existing system of domination and subordination. But to deny the reality of ethnicity and thereby disdain its investigation, I would argue, is to forgo a critical understanding of the relationship between the tool and its effectiveness.

An important example of successful analysis of Malaysian politics in class rather than ethnic terms is Kessler's trenchant study (1978) of the success of the Pan-Malayan Islamic Party (PMIP) in Kelantan.[3] But it is the exception that proves the rule. Kessler explicitly acknowledges that the lack of communal cleavages in the predominantly Malay state has facilitated both the uninhibited development of class differences among Kelantanese Malays and the expression of class antagonisms in intra-Malay politics: "Since their perception of local class antagonisms was not blurred by communal issues, the Kelantanese could discern, in at least a rudimentary manner, the basic antagonisms from which their grievances stemmed: between noble, government employee, or trader and peasant, between landlord and tenant, between town and country" (1978: 163-164). Thus

---

3. The Malay name of the party is Parti Islam se-Malaysia (PAS); it is also known as Parti Islam (PI).

the careful empirical study of a particular Malay rural community within its own specific historical setting, shaped by the colonial past and by contemporary conflicts of interest pitting Malay against Malay, allows Kessler to assert that "(contrary to the contention of many observers) class thus exerts a clearly powerful influence upon Malay politics" (1978: 241).

The detailed study of a Chinese rural community and the basic antagonisms that underlie the sense of insecurity and vulnerability felt by the Chinese villager in Malaysia reveals the other side of the coin, the side that I would argue is probably more representative of Malaysian society as a whole. Sanchun has also been shaped by the colonial experience; in its current political context, however, power inequities between village and state and between Chinese and Malay override the economic imbalances that exist between Chinese and Chinese, between labor and capital. Class antagonisms as such play a relatively small role in a community that, in part in response to its political environment, is to some degree vertically integrated, as Chinese villagers are bound, though loosely, to Chinese local leaders who mediate for them with the outside political system. Incipient class antagonisms underlay the enthusiastic response villagers gave to the 1971 MCA task force mobilization throughout Perak (to be discussed in chapter 7), as they began tentatively to express opposition to the old-guard urban capitalist MCA leadership in ideological as well as factional terms. But while Kelantanese peasants may formulate grievances against Malay elites with some clarity, Chinese villagers must deal in addition with a second level of power hierarchy controlling their lives, for Chinese elites are in turn politically subordinate to Malay elites. Communal issues cannot be conveniently "held constant" in the observer's model in Perak, as they can be in Kelantan. Class analysis, if it neglects or underestimates the salience of communal power structures, can offer only a partial understanding of social and political reality.

A Case Study of Encapsulation

The political encapsulation of Sanchun is effected along two lines, through the bureaucracy and the political party. Administratively, Sanchun comes under its own local council, a form of elected local government originally established in 1952 to provide people with a sense of direct involvement in order to encourage their support of the military effort against the insurgents. Even then councils provided little more than a taste of participatory democracy, and over the years they have been emasculated further. Since 1964 councillors have been appointed by dominant parties rather than elected. All but the most mundane actions taken by the council must be approved and often carried out at higher levels, and very little power is left

18

in local hands. Not surprisingly, positions on the council, offering few attractions and few rewards, are not widely sought after in Sanchun, and vacancies are not quickly filled. Nonetheless, a few public-spirited men do eventually come forth to serve, sometimes only reluctantly, after much urging by friends. The council has been easily controlled by a small number of strong-willed and entrenched activists who have long dominated the scene, but council politics, since the end of the Emergency at least, have been of little interest to either townspeople or the councillors themselves. Before independence in 1957, structural ties linking Sanchun leaders to the power center varied, being relatively weak under indirect rule before World War II but appreciably stronger during the Emergency. The bureaucratic encapsulation instituted under the new constitution in 1957 has unremittingly consolidated its lethargic but firm grip over the local system.

Sanchun and similar local systems have no leverage within the ponderous bureaucracy and must submit passively to the structure it imposes. But the second dimension of encapsulation—political party organization—is potentially more volatile and occasionally permits or even demands energetic local participation. The Malayan Chinese Association (MCA), formed during the Emergency, first established itself through the important welfare work it carried out for the new villages, and then joined the UMNO as the Chinese partner in the Alliance. Sanchun had been since the days of the Emergency an MCA "party" town, though until 1971 that had little significance for most people. It meant that the councillors were all MCA men and that there was a formally registered MCA branch, but paper membership in the party never exceeded a few dozen, and active participants were even fewer in number. In 1971-1972, through a well-organized statewide grassroots mobilization movement in Perak, the MCA attempted to recoup the serious losses it had sustained in the 1969 elections. The movement achieved notable success, but the price of success was eventual suppression by national MCA leaders, including mass expulsions from the party. By 1974, the ousted reformists had aligned with the "multiracial" Gerakan Rakyat (formerly in opposition but co-opted by the Malay central leadership into the government alliance in 1972—see chapter 2), and a new Gerakan party branch had been established in Sanchun.

Although post-Emergency local council matters never aroused real interest or rivalry in Sanchun, the activist MCA organizers drew enthusiastic response when they rallied village Chinese—farmers and laborers—in support of what villagers perceived as their interests and rights in the larger national arena. The ensuing split within the party at state and national levels was based in factional divisions as well as ideological differences, but it was also facilitated and furthered by the encapsulated position of Chinese politics within the Alliance/Barisan Nasional dominated by the UMNO. In Sanchun, both political and social effects have been felt; some

19

men gained stature in the course of local political upheaval and others lost it. A strong sense of general unease and sadness persists today as Sanchun people contemplate the new and public line of division in the community.

A family metaphor, powerful in Chinese society, has been offered spontaneously by more than one Sanchun informant discussing the party split. As one man put it, "We used to be one big family (*yidajia*), but now we have divided the hearth (*fen le jia*)" — for traditional Chinese, a sad state of affairs indeed. Sanchun remains in many senses a Chinese community, despite its location in Malaysia. The style of personal interaction, political as well as social, reflects traditions and values that are Chinese, though they may bear similarities to those of peasant societies everywhere. The common man in Sanchun turns to more sophisticated, better-educated, and better-connected merchant leaders to serve as intermediaries for him with the government. Local leaders, in turn, rely on Chinese party officials within the state and federal governments more often than on appropriate district-level bureaucrats (who are generally Malay) to use their influence within the government partnership in order to accomplish local administrative ends.

These higher-level Chinese leaders, however, must move in circles of power dominated not by Chinese but by Malays, and they are constrained in the support they can give their Chinese constituents on any given issue by calculations of possible costs in terms of UMNO support, whether on other issues of community concern or in factionalist fights within the elite. Chinese leaders hold their positions as much through support proffered by Malay elites as through that given by the Chinese community at large, and there is no question in anyone's mind at present as to which of these two sources of "legitimacy" is the more powerful. The Chinese mass base mobilized by the Perak task force in 1971-1973 supported an emerging rival Chinese faction, thus threatening to unbalance the carefully constructed national-level *modus vivendi*. Both the challenged Chinese leadership and their Malay alliance partners shared the conviction that the upstarts had to be contained. Failing that, the MCA favored their political elimination, but the UMNO's Malay leaders opted to permit accommodation, with the result that Chinese government leadership is now split between two parties and the strength of each is thus undermined. The rise and fall of the Perak task force deserves careful analysis at all levels, but in this book it must be seen merely as the most recent of a number of illuminating events in a study of local-level encapsulation over time. As such, it will be examined in terms of its implications for the local system, Sanchun.

Collectively, Chinese-Malaysian rural communities such as Sanchun are the homes of a significant minority of an ethnically distinct population that is itself a significant minority in a multiethnic nation. Parallels extend readily to a large number of the ethnically fragmented situations found around the world, where no majority group is large enough realistically to expect minority assimilation or even full minority acculturation. Instead, mutual accommodation offers the best hope for national harmony. Moreover, such large minorities are more likely even within the context of accommodation to be able to preserve significant elements of their own unique cultural heritages.

Although this book will provide insights into facets of such issues as ethnicity and cultural persistence, its focus is unabashedly political. Its primary aim is to illuminate an aspect of the political situation in new nation-states, specifically in Malaysia, that has heretofore received too little attention. Political information too often flows more smoothly and freely from the top down, especially in highly centralized political systems such as Malaysia. This book, by contrast, presents one of the several possible views from the bottom, that from the perspective of a Chinese rural community as it is caught up in and affected by the ebb and flow of power and dominance in a national political arena moving from colonial to communal politics.

2

Politics and Power in Malaysia

The communal structuring of contemporary politics in Malaysia emerges out of a colonial history that wrought not only economic but also demographic transformation of the Malayan peninsula. As the British rulers sought to exploit the rich resources of the land, a major component of labor policy was the attraction, by a variety of means, of an immigrant labor force to assist in the task. The political relationships that have developed over time between the immigrant groups and the politically dominant elites — first the British and later the Malays — have reflected cultural orientations and economic conditions as well as the realities of power.

Chinese who took part in the great waves of emigration from the homeland in the nineteenth and early twentieth centuries did not, for the most part, conceive of themselves as permanent settlers in new lands. In this they differed significantly from the people who made up most other major historical immigrations, for example, the European settlers of the North American continent.[1] Chinese were, or wished to be, sojourners rather than immigrants. They were men who left families behind temporarily to seek their fortunes in what they hoped would be richer pastures, always with the intention of returning home successful and investing hard-earned savings in the native place. In keeping with these goals, pursuing them with single-minded intent in order to be able to return home all the sooner, they

---

1. The Chinese case is of course not unique. Indians who went to work in Southeast Asia, the South Pacific, Africa, and the West Indies, for example, usually intended to return home. Moreover, Indian-Malaysians today are more likely to maintain close ties to ancestral communities than are Chinese-Malaysians, for whom the "homeland" has effectively been closed since 1949. Migrations of this sort should be conceptually differentiated from, for example, the European settlement of North America and parts of Africa, or the Han Chinese settlement of Taiwan in the seventeenth century.

22

tended to occupy themselves in cash-producing pursuits — commerce, wage labor, cash-crop farming. And in keeping with their status as temporary sojourners, most showed little concern with the workings of the political structures within which they happened to alight, beyond aspects that pertained directly to their own immediate goals.

It has often been remarked that a lag may occur between the rates of change of objective conditions and of certain attitudes and values that relate to those conditions. Such a culture lag has been clearly evident among Chinese in Malaya and in most of the *Nanyang* (literally, southern seas), and it has been fostered by the environment in which the objective changes have taken place. By the fourth and fifth decades of this century, greater numbers of Chinese "sojourners" no doubt accepted the likelihood that they would not return to China, a likelihood that became nearly a certainty after the change in government there in 1949. It would then have been appropriate for them to take a greater interest in the politics of their new home, but by that time the political environment of colonialism was effectively doing its part to perpetuate apolitical attitudes. Power was firmly controlled from above, and formal political recognition and encouragement were given largely to Malays — sultans, aristocrats training in the Malay College in the royal town of Kuala Kangsar for posts in the Malayan Civil Service, and *penghulus* (headmen of the lowest-level units of civil and religious administration, *mukims*). Chinese, by contrast, were encouraged simply to continue about their business of making money, performing vital economic functions in the colonial economy. Unofficial links to power were formed quite early by the more successful Chinese capitalists, who served as informal middlemen and mediators for the community as a whole, but Chinese participated only minimally in formal government and administration.[2] No groundwork was laid for the radical revision of attitudes that was soon to be required of both Malays and Chinese, when independence and the formation of a territorially, rather than culturally, defined nation-state demanded new political attitudes and patterns of cooperation between the two groups.

With the approach of independence, or *Merdeka*, Malay leaders could tap generations of traditional cultural identification with the land of Malaya and the leadership of the sultans, a tradition that had always received full British support and sanction, in stirring the Malay populace to take on the new mantle of citizenship.[3] Some Chinese leaders perceived the need for equally enthusiastic involvement on the part of the Chinese community

2. See Skinner 1968 for a detailed discussion of Chinese elites serving as links to colonial governments elsewhere in Southeast Asia.
3. A valuable and thorough treatment of the origins and development of Malay nationalism is found in Roff 1967.

in the new political endeavor. But they faced apathy from the Chinese populace, who lacked traditions both of civil participation and of cultural ties to this particular territory, and antipathy from the Malays, who feared they might lose out as drastically politically as they felt they already had economically, if the Chinese were welcomed into politics on an equal basis. Compromises were worked out that gave the preponderance of power in the new state to the Malay leadership. Chinese apolitical attitudes were once again reinforced by the structure of the political environment in which they found themselves, and Malay assumptions of their natural rights as *bumiputras* ("sons of the soil") to political supremacy were upheld. Though both attitudes are now objectively outdated in the context of a civil democracy in which all citizens are in principle equal, neither is in fact eradicated.[4]

The forms and structures of politics in Malaysia as they were established at Merdeka, and as they were manipulated by the power holders in the nation's early years, have had direct implications for Chinese local systems within the young nation. From the outset, real power has been centralized in the federal government institutions. From the outset, despite an ostensible sharing of that power among members of an intercommunal Alliance Party, control in fact has been wielded by Malay UMNO leaders not only over the government, but also, to a significant extent, over the Chinese party in the "partnership." The relative weakness of the MCA at the upper levels, I would suggest, is a major contributing factor in the apathetic reception it receives in lower-level peripheral systems such as Sanchun.[5] The party organization in the small town meant little more than just another committee membership for the established local leaders who already manned school, temple, and native-place association committees. It did not offer a modern alternative to existing patron-client forms of local-level Chinese leadership; it merely added one more strand to the rope of tradition that bound the status quo of political noninvolvement firmly in place.

To the extent that the Chinese of Malaysia are apolitical, it is no simple accident of genetic or cultural predisposition that makes them so. To the extent that they are not, it is in brave or foolhardy defiance of an encapsulating political environment that contrives to limit the range of political action available to them. This environment both dictates tightly bounded

---

4. Historical background for the generalizations given here can be found in, for example, Jackson 1961, Groves 1964, Purcell 1965 and 1967, Roff 1967, Enloe 1970, Vasil 1971, Means 1976.

5. Heng Pek Koon, who is currently working on a history of the MCA, contends that in the 1950s there was somewhat greater balance within the Alliance between the MCA and UMNO than there is now, and that the MCA was then strong at the grassroots (personal communication). Her view seems to differ somewhat from that expressed in other studies of the period, such as Miller 1959. Oral history collected in Sanchun supports Miller's perspective.

definitions of their rights and duties and more subtly invokes psychological limits of tolerance, as public examples of the unsuccessful, beaten champions of "Chinese rights" multiply over the years. At the same time, an acceptable level of economic well-being and elements of cultural tradition provide positive support for the persistent prevalence of a passive acceptance of the "apolitical" status quo.

The Constitutional Structure

As independence approached, the constitutional issues subject to most heated debate pertained to communal interests. The final product in 1957 embodied considerable compromise from both sides, though subsequent amendments and interpretations have shifted the original balance somewhat. Questions of federalism versus state autonomy, which were theoretically above communal interests, were largely resolved in favor of centralization. This centralization in turn directly limited the debate on subsequent modifications, some of which related to communal compromises, to a narrow circle of central power holders. The political insecurity felt by many Chinese-Malaysians thus derives not only from the present actual legal disposition of communal issues, but, more importantly, from the legal disposition of power, centralized in the hands of a federal government dominated by Malays.

The constitution explicitly defines the balance of power between the federal and state governments. The list of federal responsibilities includes external affairs, defense and internal security, the administration of justice, citizenship and naturalization, finance, trade and industry, communications, education, health, labor and social security, and a number of minor subjects. The state list includes only territorially circumscribed subjects such as land, agriculture and forestry, mining and natural resource development, local government, and certain public works. However, land and local government are also legitimate areas of federal legislation for purposes of ensuring uniformity, although state governments must approve such legislation.

The tax system ensures federal control of the purse strings, which is translated into control of significant rewards and sanctions that can be offered to or leveled against state governments. All customs and excise duties, income taxes, and certain license fees including radio, vehicle, and driving licenses are credited to the federal government. State income derives primarily from land taxes and other forms of license fees. It is estimated that the federal government takes about 85 percent of all revenue collected (Smith 1963: 35). State revenues are seldom sufficient to meet state needs, and deficits are covered through balancing grants and allocations from the federal government.[6] Serious frictions do sometimes arise between state and federal governments, but power is concentrated in the center, and resolution of any real conflict of interests is easily predictable.[7]

As to communal issues, concessions to Malay demands for formalization of "special rights" resulted in provisions couched in terminology of a sort very much open to interpretation. The *Yang di-Pertuan Agong* (king) is charged with the responsibility "to safeguard the special position of the Malays and the legitimate interests of the other communities" (Article 153). Special rights for Malays include reservation of certain lands and provide for favorable quotas in the granting of business licenses, scholarships, and civil service positions. Islam is declared the "religion of the Federation; but other religions may be practiced in peace and harmony" (Article 3) as long as proselytism among Muslims is avoided (Article 11). Malay is given the status of sole official language, though a period of ten years' inital grace was given to the use of English in parliament and in other official contexts, and it is clearly stated that "no person shall be prohibited or prevented from using (otherwise than for official purposes) or from teaching or learning, any other language," and that federal and state governments have the right "to preserve and sustain the use and study of the language of any community in the Federation" (Article 152).

Language policy, still one of the most critical and volatile problems in Malaysia, illustrates the powers of constitutional interpretation open to the government. The safeguards embodied in the constitution are implemented at the level of primary education, but policy and practice in the context of higher education are not so satisfactory to the Chinese. For example, English is currently being phased out as a language of instruction at all levels. Chinese students are faced with de facto quotas severely limiting their access to the government universities, but are deprived of the alternative of education in Commonwealth universities in part by the decline in the standard of English now attainable in the Malaysian education system — at least that is their perception of the situation. Chinese leaders have proposed, as an alternative, to establish a private university with Chinese as the chief language of instruction and Malay required as an ancillary subject. The Ministry of Education, however, has declared that private tertiary education is not in keeping with the government's education policy

6. In 1959, for example, eleven states were indebted to the federal government for a total of M$223 million (*Berita Harian*, January 18, 1969, cited in Kessler 1978: 10).

7. Kessler's excellent study (1978) of Kelantan during its ten years of opposition (PMIP/PAS) rule provides examples of deadlock and mutual immobilization in PMIP-UMNO conflict. But in 1972 the central government prevailed, as the PMIP joined its expanded government alliance, and in 1978, once again in opposition, the PMIP suffered serious electoral rout.

and thus will not sanction the plans.[8] Interpretation of constitutional phraseology such as "legitimate interests" is thus very much a province of the cabinet.

Concessions won by non-Malays in 1957 regarding citizenship were more concretely stated, and were then concretely amended in 1962. The principle of *jus soli* (citizenship by birth), a major demand of non-Malays, was incorporated from Merdeka on, but was not made retroactive. A special category of people, the subjects of the sultans (by definition, all Muslims), were declared citizens by operation of law regardless of birthplace, but others (that is, non-Malays), even those born in the federation before independence, had to apply for citizenship by registration (Article 16) or by naturalization (Article 19) and were required to meet residence requirements, swear an oath of loyalty, and show "an elementary knowledge of the Malay language." The constitution thus disenfranchised a large proportion of the population. Nonetheless *jus soli* ensured that in the long run citizenship would be equally available to all communities.

A constitutional amendment passed in 1962 reintroduced a degree of uncertainty. Citizenship based on birth in the federation was restricted to those cases in which one parent was already a citizen or permanent resident at the time of the birth (Second Schedule, Article 14). Moreover, a person holding citizenship by registration or naturalization rather than operation of law, and, by extension, his or her children or spouse, may be deprived of citizenship by government fiat, with appeal before a government-appointed board as the only recourse, an appeals system that has aptly been described as less effective than "the judicial safeguards that customarily surround a trial for a petty crime" (Groves 1964: 362). Although the vast majority of Chinese-Malaysians do now hold citizenship, it might appear that it is given to them as a privilege for which they owe gratitude, rather than something that is theirs by natural right.

Citizenship is not the critical issue today that it was twenty years ago, but many non-Malays feel that the perpetuation of Malay special privileges reduces their citizenship to second-class status. It would be illegal, however, to express such a view. Racial violence erupted in 1969, to be followed by a state of emergency under the rule of a small central committee for some twenty-one months. When parliament reconvened in February 1971, one of its first acts was to pass a constitutional amendment limiting freedom of speech on "sensitive issues" — national language, special rights for the native peoples, the status of the sultans, and citizenship rights for immigrant

8. "Government policy has been not to allow independent or private tertiary institutions to exist," according to Datuk Musa Hitam, minister of education, quoted by M. G. G. Pillai, *Asiaweek*, June 23, 1978: 14.

peoples — not only for the general public, but also for members of parliament and state legislatures both on the floor and off.

UMNO and the Alliance "Partnership"

The intercommunal party that ruled as the Alliance from independence until it was expanded in 1973 to the Barisan Nasional was, by its own constitution, very clearly an alliance but not a union. Individuals could hold membership only in one of the three constituent parties — the UMNO, the MCA, and the Malayan Indian Congress (MIC) — but not directly in the Alliance Party itself. A national central committee formulated policy, but joint committees at the state level served only as election machines. State and local bodies of each constituent party operated independently, responsible to separate higher-level organizations. At the national level, however, the Alliance took precedence over central committees of constituent parties, and the prime minister, invariably the leader of the UMNO, chose his Alliance cabinet personally, not bound by the leadership hierarchy of the other parties. The biographer of Tunku Abdul Rahman, first prime minister of Malaysia, wrote: "The Alliance is really made up of one principal party, the UMNO, with the MCA and the MIC as branches clothed with the intelligentsia and the capitalist classes of each community. The MCA is not representative of the two and a half million Chinese in the Federation, neither is the MIC of the six hundred thousand Indians. Neither of them has roots in the villages and small towns" (Miller 1959: 216).

The centralization of power in the UMNO's hands and the weak support base of the other parties in their own communities precluded independent action even within the other parties, which were in effect "encapsulated" by the UMNO through its decisive control of greater political resources. The details of an MCA party crisis in 1959 illustrate the means at the UMNO's disposal and to what ends they could be used.

The control of the MCA from its founding rested firmly with Tan Cheng Lock, the senior statesman of the Chinese business community, and his son, Tan Siew Sin. They were Straits Chinese who, like most of the Chinese leaders of the time, were English-educated. A segment of the party was convinced that Tan Siew Sin, in constitutional negotiations and in subsequent debates on educational policies, had failed to uphold Chinese interests successfully. In 1958 party elections, Dr. Lim Chong Eu wrested the leadership of the party from Tan Cheng Lock by a vote of 89 to 67, and all of the other important party offices were won by Lim's followers. Tan's clique, however, retained their positions in the government cabinet.

Preparations were made in 1959 for the first national elections in an independent Malaya. The Alliance National Council, whose MCA representatives, headed by Tan Siew Sin, remained unchanged despite the election of a new party leadership the year before, informally agreed to an allocation of 74 seats to the UMNO, 28 to the MCA, and 2 to the MIC. The new MCA Central Working Committee under Lim Chong Eu, however, proposed to nominate not 28 but 40 MCA candidates on the Alliance ticket, since they wanted to prevent the UMNO from controlling the two-thirds parliamentary majority required for constitutional amendment. Moreover, as Chinese comprised 35.6 percent of the electorate, they felt their proposal was justified (Means 1976: 212).[9]

The UMNO stood firm, however, and faced with a threatened breakdown of the Alliance system, Lim capitulated and accepted 32 seats. The nominees of all parties were to be chosen by Tunku Abdul Rahman, prime minister and president of the UMNO; Lim was not consulted as to the final MCA list (Vasil 1972: 31). The Tunku, not surprisingly, selected as candidates only men who were firmly in his camp, including the former leaders of the MCA, who still held their cabinet positions. Because it was feared they lacked support from the Chinese, Tan Siew Sin and his faction were given "safe" Malay-dominated constituencies, where the UMNO was strong enough to guarantee that the vote would go to the Alliance candidate, regardless of his ethnicity. Lim and his supporters, who made up the formally constituted leadership of the MCA, were conspicuously absent from the list of candidates and were thus denied membership in parliament or access to any cabinet positions.

The new MCA leadership, beaten, withdrew from the party. The MCA, purporting to represent the Chinese community, won only 19 of the 31 seats eventually allotted to it, and two-thirds of its losses were in constituencies that were 75 percent or more Chinese (Vasil 1972: 39). Following the crisis, UMNO leaders and those remaining in the MCA drew closer together. Both parties strengthened their centralized structures to increase party discipline and minimize the threat of regional revolts. In 1961 Tan Siew Sin was elected to the presidency of the MCA, much to the satisfaction, one might imagine, of UMNO leaders.

The 1969 Elections and Their Aftermath

The decade of the 1960s saw the expansion of the Federation of Malaya to include Sabah, Sarawak, and Singapore in the Federation of Malaysia in 1963; a state of military "Confrontation" declared by Indonesia from 1963

9. Since the Chinese electorate is concentrated in urban constituencies, however, where votes have less weight than in rural areas, the proportion of Chinese-majority constituencies is somewhat lower; hence Malays felt justified in demanding a higher proportion of candidates.

29

to 1965; and the expulsion of Singapore in 1965. Certain facets of these events could be shown to support my general argument; however, the national crisis provoked by the racial violence following the 1969 elections has more immediate relevance to the configuration of the national political environment surrounding Sanchun during my in-depth study there in 1971-1972, so I will describe that period in detail. Even in the face of temporary setback and of unanticipated and tragic turmoil, UMNO leaders maintain their tight grasp on the reins of power, as this case amply demonstrates. Opposition, whether non-Malay or Malay, is co-opted, controlled, or obliterated through a variety of means, most of which fall within the normal range of political wheeling and dealing from a position of power. They are not particularly admirable means, but they are effective in avoiding a transfer or even a dilution of power, and, as a side effect, they help to create a pervasive psychological climate of impotence and futility that envelops communities, groups, and individuals, especially non-Malays, in the lower levels of the political system.

The Alliance Party went into the 1969 elections with great confidence. Its success in the two preceding elections, 1959 and 1964, had rested partly in certain advantages accruing to the party in power and partly in the disarray of the opposition. The Alliance was identified as the party that had brought first Merdeka, then an expanded Malaysia. As party cum government the Alliance had retained a monopoly over both the distribution of patronage and favor and the use of the government-controlled media. An additional factor in 1964 was Indonesian Confrontation; support for the ruling party was equated with loyalty to the country, and under the internal security act several leaders of the opposition parties had been detained (Enloe 1970: 224).

In 1969 there were some critical differences that went unnoticed by Alliance strategists. For one thing, opposition parties were fewer. Moreover, though far from agreed on many of the major issues, they shared a strong common fear of the continued dominance of the Alliance. The non-Malay parties were all based on the west coast: the People's Progressive Party (PPP) in Perak, the Democratic Action Party (DAP, successor to Singapore's People's Action Party), and the Gerakan Rakyat Malaysia (Malaysian People's Movement, a multicommunal party of intellectuals), strong also in Selangor and Penang. The most crucial aim shared by these parties was voiced by a Gerakan leader, Dr. Tan Chee Khoon, in a preelection speech: "The simple message that I wish to put across to the voters of this country is this: DENY THE ALLIANCE PARTY THE TWO THIRDS MAJORITY IT NEEDS TO CHANGE THE CONSTITUTION. If the voters do just that, then there is hope that the democracy can stand the stress and strain of a multi-racial society" (quoted in Vasil 1972: 35; emphasis in the original). There was no formal tripartite agreement, but each party entered into separate agreements with the other two, with the effect that both parliamentary and state constituencies were allocated to each of the three on the basis of its organization and an estimate of electoral support in the constituency. For the first time the opposition had taken positive steps to avoid a wasteful splitting of its vote.

The Alliance system, and in fact the fabric of politics throughout the country, was premised on a strong UMNO drawing full Malay support, and the UMNO was more sensitive to the growing strength of Parti Islam se-Malaysia (PAS or PMIP; see Kessler 1978), a Malay theocentric party based on the east coast, than to the threat offered by non-Malay opposition. Alliance (that is, UMNO) strategists thus emphasized attracting Malay support, which could be done only at the risk of a certain amount of alienation of non-Malays. As the Alliance acquired an increasingly pro-Malay image, the fears of the non-Malay communities grew accordingly.[10]

The Alliance's miscalculation was of major proportions, as the national election results make amply clear. The government majority fell from 89 to 66 (out of 104 West Malaysian parliamentary seats), and it received less than half of the popular vote (see table 1). Even more appalling from the Alliance point of view were the state results. Heretofore the Alliance had controlled all state legislative assemblies with the exception of Kelantan, ruled since 1959 by the PAS. Now three of the eleven West Malaysian states had opposition majorities, and Alliance power was seriously undercut in two more.

In Penang, the Gerakan took a clear victory, winning 16 of the 24 seats, to the Alliance's 4, while 3 went to other opposition parties. In Trengganu, a predominantly Malay state, the PAS won 8 seats away from the UMNO, giving the Alliance a slim 13-to-11 majority. In Kelantan, the PAS retained its majority easily, winning 19 seats to the Alliance's 11. In Selangor, the site of the federal capital, Kuala Lumpur, the assembly was split, 14 Alliance and 14 opposition, while in Perak the opposition totaled 21 seats to the Alliance's 19. Thus in five of the eleven states, the Alliance suffered serious losses. The winners in two relatively predictable cases were the PAS, and in three total surprises, the Gerakan (Penang), the PPP (Perak), and the DAP (Selangor), although in the latter two states no party had a clear majority.

10. Certain specific actions of the Alliance government between elections contributed to these fears. In 1965, for the first time, the Alliance Party constitution was amended to state as one of its explicit objectives the promotion of the economic and social well being of the "indigenous people." In March 1968, in a move to aid Malay petty contractors in an industry long dominated by Chinese, the government decreed that government contracts for works amounting to less than M$10,000 should be given to Malay contractors only, with specified preferences given to Malays for contracts between M$10,000 and M$50,000. During the election campaign it was indicated that all existing English-medium schools would soon be converted to Malay-medium (Vasil 1972: 26n).

31

TABLE 1.   Peninsular Malayan federal election results by party, 1959, 1964, and 1969

Party	1959			1964			1969		
	Seats contested	Seats won	% of vote	Seats contested	Seats won	% of vote	Seats contested	Seats won	% of vote
Alliance									
UMNO	70	52	35.9	68	59	38.1	67	51	33.7
MCA	31	19	14.8	33	27	18.7	33	13	13.5
MIC	3	3	1.0	3	3	1.6	3	2	1.2
Total	104	74	51.8	104	89	58.4	103	66	48.4
PAS	58	13	21.2	52	9	14.4	59	12	23.7
PPP	19	4	6.3	9	2	3.6	6	4	3.9
DAP	0	—	—	11	1	2.1	24	13	13.7
Gerakan	0	—	—	0	—	—	14	8	8.6
Others	76	13	20.7	102	3	21.5	7	1	1.6
Total	257	104	99.9	278	104	100.0	213	104	99.9

Source: Vasil 1972: 85.

Although the PAS made some strong gains against the UMNO, the major losses were sustained by the MCA. Vasil (1972) has broken down the parliamentary results in MCA constituencies having more or less than 30 percent Malay vote (presumably loyal UMNO supporters, as Chinese candidates would not be fielded in PAS strongholds). With a 30 percent or more Malay vote, MCA candidates won 9 seats and lost 2; with less than a 30 percent Malay vote (that is, roughly a 70 percent or more Chinese vote) MCA candidates won only 4 and lost 18 (Vasil 1972: 39). Opposition non-Malay parties were understandably elated, for they perceived their successes as signaling the dawn of a more open democracy no longer under one-party rule. Moreover, Chinese would no longer have to rely exclusively on the UMNO-dominated MCA to support their interests.

Following the announcement of the election results, victory parades were planned in Kuala Lumpur first by the opposition parties, the Gerakan and the DAP, and then by the UMNO. Tension was high, and participants in the opposition parades allegedly hurled scathing insults at Malays heralding the fall of Malay supremacy, which of course infuriated Malays and fed their resentment and fear of the successes won by the new parties. On the night of the UMNO parade, May 13, violence broke out, and turmoil and destruction continued throughout the capital for the following four nights. By royal proclamation a nationwide state of emergency was declared on May 15, suspending parliament and certain civil liberties. Serious incidents continued sporadically for several months, some reaching up and down the entire west coast of the peninsula. A National Operations Council (NOC) was set up to act in place of parliament, which did not convene until February 1971. The NOC consisted of eight Malays (including two from the military and one from the police), one Chinese, and one Indian.

The government has been severely criticized for its handling of the emergency. Its immediate police and military response was considered by many to be far too slow and too weak. Its suspension of the public news media left the wildest of rumors free to spread uncontradicted. Most seriously, the predominantly Malay military forces were alleged to have been less than unbiased in their handling of violent clashes between Malays and non-Malays.[11]

Moreover, the general tenor of the two official reports released later in the year (Abdul Rahman 1969; NOC 1969) did not inspire confidence in their impartiality or candor. Official casualty figures, for example, for the period from May 13 to July 31 listed the total dead and missing as 235 (NOC 1969: 88), while unofficial estimates of the death toll alone range

---

11. Police forces, which include higher numbers of Chinese than do military forces, inspired somewhat greater confidence among the general population. See Enloe 1979 for a discussion of ethnicity and Malaysia's military.

from 300 to 700 (Gagliano 1970: 1). The government reports tend to place the blame for the disturbances on convenient scapegoats — the largely Chinese Communist Party, Chinese secret societies, and extremists in non-Malay opposition parties.

The official breakdown of casualty figures by ethnic group is revealing (see table 2). Gunfire injuries, it should be noted, would probably have been inflicted largely by military and police forces, as possession of firearms is severely restricted in Malaysia. Most of these casualties occurred in and around Kuala Lumpur, where Chinese outnumber Malays by more than two to one. It is intriguing to note that Chinese figure in disproportionately high numbers not only as victims (almost three to one, compared to Malays), but also as officially charged aggressors (five to two), except in the category of the most serious offenses, where Malays outnumber Chinese eight to one. While it cannot be said that there were any winners in this conflict, it is apparent that some were bigger losers than others, and the lesson was no doubt not lost on the Chinese community.

Official pronouncements notwithstanding, the most important of the policy directives initiated under NOC rule gave some indication of the government's real views on the underlying causes of the disorders and constituted realistic attempts to counteract some deep-seated economic problems. The New Economic Policy that was launched appeared to be specifically designed to pacify Malay dissatisfaction. It included programs for training the unemployed in industrial skills, special incentives for industries willing to locate in depressed rural areas, new land schemes to absorb the jobless in agricultural activities, and new direction given to employment practices in industries (Gagliano 1970: 24). The apparent aim was to cool Malay economic resentment with government-initiated programs that would increase Malay participation in both public and private spheres.

While economic policy was given priority, politics was held in abeyance

TABLE 2. Official casualty figures, May 13-July 31, 1969

	Malay	Chinese	Indian	Other
Dead	25	143	13	15
Missing	7	25	7	—
Injured by gunfire	37	125	17	1
Other injuries	90	145	9	15
Arrested (charged with murder or arson)	40	5	—	—
Arrested (other charges)	2,077	5,126	1,874	66

Source: National Operations Council 1969: 88.

(Gagliano 1970: 23). "Normalcy" gradually returned, however, and by June 1970 it was deemed safe to hold elections in East Malaysia, which had been postponed because of the May 13 violence. Sabah, ruled dictatorially by Tun Mustapha, a Malay in a predominantly non-Malay state, returned all 16 parliamentary seats to the Alliance (11 were returned unopposed). In Sarawak the Alliance won only 10 of the 24 seats. The Alliance parliamentary majority thus stood at 92 out of 144 seats, less than two-thirds.

In September 1970 Tunku Abdul Rahman stepped down from the leadership of the UMNO and of the country, to be succeeded by Tun Abdul Razak as UMNO president and Malaysian prime minister. The ban on party politics was lifted a few months later, but not before the NOC had amended the existing sedition laws to introduce the limits of freedom of speech on "sensitive issues" that were later enshrined in the constitutional amendment described earlier.

Return to "Parliamentary Democracy"

The 1957 Merdeka Constitution embodies principles of democracy as practiced in Western nations, particularly with regard to free speech and free enterprise. Since the May 13 incidents, however, Malaysian government officials have referred repeatedly to a different democracy perhaps more appropriate to the Malaysian case. As one writer notes, "Until May 1969, democracy was accepted without murmur—in that it was extolled by the modern-minded leaders of UMNO—because its operation in practice did not hinder UMNO from enjoying and exercising a preponderance of political power. As soon as signs appeared that suggested that this enjoyment might not be permanent, doubts as to the equity and efficacy of democracy began to emerge" (Goh 1971: 40). A parliamentary speech delivered in 1971 by Ghazali bin Shafie, then minister of information (now minister for home affairs), and reproduced and distributed mutilingually in pamphlet form, is entitled "Democracy: The Realities Malaysians Must Face." In it he discusses the need for a solid middle class, still lacking in Malaysia, as a basis for "Westminster type" democracy, and the necessity for full cooperation of all groups with the New Economic Policy in order to create these conditions for democracy. He maintains that partial curtailment of freedom of speech is "a small price to pay" for "the restructuring of society." In his view, "even that is not an absolute restriction, since the Prime Minister has announced the formation of the National Unity Council in which the problems of national unity may be discussed behind closed doors" (Ghazali bin Shafie 1971: 17). One can only ponder in awe the double-think involved in the concept of limited "free" speech available to a specific few when they are behind closed doors.

As the ideological climate of politics in Malaysia was tightening, practical moves to consolidate power once again in the UMNO-dominated center were not neglected. While the country was still under NOC rule, maneuvering had been initiated to regain control of recalcitrant state governments not firmly dominated by the Alliance. Defections, not uncommon in politics, returned the Alliance to power in two of the problematic states. In Perak three opposition assemblymen came over, giving the Alliance a majority of 22 to 18; in Selangor two more converted, providing a 16-to-12 majority. That left Sarawak, Penang, and Kelantan, where coalition governments were eventually formed, precursors of the subsequent federal-level coalition, the Barisan Nasional. In Sarawak, the opposition party won itself a federal cabinet seat through coalition. In Penang, by summer 1971, the Gerakan was beset by internal dissension, held by the deputy chief minister to be in no small part fostered by Alliance intervention (personal communications, June 1971). The party eventually split, losing its majority, and the chief minister Lim Chong Eu had little choice but to accept the Alliance's terms for coalition. The Kelantan coalition was of a somewhat different nature, for the UMNO was welcoming into the fold a rival Malay party. The PAS held out for some time, but eventually accepted the federal government's largesse in the form of much-needed development funds, and the coalition was announced late in 1972.

The Alliance had originally been intended as a complementary union of parties whose natural constituencies did not overlap. The coalitions of 1971-1972 and the ensuing Barisan Nasional contradicted the impeccable logic of that formula, by incorporating parties in direct competition for the same support base. The eventual extrusion of the PAS from the Barisan in 1978 and the open squabbling between two Barisan partners, the MCA and the Gerakan, during the 1978 general elections (Strauch 1980; Lee 1980) testify to the weaknesses of the new arrangement. It is perhaps curious, then, that the Alliance formed not only coalitions necessary for taking control of certain states, but an extra one in Perak as well—it took a minority opposition party, the PPP, into the state government in the spring of 1972. A possible explanation lies in the fact that the Perak coalition, like the Penang coalition before it, brought into the government multiethnic parties that drew most of their support from the Chinese. Thus the MCA, and not the UMNO, was likely to suffer from the rivalry within the partnership, a situation that could strengthen the UMNO's domination even more. The Gerakan leader, Dr. Lim Chong Eu, had broken with the MCA after a bitter fight in 1959, and it is not likely that MCA leaders were happy to share power with him in the new alliance. In Perak, the state MCA leaders, who maintained that they had not been consulted prior to the announcement of the coalition, saw it as a gratuitous insult designed to undermine their own efforts at grassroots revitalization of the MCA. They were incensed, but MCA president Tun Tan Siew Sin went along with the UMNO and eventually expelled two state leaders from the party for insubordination. This was just the opening round in a factional controversy that was to do serious damage to the MCA (see chapter 7). It could not be argued that the UMNO engineered the split from its inception, for the roots of dissension are deep within the Chinese community. But, as will be seen below, through a calculated balance of action and inaction, the UMNO played an important role in determining the eventual course of politics within the MCA and within the Chinese community.

Implications of Malay Political Supremacy

It is a widely accepted fact that the prime minister and the leaders of the UMNO are the controlling forces in political decision making in Malaysia. The material presented above shows that channels for articulation of non-Malay demands and for the development of strong and effective non-Malay interest groups are severely restricted. Through manipulation of government favors and sanctions, providing access to or exclusion from funds and high positions, Malay leaders have co-opted or crushed attempts to inform non-Malay political representation with real strength and independence. Serious efforts to form viable political groupings based on noncommunal principles have met with both similar subversion and even more direct harassment and suppression, including long-term imprisonment of party leaders (see, for example, *Southeast Asia Chronicle* 1980). Thus the communal formula is maintained.

Malay political supremacy within a communal framework is thus the dominant reality in Malaysia, the political environment within which Chinese local systems must exist. Though the effects of this monopoly of power are often felt most sharply by individual high-ranking Chinese politicians, the implications cannot be missed by the Chinese at large.[12] They are likely to see, for example, the steady pressure on vernacular education and language issues as threatening to their interests. Moreover, though the government policies directed at the alleviation of the have-not status of rural Malays have to date met with only qualified success at best (see, for example, Snodgrass n.d.), even less attention is given to the similar plight of many

12. The latest of many examples of government treatment of non-Malay political leaders who evidence strong support among the citizenry is the recent conviction of DAP president Lim Kit Siang on charges that he violated official secrets acts in making public allegations of government corruption involved in the purchase of patrol boats by the government (see news reports in *Asiaweek* and *Far Eastern Economic Review*, summer and autumn 1978).

non-Malays.[13] Chinese at all levels of society are equally subject to the effects of Malay political hegemony.

The common Chinese folk who follow national events can hardly be inspired with trust and confidence in the ability of their elected representatives to protect their interests. They are unlikely to view political participation at any level as a particularly meaningful activity. This climate of political apathy percolates down to the local community, where Chinese are likely to withdraw into private family concerns rather than enter politics either as prime actors or active supporters. Entrenched local-level political leaders are almost by definition backed by higher powers and are thus invincible—or so it seems to the common villager. The overall political climate in Malaysia does not encourage active participation on the part of the non-Malay or provide examples of permissible styles of involvement and expression that could influence local systems toward anything other than political passivity.

The Attainment of Government Goals

Like all national planners, Malaysian leaders project goals for the future development of their country and offer inducements to attract the cooperation of the population in working to attain these goals. Not all nations are faced so starkly, however, with a set of internal contradictions as potentially explosive as Malaysia's ethnic mixture and ethnic distribution of political and economic security. It is an extremely complex situation; there are more poor Malays than poor Chinese, and indeed the government has every reason to try to use its power to bring the economic situation more into balance.[14] Yet most Malaysians, power holders and masses alike, share a "constant-pie" ideology, which holds that since the pie always remains the same in size, any gain for one inevitably means a loss for another (Scott 1968: 11-13). Chinese understandably feel threatened by national development plans aimed at "restructuring society" in such a way as to threaten

13. The implementation of federal land schemes is a case in point. In 1972 an MCA cabinet minister called for Chinese villagers to show their commitment to the future of the country by participating in the land programs, but the next day the program director, high ranking in the UMNO, announced that because of a backlog further new applications would be frozen indefinitely. The Chinese leader was thus humiliated by his Malay "ally," and Chinese were made to feel excluded from the government-funded self-help program. As of 1977, 96 percent of the 46,000 families settled on the schemes are *bumiputras* (*Asiaweek*, September 22, 1978: 31).

14. According to 1970 figures, 65 percent of all Malay households fall below the government-defined poverty line, compared with only 26 percent of Chinese households and 39 percent of Indian households. Of the total number of Malaysian households that fall below that line, 74 percent are Malay, 17 percent are Chinese, and 9 percent are Indian.

their economic interests while offering them no increased political security. Malays are reluctant, equally understandably, to share out the political power that to their way of thinking is their only weapon against Chinese economic voracity.

The real power holders in Malaysia are Malays, but the policies they formulate and implement are directed at both Malays and Chinese (and others). Since the objects of policy experience significantly different relationships to the center, as argued in chapter 1, it is logical that more than one pattern of policy must be developed. A "compliance" model set out by Etzioni (1961), analyzing the relationships among goals, power, and compliance in organizations, can be useful here in sorting out the complexities of the Malaysian case.

In general terms, compliance theory holds that certain types of power applied by the superordinate in a power relationship will elicit certain corresponding types of involvement (orientation) on the part of the subordinate. Further, certain types of involvement are most effective in achieving particular kinds of goals (directives). Thus, the pursuit of certain kinds of goals is best served by the use of corresponding types of power, which elicits corresponding modes of involvement. A high degree of congruence of power, goals, and involvement is desirable for maximum effectiveness in attaining goals, so "when environmental constraints allow, organizations move from incongruent goal-compliance combinations to congruent (effective) ones" (Etzioni 1961: 88). Essentially, three types of goals (*ideological, order,* and *economic*) are seen to be most amenable to the use of three corresponding types of power (*normative, coercive,* and *remunerative*). If the goals and power are congruent, subordinates in the compliance relationship can be expected to be motivated toward compliance through corresponding modes of involvement (*commitment, alienation,* or calculative *indifference*).

Etzioni's model was developed with formal organizations in mind, but it has since been modified and applied to larger units that are organizationally integrated — total societies, with governments in the roles of power holders (see Skinner and Winckler 1969). Governmental goals of course do not at any one time fall neatly into only one of the above ideal types: a government is concerned about national unity, national security, and economic development concurrently. But the predominant goal pursued at a given time or in a given circumstance is likely to determine the weight each form of power is given in the "power mix" chosen to serve the pursuit of these unevenly weighted multiple goals. As more than one type of power is used simultaneously, mixed reactions or forms of involvement are likely to be elicited among subordinates. When forms of goals, power, and involvement do not correspond, strains and stresses are set up in the system. When contradictions among goals and compliance structures become severe, the

39

situation may be eased by compartmentalization, which can be either *spatial* or *temporal*, or, in Etzioni's terms, *concomitant* or *successive*.

Concrete examples will make the paradigm more comprehensible. When a country is involved in a civil war such as the Malayan Emergency of the 1950s, order goals are of high priority, and the government is impelled to use a good deal of coercion on those members of society of whose loyalty it feels the least certain: hence the forced relocation program resulting in Malaysia's new villages. If the government hopes to win cooperation and commitment on the part of the people at such times, however, it cannot seek support for its objectives exclusively through coercion. Force, if unmitigated in some way, would only alienate the populace at large. Instead, patriotism or nationalism becomes a widely touted theme as the goverment attempts to rally its supporters around ideological goals through the use of normative inducement, making people feel good as they do their part in the war effort. People will work over the long run, however, for neither normative nor coercive inducements alone; the former lose their validity without some sort of renewal, and the latter drive subordinates toward total alienation. Thus the government is eventually impelled to include remunerative inducements: soldiers receive pay; new villagers receive a promise of land, electricity, water, schools; and so forth.

The general example presented draws on a historical situation representing a single period in which strains in the compliance system were mitigated by a combination of temporal and spatial compartmentalization. The establishment of the new villages can be seen only as coercion, but that coercion was followed by attempts at securing more positive involvement and even commitment to government goals. The government offered the remunerative inducements mentioned above and made more tenuous attempts at helping the relocated Chinese to identify normatively with the government goals through various education and training courses and the establishment of local home guard units (see Short 1975). Even in the jungle warfare, while coercive power naturally predominated, some remunerative and normative inducements were leveled at the insurgents and their supporters as leaflets were scattered promising rewards and future favored treatment for any surrendering rebels or informers who could aid the government forces in locating Communist troops. Moving spatially away from the jungle war and the relocation settlements to the presumably loyal Malay *kampong*s, the government shifted to normative inducements but again included some remunerative incentives. Loyal citizens were exhorted to join the war effort as soldiers for both ideological and economic reasons: the soldier serves his country, earns a salary, and ultimately, as the war is won, contributes to the eventual reestablishment of peace and order and new economic stability for the nation.

Largely as a result of the Emergency and the ghettoization of rural Chinese, Malay and Chinese rural local systems still tend to be spatially and

administratively distinct, especially at the lowest levels. The federally designed administrative structures of local government cut nucleated Chinese
islands out of dispersed Malay settlement patterns across *mukim*s to make
separately governed local council areas (see, for instance, Beaglehole 1976:
71-72), which makes possible the neat spatial compartmentalization of
compliance structures.[15] Each ethnic community bears a distinctly different relationship to the central power holders, both formally and qualita-
tively. The analysis of goals and compliance structures of the Malaysian
leadership in these terms sheds much light on what appear to be contrasting modes of involvement or orientation, expressed in contrasting styles of
political activity, in Chinese and Malay local systems (see chapter 8). It
provides a greatly refined clarity to Bailey's notion of the relative "severity"
of encapsulation, discussed earlier.

The general body of goals publicly espoused by Malaysian leaders is reasonably coherent, but as it is translated into specific policies and programs
directed at a populace bifurcated by the definition of a specially privileged
class of *bumiputras* (logically opposed to non-*bumiputras*), irreconcilable
strains and tensions materialize. Since the meaning and implications of
various goals are different for each group, the orientations of the group
members toward the goals differ, and the forms of power, or power mixes,
that must be used to induce compliance with the stated goals also differ. A
given power mix is not determined by power holders independently of such
considerations. As Skinner and Winckler note, subordinates may "tend
uncontrollably toward a particular mode of involvement, forcing superordinates to change their power mix, and eventually also their immediate
goals" (1969: 412). Stated long-range goals of harmony and equal prosperity for all appear to be pushed out of shape by immediate pressures that
arise out of the modes of involvement of the two groups, sometimes in direct opposition to one another. The leadership may attempt to increase its
short-run effectiveness through communal compartmentalization of its
goal-oriented policies and its compliance relationships. The success of the
strategy in the long run, however, is by no means assured.

Malaysian Goals and Their Inherent Ethnic Contradictions

Economic goals are relatively clear-cut and can be summed up succinctly.
Like most of the developing world, Malaysia is concerned with growth and

15. It is likely that temporal cycling of compliance structures could also be charted in Malaysia, but that complex task is beyond the scope of the present study. The events discussed in
Strauch 1975, chap. 2, indicate sharp alternation in policy as political successes achieved by
one ethnic group are feared and opposed by the other.

prosperity. Since by most evaluations (see, for instance, Tilman 1964: 587; *Far Eastern Economic Review*, 8/31/79: 61-65) Malaysia ranks high on the scale of development, the concern is for continued growth, continued prosperity, and the avoidance of economic setbacks that might grow out of political causes.

A second major focus of economic goals, however, is in some ways directly contradictory to the first, as it is in fact based on political considerations. The government is committed to finding means to advance the rate of Malay participation in the economy of the country. Much economic policy is formulated and implemented to that political end. Quotas, both compulsory and "voluntary," are set in many categories of commercial enterprise, requiring businesses to hire certain percentages of Malay employees at all levels. Government programs make available special financial assistance and incentives to Malay-owned enterprises and offer special training facilities to Malays interested in preparing for business and sales careers. It is not surprising, in the context of constant-pie ideology, that despite real economic growth, Chinese businessmen perceive government manipulations favoring Malays as a threat to their own interests. The Malaysian form of affirmative action subsidizes the economic advancement of one ethnic group and requires what some Chinese perceive as a considerable abridgement of the laissez faire capitalism that prevailed in the past.[16] Whether economic setbacks or recessions for the nation or for any group within it will indeed result is a moot point. The political effects of this economic policy, nonetheless, are very real.

The ideological goals pursued by the Malaysian leadership are even more difficult to present with equivalent appeal to both *bumiputras* and non-*bumiputras*. Most simply stated, the goal is unity, but political symbols of unity equally acceptable to all communities are hard to come by. The call is for united support of the government and the nation, but the appeals are disproportionately couched in Malay terms, implicitly ignoring non-Malays. The symbols are almost exclusively Malay and Muslim, highlighting divergence rather than unity, honoring one culture, the Malay, over the others.

State ritual focuses on Islam and the sultans, the state religion and its prime defenders. Chinese and Indian religious festivals are also national holidays, but public media such as broadcasting networks and newspapers give more fanfare to Hari Raya than to Chinese New Year or Deepavali. Weeks in advance of any Malay holiday, news photos appear daily of some pretty *kampong* wife preparing special cakes to send to her patriotic hus-

16. Stenson (1976: 49-50) points out that this affirmative action does not benefit all Malays equally, but rather has acted to increase class polarization within Malay society, as a small number of well-to-do Malays gain while peasants' real income drops.

band serving away from home in the Royal Malay Regiment. The national mosque and the palaces of the king and the sultans are sources of pride to the Malay community but tend to be resented by non-Malays as a pointless economic drain (Scott 1968: 11). Public service is rewarded yearly with the announcement of Birthday Honors Lists proclaimed by each sultan and by the king; non-Malays as well as Malays are dubbed "Dato" or "Tun"—but the titles derive from Malay tradition, and are bestowed by Malay rulers.[17]

National political symbols ostensibly proclaim multicommunal unity. Everyone can take pride in the modern parliament buildings and in the multicultural body that labors there for the good of the nation, under the leadership of the Barisan Nasional. But the Barisan Nasional is clearly dominated by the UMNO, as are the government and the country. The "alliance" of the several parties is in fact a union formed and existing as a result more of pragmatic considerations than of shared commitment to ideological goals. The functions described, for example, in the 1958 constitution of the Alliance (on which the present Barisan Nasional is based) deal almost exclusively with procedures for general elections (Vasil 1971: 22-24). The original alliance and the current one serve the purposes of getting elected and forming a government, but mutual cooperation and agreement do not necessarily extend to policy decisions. The observation of one pre-Barisan Nasional observer is by no means out of date. Although the UMNO has made some real concessions to the MCA and the MIC, he notes, "the price exacted has always been non-Malay acceptance of UMNO-led Malay political paramouncy within a Malay political culture. To UMNO these issues have been non-negotiable. This setting has assured the maintenance of a Malay preponderance of political power, and a virtual Malay monopoly upon the symbols and framework of political life" (Gagliano 1970: 6).

Issues of citizenship and national language also divide rather than unite, as has been noted above. Citizenship is seen as a natural right for all of Malay stock, including first- and second-generation Indonesian immigrants who as Muslims are considered to be subjects of the sultans, but is less easily accessible to other immigrants and even many second-generation non-Malays. National language policy moves steadily toward virtually exclusive use of Bahasa Malaysia; English, despite its deep local roots and indisputable international utility, is being discarded along with locally

---

17. Some degree of Chinese identification with these titles is seen in the common Chinese name for local-place spirits who often reside in tree trunks or big stones. Chinese set up small shrines and burn incense regularly for these spirits, called in Cantonese *natogung*. Though the spirits are honored by Chinese, they are usually thought of as Malay; one in particular that I know of was seen wearing a Malay *songkok* (a hat) and spoke Malay to the several Chinese who saw him.

used vernaculars. Non-Malays generally pay lip service to the use of Malay, but in fact feel threatened by the changes.

In sum, though the ideological goal — national unity — is clear, the practical implementation that the government envisions remains murky: to what extent is Malaysian nationalism in fact still Malay nationalism? However genuine its intentions to create a multicommunal unity might be, the government is clearly hindered by the fact that the normative inducements it controls and emphasizes are likely to hold far more attraction symbolically for one segment of the population than for the other.

Finally, order goals in Malaysia are directed toward two chronic problems: the continuing communist guerrilla activity and the latent threat of the eruption of communal violence. The communist problem occasionally becomes acute, as it did in 1971, when a large jungle camp was found in Perak and four Chinese new villages were refenced and put under curfew for several months. Curfews were widespread in northern Perak again for a time in 1976. The continued potential for racial violence in Malaysia's plural society was made only too clear in the 1969 riots. Tension remains latent, but it does not fade away completely. Government order goals are concerned primarily with these two issues, for individual crimes against persons or property are considerably less prevalent than in many Western countries. Government policies designed to maintain order tend to be directed at groups rather than individuals, and ideological groupings are assumed to coincide to some extent with communal groupings: Chinese are considered to be the backbone of the communist movement, despite the increasing involvement of Malay dissidents from southern Thailand.

Government goals, while conceptually separable, are of course in practice intertwined. Economic development and national solidarity are emphasized jointly, but it is recognized, and lamented, that the two major communities do not share jointly the benefits and responsibilities of either. The government is faced with the difficult task of balancing the two, trying to avoid alienation on the part of either community, and if possible, win the commitment of both. A 1967 statement of the government's understanding of the dilemma it faced then (and now), however, could hardly be very reassuring to the Chinese. The late prime minister, Tun Haji Abdul Razak bin Hussein, made the following statement as deputy prime minister in an interview broadcast in New Zealand: "It is true at the moment that political power is in the hands of the Malaysians and economic power is in the hands of the Chinese. That is why we must try and balance things out. That is why we are doing our best to try and give the Malays a little bit of a share in the economic life to enable them to feel safe in the country. After all, they were the original settlers" (quoted by the interviewer, Vasil 1971: 5). Two points are troublesome. First, Razak contrasts "Malaysians" with "Chinese," thereby depriving the Chinese of a legitimate national label of identification. The semantic, but highly symbolic, slip pales, however, beside the firm expression of a conception of "balancing things out" that would mean added economic power for Malays without any suggestion of increased political power for Chinese.

Malaysian Compliance Structures

The power mixes chosen for use in inducing compliance will depend in part on what the power holders have available to them, what incentives in their control will work most effectively with the subordinates from whom they seek compliance. Skinner and Winckler define normative power as that "based on persuasion, promises, and the manipulation of symbolic rewards." The effective use of such power ideally generates strong positive commitment, and it is especially appropriate to ideological goals. Remunerative power, by contrast, "rests on the rationalized exchange of compliance for material rewards," and tends to generate calculative indifference, involvement of a low intensity, but it is effective in inducing people "to produce and exchange goods and services" (1969: 412).

Normative power is thus premised on a degree of commonality, a sharing of symbolic values that is a prerequisite if symbols offered as rewards are to be accepted and received as rewards rather than with indifference. Remunerative power, on the other hand, is based on the principle of exchange, offering rewards of material rather than symbolic value. Affinity between partners in exchange is neither required nor precluded. I have argued that Malay local systems — that is, Malay subordinates in the political system of Malaysia — have relatively more in common with the center in terms of cultural and symbolic values, while Chinese are closer to the center in terms of orientations toward modernity and the sort of rationality that is congruent with economic development. Thus the center readily controls normative power vis-a-vis one group only, Malays, with whom a strong sense of community exists, while its remunerative inducements can be expected to be effective vis-à-vis both groups at the periphery, though Chinese may weight them more carefully, calculating the degree of involvement or indifference given inducements may be seen to merit.

The Malay-dominated federal government has hardly attempted to dilute symbolic rewards in such a way that they might have some meaningful attraction to both subordinate groups. Instead, it has opted for a concentration of Malay-oriented symbolic inducements aimed at enlisting full support from the Malay half of the population, rather than risking a wider appeal that might succeed in arousing only an unstable partial commitment from a broader representation of the Malaysian cultural spectrum. This choice has not proven entirely successful, for PAS support continues

to be fairly strong in popular vote, despite its 1978 electoral defeats as measured by seats won and lost.[18] But the pattern is firmly set, and could not
be easily reversed: normatively, the government is consistently backing the
bumiputra horse. In remunerative terms, the government controls rewards
that are attractive to all communities. Coercion, if used at all, must be
used with care, or resulting alienation could nullify both the commitment
demanded of the Malays and the indifference tolerated on the part of the
Chinese.

Malays.
Ideological and economic goals are strongly emphasized with Malays, and
there is a tacit expectation that the positive commitment generated by a
judicious combination of normative and remunerative rewards will obviate
any need for coercion. The New Economic Policy coincides in principle
with Malay demands for an improved standard of living, but Malay expectations of immediate results tend to be somewhat unrealistic. There is a
legacy of paternalistic nurturance of the *bumiputras*, which was part of
British colonial policy and is now enshrined in the concept of Malay "special rights." The land reservations, rural resettlement schemes providing
government-planted rubber or oil palm land, favored status for Malay
businesses, easy loans, quotas for licenses, and so forth, that are in fact
forthcoming seem to indicate that the government accepts responsibility
for the welfare of the *bumiputras*, at least in principle, although their notion of "welfare" may be seen to be colored by class interests.

To counteract inflated expectations, the government makes use of normative calls for support for its programs and understanding of its difficulties. Malay peasants and small businessmen are exhorted to adopt new
attitudes and to improve work and saving habits. They are assured that Islamic law does not prohibit good business practice, and are reminded that
the government, although it is doing its best, cannot spoonfeed the people
forever; the people must accept some responsibility for improving their
economic lot by following the government's lead, making full use of the
opportunities it gives them, and changing their ways. The real economic
gains accruing to the diligent Malay farmer or shopkeeper are thus supplemented by the good feeling of government approval. He is assured that in
serving the economic interests of himself and his family he is also serving
his people and his country.

Some Malay critics of the UMNO feel that land reservations and license
quotas are insufficient, that Islam should be not the favored religion but

---

18. In the 1978 West Malaysian parliamentary elections, the ten-party Barisan Nasional
won 94 of a total of 114 seats (82.5 percent) though it polled only 55.14 percent of the total
vote cast; the PAS won only 3 seats but 17 percent of the vote.

the only religion, that Malaysia should belong solely to Malays, and that until non-Malay infidels can be driven out they should at least be restricted to definitely second-class status in as many areas as possible. The government considers these critics hotheads, dangerous in their propensity toward radical and if necessary violent solutions to Malaysia's problems, in direct contradiction to government order goals. But because of their positive appeal to Malay sentiments, their leaders must be placated rather than controlled through coercion. However, the normative appeals, coupled with political concessions and economic favors, that initially induced the strongest of these opposition leaders to bring the PAS into the coalition in 1972 showed declining efficacy in Kelantan in November 1977. Martial law was temporarily imposed, and the PAS eventually left the government coalition. The UMNO then went directly to the people with the normative persuasions and, more importantly, promises of massive economic investment. The UMNO's success in the 1978 elections indicates that at present a remunerative-normative power mix, heavy on the former, has more appeal than the primarily normative power PAS has used as its staple over the years, having little else at its disposal.[19]

Malay extremists within the ranks must also be dealt with from time to time. One UMNO man considered valuable to the party, who was guilty of indiscretion in intraparty power maneuvering in the aftermath of the May 13 riots, was allowed to retain his parliament seat but was advised to go off to England for graduate study. He was brought back a year or so later and has advanced through the party hierarchy to an important position in the cabinet. Another, the author of a pro-Malay book banned in Malaysia as racially inflammatory, was publicly dishonored by expulsion from the party for a time, but he has since been reinstated and now holds the position of deputy prime minister. In these cases a touch of coercion is followed (after a change of top leadership in the UMNO) by a reminder of the pleasant reward awaiting those who show restraint in accordance with the government line, and these men now in fact help to set that line.

The government does not totally eschew coercive power in dealing with Malays, but when possible its use is greatly minimized. Non-Malays tend to believe that allegations of exaggerated restraint shown by Malay forces toward Malay rioters during the May 13 disturbances are true, constituting proof that the government is unwilling to use coercion against Malays in defense of non-Malays. The New Economic Policy can be seen as a pure case of the use of economic inducements to pursue order goals (see, for example, Gagliano 1970: 30). The normative-remunerative mix extended to Malays is problematic because promises of material benefit offered to induce positive commitment may sometimes exceed the economic rewards

---

19. See Kessler (1978) for a thorough analysis of pre-1969 PAS support in Kelantan.

available to be handed out. Class tension and strain are exacerbated when raised Malay expectations are not met, and these may too readily be diverted to ethnic conflict.

Chinese.

The compliance relationship between the Chinese community and the government contrasts sharply with the relationship outlined above. Chinese attitudes toward the Malay political and religious symbols meant to serve as focuses of national unity fall understandably short of positive commitment. The MCA, charged with the task of rallying Chinese loyalty to the government, has been hindered by the UMNO's insistence on an MCA leadership dependent more on UMNO support than on support from the Chinese community. Since the government has little normative appeal to offer the Chinese, it must concentrate heavily on remunerative power, wielded effectively to maintain calculative involvement in the economic sphere, the area in which Chinese compliance is of most concern. The government seldom employs overt coercive power—except in the case of the Communist guerrillas, a group apart—but Chinese feel an implicit threat, particularly since the May 13 incidents.

The government strategy aimed at indirect recourse to normative power that might be effective in relation to the Chinese community is so complex as to be self-defeating. Accepting the present impossibility of direct positive Chinese involvement with the dominant Malay political culture, the UMNO posits a communal solution whereby the government creates and controls Chinese leaders, who are then expected to manipulate normative appeals to win support directly for themselves, and thus indirectly for the government. This was done until 1974 within the context of the UMNO-MCA Alliance. As Vasil sees it, "The general pattern is that a Chinese politician first becomes a leader in the Government and the Alliance, and only later emerges as a leader of the MCA. Association with the Government gives him a position where he can distribute favors and gather support for himself within the party" (1971: 35).[20] MCA power holders claim their right to unquestioned leadership of the Chinese on the basis of their good contacts with the UMNO. They plead with their community to accept the political necessity of a degree of appeasement and subservience within the Alliance. Many Chinese workers and farmers, however, feel that the MCA leadership has sold out to the UMNO and does not represent their interests. Widespread disillusionment of this sort led to the heavy MCA losses in the 1969 elections and the success of the MCA task force in 1971-1973.

The UMNO delegated responsibility for control of normative power to

20. The current MCA national chairman, Lee San Choon, seems to be an exception in that when he came into office in 1974 he did not have strong links to the UMNO; his position in the government has been correspondingly weak.

the MCA, but at the same time it undermined any real potential the MCA might have had for fulfilling that responsibility. Control of normative symbols has thus been an open prize to be fought for within the Chinese community. However, organizations that begin to present effective appeals for unity and loyalty tend to be successfully subverted in one way or another by government leaders, both Malay and Chinese. The 1971-1973 conflict between the MCA old guard and new challengers for leadership of the Chinese will be discussed at length in chapter 7.

Chinese compliance with economic goals is of utmost importance. The government indicates its concern for this in its somewhat more judicious and successful manipulation of remunerative power. A certain amount of recognition is given to the historical role played by Chinese laborers and entrepreneurs in the development of Malaysia to its current high standard, and to their continuing central position in the economic sphere of the country; Chinese dominate the distribution network, though they still rank far behind foreign interests in share capital investment. If Chinese businessman are to persist in financing and managing a significant portion of the economic expansion in the locally based private sector, sufficient economic rewards must continue to be forthcoming. Here remunerative power plays its standard role.

However, the Malaysian government must obtain the further cooperation of the Chinese to effect increased Malay participation in the private sector of the economy, a quasi-political goal that many Chinese tend to see as contrary to their own interests. Chinese are required to employ and train Malays in management, often to see them leave to start their own rival businesses with government-granted favored status. At all levels of business, even down to the small family shops, Chinese must hire a certain token percentage of Malay workers. As a group, Chinese are asked not to be resentful when quotas are established and strictly observed in the issuing of various licenses and permits.

Chinese compliance in these economic matters is obtained primarily through manipulation of remunerative power, as is appropriate. Chinese businessmen do, of course, continue to make money, if not quite at the rate they might have under the British and in times of higher rubber and tin prices. Still, fortunes are made and increased. Remunerative power in its negative form may be used in the economic sphere as well, as action is occasionally taken against "pirate" taxi drivers and peddlers unable to obtain licenses because of quota restrictions.[21] Sanctions could similarly be

---

21. An example of the consequences of this policy was the hopeless overloading and consequent disruption of public transportation in the predominantly Chinese city of Ipoh in 1972 when a police crackdown removed hundreds of unlicensed Chinese taxi drivers from the streets, despite the dependence of workers and school children on these taxis for daily transportation, and the lack of sufficient Malay applicants to fill their quota.

employed against a businessman refusing to hire Malays, depriving him of his means of earning a living.

Coercive power is also a component of this power mix, in a more indirect but constant form—lightly veiled threats by the government of unstated consequences should the Chinese business community fail to cooperate with government goals. Government officials, such as the late deputy prime minister, Tun Ismail, have periodically made public statements to the effect that the Chinese "had better cooperate," often in the context of a speech to the Malay Chamber of Commerce, the Malay business college, or some similar body (for example, *Straits Times*, August 14, 1971). The implication is that the government cannot be responsible for righteous Malay outrage, and its logical outcome, if the Chinese should appear in any sense to be holding back rather than extending a helping hand to their Malay brothers.[22]

Control over coercive power is virtually monopolized by Malays. Though precise figures are not available, both the police force and the army are manned disproportionately by Malays, and an entire regiment of thirteen battalions is exclusively Malay. Although a significant minority of the current underground communist force is thought to be Malay, largely dissidents from southern Thailand, coercive measures such as those used against Chinese villagers in upper Perak, who were suspected of supporting communist guerrillas presumed to be Chinese, tend to be leveled only at Chinese villagers. Malay villagers, it appears, are deemed more susceptible to a heavy application of normative power, administered through local religious leaders who remind these staunch Muslims that Islam is incompatible with communism. Although normative power in the form of calls for loyalty is also applied to Chinese, its value as normative power per se is very likely neutralized by the concurrent application of coercion in the form of fences and curfews.

Maintenance of order across the national arena probably rests primarily on the generally high standard of living and well-being in Malaysia. Chinese seem to be willing to bear a great deal of political pressure as long as their rice bowls are not seriously threatened, and as far as is currently known, new recruits to the guerrilla cause are relatively few. If the pressure on Chinese political and cultural rights continues to increase, however, or if economic prosperity declined and the government were unable to sustain remunerative power, the situation could change. The Malaysian powder keg could eventually explode, calling for strong coercive response by the

---

22. When statements of this sort are seen in the light of the May 13 riots—when Malay anger, righteous or not, caused scores or perhaps hundreds of Chinese deaths while official response, as the Chinese see it, offered inadequate protection at best—such an inference comes easily to the Chinese mind.

government. In the meantime, the government power mix toward the Chinese, essentially remunerative-coercive, is effective in maintaining economic output with minimal disturbance.

The foregoing model of government strategies is, like all models, useful only as a guide rather than as a perfect reflection of a complex reality. It offers an interesting perspective on the issue of encapsulation. Discussing the role of the external political context in shaping local-level political activity, Bujra poses a number of cogent questions about the ideological thrust of government policy regarding local systems: "What is the national policy in relation to rural areas, and who has to explain and implement this at the local level? Do government policies threaten (or alternatively reinforce) the position of any particular local class or category of people, or do they affect all equally? To what extent is government action motivated toward creating a local-level political consciousness so that demand for change comes from the grass roots? Alternatively, is the government simply interested in a passive and loyal electorate?" (1973: 150).

In Malaysia, national policy toward Malay and Chinese rural systems differs. The government would like a loyal electorate, but if loyalty is at all in question, passivity is accepted in its place. The Malay masses, despite increasingly significant factionalism within the UMNO, continuing problems between the UMNO and the PAS, and periodic eruptions of peasant unrest, are on the whole assumed with little question to be loyal to the nation and to the government — and the two are too often equated — if occasionally "misguided."[23] The Chinese masses, by contrast, are still exhorted to prove their loyalty, as if it were a matter of doubt.[24] Malays are not only encouraged to participate actively in the variety of government economic

23. Recent anti-government disturbances have included a Malay squatter protest in Johore in 1974 and Malay peasant demonstrations in Kedah against low rubber prices in 1974 and again against low rice prices and a forced savings scheme in 1980. Students have demonstrated in active support of these peasant movements as well.

24. The loyalty of Chinese Malaysians is often questioned by innuendo, not only in specifically political contexts, such as the Perak task force mobilization program to be discussed in chapter 7, but in other contexts as well. For example, when the Chinese community complied with the government's wishes to keep the Vietnamese refugee issue from being fully aired internally, opposition leader Lim Kit Siang bemoaned the lack of humanitarian assistance being offered the refugees (who were largely ethnic Chinese), but praised the "conduct of the Chinese community" in avoiding any action that "could remotely be misconstrued as siding with ethnic Chinese from other countries against the welfare and interests of Malaysia," noting that such conduct "should be accepted and recognized by all Malaysians as a mark of loyalty and attachment to Malaysia" (quotations from a speech delivered in Kuala Lumpur, July 15, 1979; see Strauch 1980b). Thus, by offering a defense, the "victim" implicitly accepts the "blame," seemingly acknowledging the legitimacy of fears of "disloyalty" — though such legitimacy would never be granted should the question be raised explicitly, which may be why it seldom is. Such protestations of loyalty would never be offered on behalf of the Malay community as a whole, for it would never be questioned in a similar manner.

programs established as part of the New Economic Policy and "restructuring of society" begun under the Second Malaysia Plan and continued under the Third, they are also urged to take an active political role, through the UMNO and UMNO Youth branches that cover the countryside. But Chinese are explicitly excluded from many government economic programs and are offered somewhat less incentive to political activism as well. The government appears less than sanguine, perhaps realistically so, about the measure of enthusiastic support that spontaneous Chinese public sentiment might embody for a Malay political culture.

In small Chinese communities such as Sanchun, a holding pattern, both economically and politically, seems to be all that is expected or desired by the superordinate powers. Sanchun's economic well-being is secure, though little surplus is produced to be either fought over internally or drained off by external interests. Sanchun is neither expected nor required to play an active role in meeting any national development goals of the sort that tend to affect Malay local communities at one end of the scale and big Chinese capitalists at the other. The outcome of the MCA mobilization of the early 1970s suggests that in political terms Chinese are considered better citizens if they maintain their long-standing passive low profile than if they join together to participate in active party politics, expressing political consciousness motivating a demand for change within their own Chinese party.

The extended case study provided in the following chapters supports the argument that so far has been defended only from a macrolevel perspective, and applied by inference to the microlevel. The Sanchun historical and social background provides the setting for the introduction of personalities and cliques who, as local-level leaders, find themselves caught up in the political developments of the 1970s, and respond within the limited parameters described for them by an encapsulating political environment firmly committed to the maintenance of the status quo.

3

Sanchun from Origins to Independence

The dominant topographic feature of the Malayan peninsula is the high mountain range stretching more than halfway down the peninsula slightly west of center. Much of the population of West Malaysia is concentrated in the relatively narrow belt between this mountain chain and the sea, the Straits of Malacca. Two of the largest cities, Kuala Lumpur, the capital, and Ipoh, the center of the Kinta mining district in Perak, lie 130 miles apart on a line near the extreme inland extension of this population belt, about thirty miles from the coast. The major north-south transportation routes, the railroad and the main highway, follow this line, approaching the coast more closely only to the north and to the south of these two cities, also moving inland south of the mountain chain.

Located just between these closely aligned transportation routes, somewhat north of the midpoint between Kuala Lumpur and Ipoh, is the town of Sanchun. The present settlement lies about a mile north of the original market site on the Sungai Sanchun (the Sanchun River), which flows down from the mountains, meandering on a westerly course to join the Sungai Perak on its way to the sea. Thirty or so of the forty miles between Sanchun and the straits to the west are largely freshwater tidal mangrove swamps, some areas of which have been reclaimed with complex systems of dikes for wet rice and other types of cultivation. Immediately surrounding Sanchun are extensive rubber estates, forest lands, and large reserves held for tin mining. A few miles to the east are the mountains, sparsely populated by small bands of aborigines and logging teams. Traveling by road either north or south, one reaches in fifteen miles or so the eastern rim of other areas of population concentration stretching westward to the sea. In the early days the river itself was probably the most direct route to the coastal towns, navigable by *perahu* (small boats), but today it is no longer used for transport.

53

The Early Days of Chinese Settlement

Chinese settlement in the Sanchun area goes back not more than a hundred years. Ancestors of the family now claiming longest continuous residence were shopkeepers who arrived around 1895, but some Chinese laborers had preceded the merchants. Malay *kampongs* (villages often featuring dispersed settlement) dotted the area before the coming of the Chinese and Indians, but the length of earlier Malay settlement is unknown. By 1890, British rubber interests were moving into the area, employing Chinese to clear jungle tracts and plant rubber seedlings. Tamil Indians were imported as tappers, and some Chinese also tapped for British estates. More Chinese, however, acquired smallholdings of their own. The first Chinese shophouses were built adjacent to the river; in 1907, probably to take advantage of improved roads and to avoid periodic flooding, the shops were moved to their present site on higher land. Today there are eight blocks of traditional southern Chinese two-storied stone shophouses. All of the forty-eight shops were in place by 1925. There are a few Indian shops catering to the tastes of Indian tappers on nearby estates, but most of these shops have always been owned and operated by Chinese.

By the 1920s the nucleus of the present market center was firmly established. About two or three hundred Chinese lived in this market center, and nearly ten times that number were scattered throughout the area. Like *Nanyang* Chinese everywhere, the Sanchun Chinese were predominantly male. An elderly pharmacist recalls seeing only eight or ten Chinese women in the town when he arrived fifty years ago, but in any case women in those days would not have ventured out in public very often. Most shopkeepers had originally come to Sanchun as single laborers, saving their wages until they could begin small businesses. If business went well, they might eventually return to China for a bride or write for one to be sent. Since the actual selection was left to the man's parents, a mail-order bride was as good as any other, and cheaper. The round-trip passage at that time was quite inexpensive, but the more elaborate and ostentatious wedding celebration that would be necessary if the man returned to the village could use up capital needed for business investment.

The first Chinese to arrive in the Sanchun area were Cantonese and Kwongsai (Guangxi) laborers, followed later by Hokkien (Fujian) and Cantonese merchants. About two-thirds of the Chinese in the area found work connected with the booming rubber industry, either tapping or doing odd jobs for estates, or working their own smallholdings of five or ten acres. Other common jobs included clearing light jungle, heavy logging, construction, rickshaw transportation of goods, and growing vegetables for local sale. People who dealt in special items such as cloth, gold, and herbs and pharmaceutical goods usually arrived in Sanchun prepared to open

54

new shops. Sundry-goods merchants and coffee shop owners more often than not had first worked in the area as wage laborers, possibly as shop assistants, and only later managed to go into business for themselves.

Occupational specialization tended to follow social divisions based on common language and place of origin in China. Secret societies existed that offered mutual aid and protection, but according to informants membership was not compulsory. They also served as labor organizations. The two most active societies in the Sanchun area were rivals comprised of rickshaw pullers from two neighboring districts in Fujian province. In the early years there were frequent fights between the two societies over hauling contracts, but as more draft animals and eventually motorized transport came into the area, members were forced to find other types of jobs, and these two societies gradually disappeared. One informant tells of another secret society connected with the logging industry, of which his first patron was a member. When he signed on as an apprentice to this master logger, he was asked to join the society, but he maintains that he chose not to, and found that it did not affect his working relationships nor his future jobs. Logging bosses who were members of a given society never hired rivals, but were willing to employ both fellow members and independents.

Associations based on common surname played no role in Sanchun society, but some of the native-place associations (*tongxiang huiguan*) from the nearby larger towns sent representatives to the Sanchun area to recruit members. Rubber tappers and loggers showed little interest in joining. Even merchants, who were more likely to benefit from such affiliation, hesitated to join both the *huiguan* and the regional Chinese Chamber of Commerce until they felt themselves well established, for new businesses often failed within the first three or four years, and traders who failed usually moved on. The only formal organizations existing in Sanchun prior to 1930 were the cemetery committee, established in 1910, and the school, which opened in 1922 with twenty-eight pupils, expanded to thirty-six in its second year, and continued to grow rapidly. That death and education should provide the first focuses for communal effort and cooperation is an interesting commentary on the transference of traditional Chinese values to the *Nanyang*.

The early settlement of the Sanchun area is probably fairly representative of much of the country that developed primarily around rubber production rather than tin mining. Most of the early Sanchun settlers had first sought work elsewhere in Malaya, in cities or perhaps in mines, and eventually moved on, arriving in Sanchun, again seeking work, again often moving on. The Hokkien shopkeepers were exceptions. They came looking for a place to open a business and settle more permanently. It was they who could afford visits to China every few years, bringing back wives, or perhaps only sons, to establish real homes. As rubber land became available and profitable, others began to settle down as well, but there continued to be much in- and out-migration throughout the area up through the Depression and probably during the Japanese occupation, ending temporarily under the restrictions of the Emergency. Occasionally the British owners of a newly established rubber estate decided to use Chinese labor and dispatched a Chinese agent to his native district in China to recruit a group of one or two hundred workers, but more often immigrant workers drifted casually as individuals or in small groups, joining a relative in one town, someone from the same native place (*tongxiang*) in the next, or just following an urge to see what the next town might offer. Until the invasion of China by Japan in 1937, it was common for Chinese to return to China permanently. In sum, it was a society very much in flux, except for a small core, most of whom were merchants. Nonetheless, informants agree that there was rapid overall growth in the Sanchun community in the years preceding the Depression.

The economy of Malaya, based almost exclusively on rubber and tin, was seriously affected by the Depression, for both commodities dropped greatly in value on the world market. In the Sanchun area the rubber estates and smallholders suffered losses first; as tappers' purchasing power declined, the shops felt the pinch. One informant estimated that nearly half of the shops closed. Some of the owners joined the move to subsistence cultivation to get through the slump and later reopened.

In larger towns the government provided free food to those in need, as well as the offer of free tickets back to China or to India. Tin mine workers, having little access to arable or even marginal land (tin mining strips the soil and leaves barren sand), often had no alternative to repatriation. There were no mines in the Sanchun area at that time, however, and most local people were able to get by, growing their own vegetables and keeping a few chickens. Prices in the shops that remained open were extremely low. Estates gave their tappers small maintenance allowances, which was cheaper than repatriating the laborers and later having to send for them when the economic situation improved.

As things stabilized following the Depression, Sanchun, like the rest of the Nanyang, benefited from the increase in the number of Chinese women among the new immigrants. More and more families came and stayed. Women worked with men in the rubber gardens and even in logging camps, and the community, though still widely dispersed, took on a more permanent, settled nature.

In prewar years, members of different speech groups often mistrusted each other, and disputes arose in which joint mediation by leaders of two or more speech groups was required to reach resolution satisfactory to all parties. Intermarriage between speech groups was then rare, a circumstance no doubt influenced by the simple fact that most brides still came directly from the husband's native district in China, and there were still few second-generation young people growing up together. Since the war and the concentration of the population under the Emergency regulations, however, speech-group differences have become attenuated, and intermarriage is no longer uncommon. Although Hokkiens had predominated in the shop section, the more numerous laborers in the surrounding area were chiefly Cantonese, and Cantonese has now become the lingua franca in the market town as well as throughout the region.

Leadership in Sanchun, as in most overseas Chinese communities, devolved upon wealthy merchants who had proven themselves through their success and demonstrated skills worthy of respect. Since most of the original shopkeepers in Sanchun were Hokkien, it followed that the early informal headmen of the market area were Hokkien. Similarly, the temple they built was dedicated to a group of heroes legendary in Fujian province, the Nine Gods (*jiuhuangye* — literally, nine emperors). The functions of the leadership elite included serving on the temple and cemetery committees, the school board of managers, and, from its founding in 1936, the executive board of the Sanchun Recreation Club (its primary activity is gambling).

In keeping with the British policy of indirect rule, internal affairs in Sanchun were only slightly affected by the presence of the official British colonial government; "encapsulation proper" prevailed. The district headquarters, Papar, where the British district officer was stationed, was sixteen miles distant. In a town of that size or larger the Chinese Kapitan might receive an official title, such as justice of the peace or Dato. In smaller settlements such as Sanchun, no official recognition was given the headman, though he was expected to handle most local affairs himself, without calling on the half-dozen Malay policemen likely to be posted there to serve the *mukim*. Given traditional Chinese distrust of police stations and courts of law, it is not surprising that very few disputes reached official casebooks.

The Chinese headman in Sanchun from the 1920s until his death in 1937 was a Hokkien shopkeeper who was formally chairman of the school board, an important locus of power where virtually all of the wealthy local families were represented. After the shopkeeper's death the family business declined; his survivors were forced to sell out and move to Ipoh. Taking his place as the chairman of the school board and as the local headman was another Hokkien shopkeeper and rubber dealer, Tan Tien Yu. Though neither of these men was officially recognized by the British government, the district officer made direct contact with them when any problem or matter of business arose that affected Sanchun Chinese. Similarly, any local Chinese wishing a matter brought to official attention called upon this unofficial headman to act as an intermediary. British indirect rule thus extended all the way down the line, utilizing separately the leaders of Chinese, Malay, and Indian communities at the local level.

The Japanese Occupation

In 1941 the Japanese invaded Malaya from the north and pushed south to Singapore in a few short weeks. Still, there was time enough for people in the towns along the main route south, including Sanchun, to take to the jungle to avoid the expected onslaught. Most returned to the towns within a few weeks or a month or two, as the occupation settled into a regularized pattern. Sanchun suffered little during the advance. The first unit of Japanese soldiers to pass through is remembered almost warmly, at least by comparison with those who later took charge in Sanchun for the duration of the occupation. The soldiers of the first group were orderly and well mannered, and they often paid for the bicycles and tinned goods they took. The looting that occurred was at the hands of local people, both opportunists and honest but poor and frightened people, securing caches for the unknown days ahead. When the next Japanese unit arrived and settled in, the worst of their fears were realized.

Throughout Malaya, occupation conditions tended to be worse for Chinese than for Malays or Indians. Japan and China had had a long history of enmity, culminating in the Japanese invasion of China in 1937; Chinese everywhere were considered, and treated as, enemies. Malays and Indians, however, were told they were being "liberated" from the oppression of European colonialism to join the "Greater East-Asia Co-Prosperity Sphere," and were encouraged to participate in the administration of the country. The only active resistance force, the Malayan People's Anti-Japanese Army (MPAJA), was largely Chinese in makeup and was led by the Malayan Communist Party (MCP). The consequent exacerbation of communal divisions within the Malayan population was to have serious repercussions following the war (see, for example, Means 1976: 44-47).

In Sanchun, as elsewhere, Chinese men and boys were taken away to serve in labor gangs, and many never returned. More than a hundred were arrested and executed during the occupation, many of these in an incident involving the MPAJA and a Bengali police officer serving under the Japanese. The MPAJA attacked the police barracks and murdered the Bengali's wife before his eyes; he retaliated by arresting a number of local Chinese allegedly involved in providing material support to the resistance forces. All were executed by the Japanese.

Many Chinese tried to isolate their young men from the unpredictable wrath of the Japanese by establishing hideouts deep in the jungle. Smallholders and loggers who were out of work because of the general economic chaos planted small plots on the jungle fringes to maintain a subsistence living. Because of widespread food shortages, townspeople were encouraged by the Japanese to do the same. Thus large numbers of Chinese lived within reach of the jungle-based MPAJA, and although many of them tried to avoid involvement of any kind, the Japanese considered all of them likely subversives. Constant suspicion led occasionally to torture, as the Japanese tried to get information on MPAJA support sources.

One serious incident involved a merchant, Lung Sooi, and a family headed by a logger, Lee Koi, both of whom are important leaders in the Sanchun community today.[1] Lee had a house hidden deep in the jungle. His friend Lung, under brutal torture, revealed its location, but was able to get a warning to Lee before the Japanese arrived, and the house was empty when they opened fire. Lee maintains that he had no connection with the MPAJA, but he had stocked a good supply of small bombs used to stun river fish. The Japanese gunfire set off a series of alarming explosions that confirmed their suspicions of having found a resistance stronghold. The Japanese took further reprisals against local Chinese as a result, as it was "proven" that the Chinese had contacts with and supported the MPAJA.

The Chinese could not completely avoid cooperation with the Japanese authorities. The established local leaders, obvious because of their wealth and their membership on various organization boards, were ordered to form a "maintenance committee," and Tan Tien Yu was appointed its head. The committee's main duties were collecting subscriptions from merchants to be paid to the Japanese, and forming a night patrol to give warning of any further MPAJA attacks. The demands made by the occupying Japanese on Sanchun were thus somewhat more severe than the British demands had been, and the constraints imposed on local action were more stringent.

When, upon the sudden surrender and departure of the Japanese, the MPAJA took over the police station and local administration, they apparently distinguished between forced collaboration and a more voluntary type, for their reprisals did not affect any members of Sanchun's maintenance committee. Nonetheless, more Chinese were executed by the MPAJA as alleged collaborators than Malays and Indians, and their executions were often public, as a warning to Chinese who would turn against their brothers; Malays and Indians were punished more quietly, but often as severely. In addition to these police activities, members of the MPAJA

---

1. This particular incident is one of a series illuminating the relationship between Lee Koi and Lung Sooi, who through the years have been among the most influential and respected men in the Sanchun Chinese community; its import will be seen more clearly below, in chapter 5.

helped to reopen the Chinese school, which had been closed by the Japanese, and they provided teaching not only in traditional subjects but on politics as well, although the latter classes, I was told, were not well attended and apparently had little effect. The British returned to resume authority about three months after the Japanese surrender.

Informants talk about the occupation as a very difficult time, but it is now far in the past, and, they say, life has always been difficult anyway. A small market center was of prime importance to neither the Japanese nor the MPAJA; thus from neither side were demands on Sanchun excessive. Passive cooperation with the Japanese, if one lived in town, and with the MPAJA, if one lived in the jungle, proved the most effective means for personal survival.

The Malayan Emergency

Information on the brief interim between the occupation and the Emergency is sparse. People in Sanchun were grateful for the return of normal daily life, the renewed flow of goods from the outside, and the renewed demand for rubber and timber. Some shopkeepers returned and reopened their businesses. Logging enterprises began operation again, as did rubber processing factories, and large export firms were once again activated throughout the country. Sanchun families could send their children to school again. (Rich merchants tended even then to send their children to Ipoh or Penang, where the better Chinese-language primary and secondary schools were located.) Life gradually resumed its familiar pattern.

A brief three years after the end of the world war, however, there came another war of a different kind, as the MPAJA regrouped under the aegis of the Malayan Communist Party (MCP) and returned to the jungles to begin a protracted guerrilla war of independence. When, despite the support they had offered the British as a resistance force, they were refused a role in the postwar government, they once again picked up arms. In June 1948, following a series of well-coordinated attacks on European-owned plantations, police stations, tin mines, and transportation lines, the government declared a state of emergency (see Stenson 1969). The MCP strategy was to strike a sudden and telling blow at the national economy, inflicting casualties on the security forces and capturing quantities of arms and ammunition. Assassination squads murdered not only European planters, isolated on their plantations, but also Chinese Guomindang officials and Chinese police detectives in more urban areas. The overall organization and coordination of the offensive, however, was weak, and the damage inflicted was absorbed. The populace tended to be more frightened and alienated by the random terrorist activity than "awakened" and eager to follow the banner of Communism. With the failure of the initial offensive, the guerrillas retreated to jungle camps to retrench and reorganize. For the next eleven years they were almost continually on the defensive, fighting a war of attrition against increasingly well prepared government security forces.

The revolutionaries were believed to number between four and five thousand in 1948, including large numbers of ex-guerrillas from the anti-Japanese forces and teen-age recruits of both sexes from the Chinese secondary schools. All but a small minority were Chinese. The Malays and Indians on the whole supported the government, and enlisted enthusiastically in the security forces and the police. The Chinese did not necessarily support the Communists, but neither were they confident that taking sides with the government would be wise — they had been given a harsh lesson by the MPAJA after the withdrawal of the Japanese. Moreover, soldiering is not a traditionally valued occupation among Chinese, and Chinese as yet lacked a sense of commitment to Malaya as a nation; Chinese did not join the government forces in significant numbers.

In the early years of the Emergency, guerrilla forces were consistently replenished with new recruits, some of them forced into the jungle by circumstances beyond their control. People involved voluntarily or otherwise with the civilian support group, the Min Yuen, were sometimes "warned" that their activities were about to come to the attention of the authorities; their only safe course of action, in that case, was to go "inside." The guerrilla strength was believed to be at its height in 1951, numbering about eight thousand, of which perhaps thirty percent were nonfighting support and supply groups. This maximum strength had fallen to about twenty-five hundred by 1957, with a somewhat higher percentage working in various branches of the Min Yuen (Clutterbuck 1966: 87).

Although even in 1948 the government and the economy were never seriously threatened, the declaration of a state of emergency and the implementation of severe emergency regulations were seen as a necessary response to the Communist offensive. The regulations covered subjects such as the possession of firearms, powers of arrest and detention, control of food supplies, and clearing of undergrowth along transportation routes. Everyone over the age of twelve was required to register and to carry an identity card at all times. Perhaps the most drastic of these regulations was the power of mass detention and deportation, which in 1949 alone resulted in the deportation of six thousand Chinese, including a dozen or more from the Sanchun area. Powers of arrest and detention were continually expanded in the early years, as new crimes were defined and added to the books and as the imposition of curfews and food restrictions became widespread.

A primary propaganda issue used by the MCP as a justification for its continuing war was the cry for independence. When the British government in fact began making concrete plans for Malayan independence, and the MCP was in any case in an increasingly weak military position, attempts at negotiation were agreed upon by both sides. Chin Peng, the secretary-general of the MCP, met Tunku Abdul Rahman, leader of the UMNO and soon to become the first prime minister, to conduct peace talks in 1955. The Communists demanded the right to continue to operate as a legal political party following cessation of hostilities, but the Tunku, while agreeing to generous surrender terms, refused to go further, and the talks subsequently broke down.

Conditions over the next few years continued to deteriorate for the Communists. Supplies were scarce and difficult to obtain as relocation and curfew programs took effect. Guerrillas who surrendered and cooperated with military intelligence, however, were treated well and received cash rewards and assistance in establishing themselves in new lives after their periods of usefulness were over. The remaining troops, suffering the rigors of jungle life, were demoralized by increasing numbers of surrenders and were unable to revitalize themselves and renew an offensive. By 1957 "white areas," where guerrilla activity had been essentially eradicated, extended across most of eastern Malaya and across the center of the country, including the capital, Kuala Lumpur. Johore and Perak (including Sanchun) remained the final "black areas"; they eventually crumbled as the government forces concentrated their efforts, and as high-ranking Communists surrendered, urging others to follow them. By 1960, the state of emergency was at an end, although Chin Peng remained with a small force of about four hundred based along the Thai border.

Relocation and Resettlement

The Chinese population in Malaya, which until the 1930s was concentrated chiefly in the cities and mining areas, showed signs during the Depression of dispersion to subsistence farms on the edge of the jungle. Often it was wives and children who first moved away from the more populated areas, supplementing with small garden plots the meager wage income the husband was making in the city or the mine. With the Japanese occupation, the dispersion continued; men too withdrew from areas of Japanese control and often went further into the jungle than the women, either to join the guerrilla forces or simply to avoid the Japanese labor and execution squads. It is estimated that in 1940 there were about 150,000 dispersed Chinese "squatters," the number increasing to some 400,000 by 1945 (Robinson 1956: 76).

The resettlement of these "squatters," undertaken between 1950 and

1952 under the Briggs Plan, was seen primarily as a military matter, and only later were its social ramifications fully recognized. Resettlement types fell into several categories; a precise accounting of the number of sites and people affected is therefore unavailable. One writer lists seven different sets of figures from seven sources (Sandhu 1964: 164), all excluding a "regroupment" category that was carried out privately within estate or mining areas in cooperation with the government program. The Federation of Malaya Annual Report for 1952 states that 461,822 persons were relocated into 509 new villages during the two-year period. That figure may be low; of the other six sources, four report more than 550,000 persons involved in the relocation. Some 86 percent of those affected were Chinese (Sandhu 1964: 165). A later study, concerned specifically with Chinese population geography in Malaya, reports that 780,000 Chinese squatters and mine and estate workers were relocated in 574 new villages, broken categorically into 480 relocated areas (new settlements either totally detached or appended to existing market towns or cities) and 94 regroupment areas (Niew 1969: 260).

Regardless of the exact numbers involved, it is clear that massive social engineering was taking place under the urgency of military necessity. Nearly one in four of the Chinese in Malaya, and one in ten of the entire population of the Federation, was involved in resettlement. Nearly half the new villages numbered over one thousand settlers, a figure sometimes used to distinguish urban from rural populations. The Malayan relocation program has been viewed in different ways by various observers over the years. Some British writers trying to popularize the war at home saw resettlement, with all its promised amenities and experiments in grassroots democracy, as a positive boon to the Chinese farmers. Many Malays tended to resent that the amenities — schools, houselots, electricity (necessary to illuminate the barbed wire perimeter fences by night), piped or well water — were given to suspected traitors. More critical observers, both Malaysians and others, take a harsher view of the program, focusing on the hardships forced upon a frightened and threatened people.

Conditions varied greatly across the country, both in the quality of the relocation sites selected and in the actual organization of the move. Although British authorities in some cases spread advance warning of an impending move, military exigency often required that no prior notice of the exact date of the move be given. The hamlets to be relocated were surrounded before dawn by British forces; the inhabitants were rudely awakened and given only a matter of hours to gather as many of their possessions as possible and load them into army trucks. As the loading proceeded, the houses were set aflame. People gathered what crops they could to take with them, and if the relocation site was not too distant, they might go on tending the same gardens; otherwise the plots were destroyed to prevent the guerrillas from harvesting the remaining crops. If animals could not be taken along they were destroyed. The owners were given some compensation whenever possible. Ideally, each family received a houselot within a fenced new village and some agricultural land outside the fence as well, the amount depending on the area and other sources of income available to the family. In fact, this was not always feasible; even when it was, the time loss involved in bringing a new garden to fruition was crucial to people who existed at the edge of subsistence already.

Most discussions of the Malayan relocation operations outline the ideal, and make slight reference to the fact that the ideal could seldom be achieved. Outspoken condemnation of the operation is found occasionally, however. Sandhu points out that the term *squatter* is inaccurate in probably half the cases, since many of the agriculturalists were legitimate landowners or renters. He also draws attention to the fact that as postwar reconstruction brought a return of the market mechanism, many of the so-called squatters had moved from subsistence to cash-crop farming, either growing vegetables for sale or returning to tapping their rubber trees. Thus, in many cases growing prosperity was shattered by the sudden forced resettlement "crusade" (Sandhu 1964: 160).

A moving description of the plight of the resettled people, probably a more accurate assessment of the Chinese perspective of the period than most other more academic accounts, is found in a novel by Han Suyin, *And the Rain My Drink*. A French priest, recently arrived from China, describes the resettlement process as he saw it begin in a village in Johore:

> How undramatic, trivial it all was . . . and so hot too, and you know what heat does to you . . . makes you not notice, makes you forget . . . they were still putting up the wire fences, round the high ground. Some lorries had come in filled with people to be resettled, and armoured cars, and everywhere policemen with guns levelled against everyone round them, and soldiers. Then the people came out of the lorries and stood in groups there on the central square . . . and the Resettlement Officer, . . . shouting at them, waving his arm and his stick: 'Come on, get cracking over there . . .' and the quiet hard hatred seeped out of them thick, thick . . . I could smell the hate hitting us full in the face, great waves of it out of the docile people lining up in the square. (Han 1970: 96-97)

Although the resettlement program undoubtedly reversed the direction of the war, as terrorists were cut off from easy access to supplies and recruits, the program was by no means an instant success. The almost universal resentment stirred by forced relocation could not be erased immediately, and was no doubt exacerbated by the fact that the promised amenities were in many cases years in coming. By the end of 1952, for example, less than half of the villages actually had the promised schools, and most of these were poorly staffed by underpaid and overworked teachers (Short

1975). To this day most of the lots on which the settlers built houses over twenty years ago do not belong to the people outright, as originally promised, but are held on yearly renewable temporary occupation licenses. The most basic problem, however, was the continued vulnerabilty of the Chinese workers. Chinese were not permitted to remain neutral; instead they were asked for the most personally dangerous form of assistance—intelligence information. Once outside the fence for a day's work, however, the Chinese rubber tapper or tin miner was an easy target for the guerrilla assassin. During the Emergency more ordinary Chinese civilians were killed than anyone else, presumably because they presented both the greatest hope and the greatest danger to the MCP.

At least two instances of collective punishment ordered for entire communities were noted in government reports. In 1952, Tanjong Malim, a larger market town about thirty miles south of Sanchun, had such a high rate of "incidents" and such a total lack of public "cooperation" with the authorities that the entire town was put under a twenty-two-hour curfew, allowing two hours to buy food, and the daily rice ration was cut in half. Every adult was given a questionnaire to fill in, anonymously. Twenty-four hours later each house was visited by police and soldiers bearing sealed boxes into which the folded and unsigned forms were dropped. The number of blank questionnaires was not disclosed, but within the next two weeks forty Chinese in the district were arrested as food suppliers and couriers for the Communists, and the collective punishment was lifted. Pusing, a small new village near Ipoh, was placed under similar punishment, including strict curfew, cuts in rations, and a fine levied according to income level and collected by local leaders from every household and shop.

Eventually the balance shifted. As terrorism decreased and workers felt more protected and settled in their new situations, enjoying both the safety and the community spirit that gradually developed behind the fences, Chinese gave more information, and terrorism was more successfully combatted—a circular effect. Long before the Emergency was officially declared at an end in 1960, most of the fences had been opened and restrictions of movement lifted. Although a handful of the smaller, less well located villages dispersed altogether, the vast majority of the settlements have continued to the present as viable social units, enjoying most of the amenities of life once promised them. In view of present-day racial tensions it is perhaps unfortunate that the Chinese, who once mixed freely with Malays in the rural areas, were placed in virtual ghettos; a separate subculture permitting relatively little personal interchange between the Chinese and other groups was perpetuated. Nonetheless, the rural Chinese of postwar Malaya were effectively "urbanized," apparently to their benefit, as evidenced by the continued coherence of the new villages as social communities.

The Emergency in Sanchun

Sanchun's shops stretched about 400 yards along the main road, with a second block of shops and an open market to the east of the road. In 1950 the British government purchased from an Indian *Chettiar* a large rubber grove adjoining this market center to the south and east, and eventually a double row of barbed wire fencing enclosed both, an area about 500 by 750 yards. The rubber grove, about half of that area, was cleared of rubber trees and divided into houselots for the new settlers. This area was and still is termed the "new village" (*xincun*), contrasted in people's minds and speech with the "street" (*jieshang*), although the two are contiguous. Both were subject to the same curfew restrictions and home guard duties, and eventually both came under the same governing body, the local council, which in modified form is still the local authority today.

The residents of the two areas were in some respects quite different. Most of the street people were established merchants; the new settlers were for the most part uprooted poor, struggling to build houses around themselves to keep the rain off their heads. Most of the villagers knew few of their new neighbors when they first arrived. They had been living in clusters of from three to eight or ten families, widely scattered throughout the marketing hinterland of Sanchun. The older merchants report, however, that they were acquainted with most of the settlers, and many of the settlers acknowledge knowing the street people, especially those merchants they dealt with, and the leaders who ran such organizations as the school board and the gambling club. But the settlers were often strangers to one another, and they did not always speak the same languages. Most were Cantonese or Hakka, but other groups were represented in smaller numbers, and several informants admit that they had difficulties at first with the variety of languages.

I wondered, and asked, whether in such troubled times strangers might have been eyed distrustfully and avoided, and whether street people might have shared the British authorities' fear of the possibility of communist elements being among the new settlers, a threat to safety and harmony. For many years Sanchun was considered a "black area," a center of particularly heavy terrorist activity. It was cited by name in a 1951 *Straits Times* report as falling within the area of "Perak's main terrorist problem today" (Malaya, Department of Information, 1951: 27). Answers may have been tempered by time, but no one recalled such mistrust and fear, either among the villagers or between villagers and street people. Chinese were all Chinese, and all were oppressed by foreign military rulers, some more than others (villagers more than shopkeepers), but they were to be pitied more than feared. One shopkeeper expressed great sympathy for the newcomers, despite the extra burden he admitted merchants had to take on, extending credit both for basic building materials for new houses and for foodstuffs to take the place of those the settlers had been growing themselves before, now often destroyed.

By contrast, many informants stressed the mistrust that the Sanchun people, street and village alike, felt toward the government officials overseeing the relocation process. These officials, both European and Asian, tended to suspect everyone of communist leanings. They treated the resettled villagers with little respect, giving them no dignity, no "face." The assistant resettlement officer (ARO), a Chinese, but an outsider appointed by the government, was particularly disliked. As one informant put it, however, "During that particular time, you couldn't blame him [the ARO] either. He acted very proud and haughty, but he felt insecure. He thought you were Communists, so how could he dare to be friendly with you? That's why his behavior sometimes made you uncomfortable."

The government had cleared the rubber land and divided it into house-lots of fairly uniform size, but some inequity in distribution was inevitable since the site to be enclosed by the fence included low, poorly drained land as well as more desirable high land. At present the village is divided into three sections, A, B, and C. Section A extends from the shops along the road, and seven or eight wooden houses were built there sometime before the forced resettlement. A and B were settled roughly within the same period of a month or two, while space in C was available as late as 1960. Informants differ in their description of the distribution, some maintaining that the ARO simply drew a random number for each family and told them to go find the correspondingly numbered lot and begin building a house. Some, however, maintain that families could choose to group together, while others say that such choice was available only to those who had "good relations" (*guanxi* or *ganqing*) with the ARO or Lee Koi, the influential local leader who worked closely with the ARO. The village does in fact include a number of duplex houses built on adjacent lots by relatives and old friends sharing common native-place ties. Not all duplexes are currently occupied by closely related families, nor were they from the beginning. Many people simply found it cheaper to build with one wall in common with a neighbor. Moreover, since the opening of the village fences in 1958 there has been some degree of mobility, obscuring some of the original residential patterns.

In addition to appending the village, the relocation program brought about some change in the nature of occupation on the street. A number of people living on smallholdings, or squatting, moved to the street as lodgers to avoid forced relocation. Even today most shops rent out one or more rooms, sometimes to kin or to employees, but more often to whomever happens to need the space. Each shophouse has a "main tenant," not always resident, and not always even resident in Sanchun. Rents cannot legally be raised for a main tenant, but since subtenants come and go, sub-rents may be increased in keeping with the times, the main tenant realizing the profit. The origin of this system probably predates the Emergency, but the influx of people into the town undoubtedly deepened the layers of rent-ers and subrenters and opened new possibilities of profit for the fortunate. On the whole, however, informants report that most new settlers went to the village, and overcrowding on the street did not result.

Renting occurred in the new village as well. It was possible for families living on estates or smallholdings that were as yet not threatened by guer-rillas to apply for and receive title to houselots within the village, build houses, and then rent them out. The owners, many of them now living in their village houses, usually wanted the house to fall back on in case the Emergency got worse, or as a place for retirement when they could no longer live in estate quarters. Families who originally chose to rent rather than to apply for land of their own often did not intend to stay in Sanchun, though many of them have. Some are still renting the original houses, while others have moved into houses of their own. Technically, once the land had been obtained from the government it was not to change hands except within loosely defined kinship groups, but a number of my infor-mants, when looking for a house to buy, were conveniently able to find dis-tant kinship ties connecting them with someone wishing to sell.

Eight or ten new villages were being established concurrently within an area of perhaps sixty square miles, mostly to the north and west of San-chun. Some families report that they were given a choice of several villages to move to, while others say they were forced to move to Sanchun. Two shopkeepers suggested that this discrepancy was due to greater leniency shown people in settlements that were less suspect; they were given more time for the move and a choice of villages.

For all of the relocated families, the experience was undoubtedly fraught with difficulty. Many tell of finding themselves deposited, along with what belongings they had been able to salvage rapidly, on an empty lot, where they first built shacks as basic protection against the frequent tropical rains. More adequate houses were constructed as shells around the original shacks, which were then dismantled, and the shell was divided into rooms, provided with a proper kitchen, stove, bathing room, and so forth. "Origi-nal settlers," those moving in within the first few months, were given M$100 in assistance by the Malayan Chinese Association (MCA), a sum which at that time provided a reasonable start toward the purchase of building supplies for a simple frame house suitable for the tropics. A good number of the resettled families included trained carpenters, construction workers, or jacks-of-all-trades, who could provide their own labor. Over the years most of the villagers have found it possible to make some improvements. A number have demolished their original houses and built impressive new homes, a few even using concrete construction rather than the more common wooden planks.

Despite the constraints imposed by a state of emergency, the early 1950s were years of economic boom for Malaya and for many people in Sanchun. Rubber, a commodity figuring in the livelihoods of a large majority of street people and villagers alike, climbed steadily in value, spurred by the requirements of the Korean war and as yet unrivaled by the synthetic product. By 1972 the market price had dropped to a fraction of its former high, and informants nostalgically recalled the times when five or ten acres meant luxury even for a large family and stories were told of rubber tappers who drove their own automobiles to their gardens to collect the latex. Nonetheless, rubber gardens and unprotected tappers were in those years often the targets of the guerrillas, and rubber land could sometimes be bought fairly cheaply from owners who preferred hard cash to the risk of slashed trees, or worse, slashed tappers.

Local Administration under the Emergency

At the time of relocation, the market center of Sanchun was included for administrative purposes under the town board of the district headquarters sixteen miles away. Since the relocation meant little disruption for the street beyond registration of households and residents, it was decided to allow that situation to continue, rather than transfer taxation, licensing, and so on to a new local body.

As part of the government's program to make the resettled villagers feel they had a stake in their new homes, however, a village committee was created. As Lee Koi tells it, one day in 1951, when the village already had over a hundred families in residence, the district officer (DO) came around in an information van to call all adults over eighteen years of age to a meeting in the schoolhouse. No one knew just what was going to happen, but most of the men went, while the women, bound more by the norms of traditional Chinese society than by British military orders, stayed home. The DO spoke in Mandarin, which was then translated into Cantonese for those, like Lee, who understood no Mandarin, reassuring everyone that the meeting was a friendly one. He told them they were to select twenty people from among themselves to act as their representatives. Lee estimated that there were some three hundred people present, including men from the street. Nominations were taken from the floor for twenty names, which were written beside numbers on a blackboard. The twenty nominated people, who were to constitute the village committee, were then given blank pieces of paper on which to write the number corresponding to the name of their choice for chairman, or village head. Lee Koi, according to his own account, was elected unanimously.

I could find no formal record of this meeting, nor any list of the members of the original village committee. Informants concurred, however, that most were shopkeepers. In those early years, when there were perhaps higher numbers of communists and communist sympathizers still included within the new village, villagers generally chose to avoid all contact with government and its representatives. They tended to be a bit less "enthusiastic" (*rexin*) even in purely social cooperation than was considered usual and appropriate in a Chinese village. Life for them was difficult, beginning in the morning with lines at the gate where they were searched for illegal food as they left for work, which might be some distance away. By the time they returned, hungry and tired, still facing a few more hours of work on the new house, they doubtless had little energy or interest in attending meetings. Moreover, tappers and farmers who left the village daily to work in secluded areas were far more vulnerable to the threats of the communists, and understandably had little desire to be involved with the committee, whose members were labeled "running dogs of British imperialism" by communist propaganda.

Thus, the village committee, like most governing bodies in overseas Chinese society, was composed primarily of merchants. According to some informants, however, some of the wealthiest traditional leaders, like the villagers, chose to remain separate from the government, and often moved to larger, more protected towns where threats to both life and property were fewer. At least eighteen of the forty-eight stone shophouses, for example, are still owned by men who have left Sanchun, twelve of them by one particularly successful man, four by another, both of whom long ago moved up out of the small local system into larger economic arenas.

In 1952 the British colonial government passed the Local Council Ordinance. This left to the discretion of district officers the formation of local councils, somewhat advanced from village committees, which could take over the town board functions of taxation (on residences only, as land taxes went and still go directly to the state), certain licenses, and other items of administration properly left to a local body. In 1954, as a forerunner to an anticipated changeover, Sanchun held its first formal election, which included a nomination day three weeks before election day, posters widely distributed with the names and photographs of the candidates, and secret ballots. Voters were to vote in one of four wards, all non-Chinese voting with the street ward, and each voter cast three ballots. Informants report that the turnout was low; villagers were uninterested or afraid to vote, in part because a stranger, supposedly a neutral outsider, entered the booth with illiterate voters to help them mark the ballot for the men of their choice. Nonetheless, with 908 electors on the rolls and 1,664 votes cast, assuming three votes per elector (admittedly an incautious assumption, but the number of voters is not stated), possibly 60 percent of the voters eligible came to the polls. One-third of the committee was to be elected annually, but no records are available for 1955. In the 1956 election for Sanchun's first formally constituted local council, 482 voters out of 1,175 registered came to the polls, a mere 41 percent. Records of later local elections provide less detailed data, and national election records are broken down only by *mukim*, a subunit of the district that includes a sizable rural area surrounding Sanchun, so no further light can be shed on the actual electoral participation of the people of Sanchun. It would seem, however, that grassroots democracy had a rather inauspicious beginning.

Both street people and villagers maintain that the former are more interested in public welfare and more likely to merit the description of being *rexin*, enthusiastic in their participation in community social activities. Villagers, it is said, are too busy making a living, and during the Emergency were too heavily under the threat of the guerrillas outside the gates to have any interest in such participation. Election behavior bears out these contentions. In the 1954 elections, when villagers outnumbered street people approximately two to one, there were in the town ward eight Chinese candidates and six non-Chinese; in the three village wards combined, only seven Chinese candidates came forward. In the town ward 716 votes were cast, compared to 954 in the village. The top eleven vote-getters won seats on the council, four of them town Chinese, four village Chinese, and three non-Chinese.

Of the four villagers, one was Lee Koi, a longtime resident in one of the early houses in A section, manager of the Sanchun Recreation Club since its formation in 1936, and village head for three years. A second one was a classical Cantonese scholar who tutored private pupils, and a third was a shopkeeper in an area newly set aside for shops at one edge of the village. None could be said to be typical of the resettled villagers. The shop contingent included three widely respected businessmen (among them Lung Sooi and Choong Hah, Lee Koi's patron), and the son of a fourth. Tan Tien Yu, who was long known to all as the headman of the Sanchun marketing area, chairman formerly of the Japanese maintenance committee and still of several other local bodies, chose to let his son serve rather than to do so himself.

The responsibilities of the village committee from the time of its inception in 1951 until its conversion to a local council in 1957 were rather narrow, extending only to household registration, social welfare, and sanitary works. Little money was involved: a household tax of M$1 was matched, dollar for dollar, by the government. The license fees and various taxes drawn from the established shopkeepers continued to be funneled through the district headquarters rather than the committee before they came back in the form of capital works such as roads, drains, and lighting. The limited village committee funds were used mostly to support destitute families whose main breadwinner had been killed by the Japanese or the Communists or detained by the British, and to pay the salaries of a few council laborers.

The village committee met monthly, with the ARO, a British police officer, a district Chinese-affairs officer (CAO), and the DO in attendance as well as the councillors, at least ideally. District officers were subject to frequent changes in postings, even during the Emergency; such lack of continuity inevitably affected the efficiency of communications channels, a problem still present today.

Documentary data from the early years of the village committee are limited to a single file covering random business matters in the years 1953-1955. Most of its contents refer to routine telephone, electricity, and stationery bills and receipts, providing little impression of the workings of the committee or the conditions of village life. Also included are a number of propaganda notices from the Information Service, including notification of civics courses held in nearby towns to which each new village sent a few representatives, and notices of the dates of visits of the information vans with films, as well as exhortations to continued vigilance in controlling the transport of food. From the other side, there are requests from Lee Koi, as representative of the people, for relaxed curfews during the temple festival and Chinese New Year celebrations.

A second newly created local organization, also aimed at providing the new settlers with a sense of participation and responsibility as well as utilizing their labor and evidencing the government's trust in them, was the home guard. All males between the ages of eighteen and fifty-five were required to register for home guard duty, but if a given duty date was inconvient, a replacement could be substituted for a fee of M$4. Tan Tien Yu's son, Tan Siew Hing, in his mid-twenties, was appointed lieutenant commander of the home guard. The commander was the British police officer.

The village was reclassified from "black" to "white" in 1958. A number of informants felt that this effective "pacification" resulted more from the stick than the carrot, from the strictness of government policies rather than from the amenities promised the relocated settlers, which were often slow in coming. In the early years of the village some ten to twenty people were deported to China, and forty or fifty were sent to detention camps. After the supposedly "bad elements" were removed, the remaining settlers increasingly dissociated themselves from the MCP. Though fewer than ten people were killed in the Sanchun area by the Communists, and most of those were Europeans, tappers and loggers were often under pressure to smuggle food and felt that the guerrillas were being unreasonable in failing to see how difficult this was under strict government surveillance. It became common for a worker to remain in the village for a few days if he felt threatened, despite the loss in income, but the threats no longer held long-term currency. Thus gradually the MCP lost power in one of its last strongholds, as the Emergency wound down to its formal conclusion in 1960.

The Sanchun of the 1970s has grown out of the history presented above, its roots clearly traceable in the past. The families who in the old days made fortunes and established positions of esteem and respect, to be passed on, if possible, to sons, provide direct links to that past, as do villagers who participated more passively in the political life of the community, then, as now. Significant changes that occurred in Sanchun during the years of the occupation and the Emergency have continuing implications today.

The severity of the Japanese occupation suspended local action temporarily, and in the chaotic times of Emergency and relocation, patterns of power and influence failed to regain their previous regularity and form. The political game was open to all comers. Before the occupation the Chinese political middleman found himself operating within an economically oriented laissez faire power structure, but under the law-and-order goals of the Emergency, a different set of rules held sway, permitting the development of a new style of leadership. All pre-Emergency leaders of the top echelon had been wealthy and had used their wealth to establish patron-client networks of support internally. During the Emergency Lee Koi broke this precedent, and, having no wealth to speak of, built himself a position of power and respect through force of personality alone. His courage and decisiveness were qualities valued by the British military authorities, and once he had established his importance to them, he could make himself useful to villagers and townspeople in ways that permitted him to build up a firm foundation of local support — all without the benefit of a personal fortune. He was still a central figure in the Sanchun of the early 1970s.

4

Sanchun, 1972

The local-level political maneuverings that are an important focus for this book take place not only within the political environment imposed by the encapsulating state, but also within a local social community that provides a context for support formation, rivalry, and manipulation of public opinion. The broad outlines of this community can be presented in the form of basic data regarding demographic, occupational, and organizational structures of Sanchun, as they appeared in the "ethnographic present" of 1972.[1]

The 1970 government census, conducted some fifteen months before my own surveys, gives the population of the Local Council Area of Sanchun — that is, the area within the original fence of the Emergency period — as 2,704, of which 2,126, or 79 percent, are Chinese (Chander 1972: 251). Extrapolations from my own material and other local council records suggest the Chinese population to be some 15 percent higher than the government figure, however, about 2,500 (Strauch 1975: 124-125).

While Malays and Indians contribute to the marketplace mosaic of Sanchun, their social, political, and religious orientations focus elsewhere. The council area is surrounded by Malay *kampong*s and by rubber estates employing and housing large numbers of Indians, to which the twenty percent non-Chinese residents of Sanchun turn for a sense of belonging and community. Moreover, the majority of the Malays actually resident within the council area boundaries are government servants of one sort or another who tend to turn even further outward, to the district capital sixteen miles

---

1. A more complete ethnographic description of Sanchun, including its kinship patterns, ritual cycles, and similar data that may be of interest primarily to anthropologists, is given in Strauch 1975: chap. 5.

Sanchun, 1972

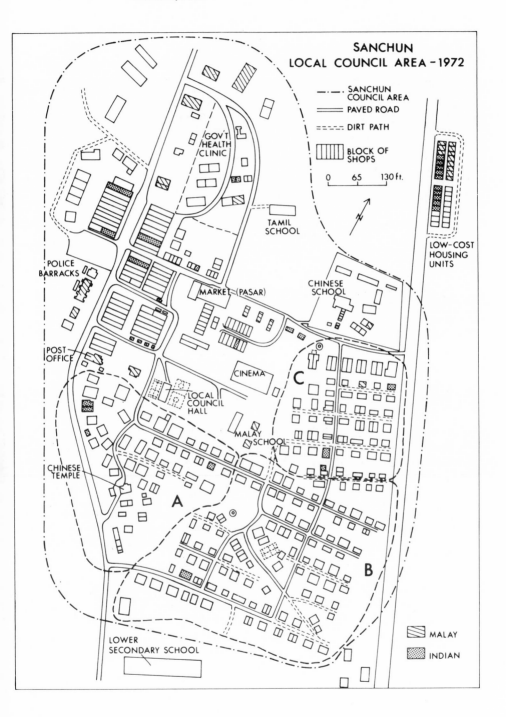

SANCHUN
LOCAL COUNCIL AREA – 1972

—.—.— SANCHUN COUNCIL AREA
═══ PAVED ROAD
===== DIRT PATH
▥ BLOCK OF SHOPS

0   65   130 ft.

GOV'T HEALTH CLINIC

TAMIL SCHOOL

CHINESE SCHOOL

LOW-COST HOUSING UNITS

POLICE BARRACKS

MARKET (PASAR)

POST OFFICE

CINEMA

C

LOCAL COUNCIL HALL

MALAY SCHOOL

CHINESE TEMPLE

A

B

LOWER SECONDARY SCHOOL

▨ MALAY
▦ INDIAN

away, in their social identification. Indian residents include a number of shopkeepers and a few laborers and their families. The three communal groups interact daily in the marketplace and less often in gatherings organized by government bodies — for example, in council meetings or in National Day celebrations. For the most part, however, no disservice is done to reality in treating Sanchun in social as well as political and economic terms as an essentially Chinese community.

The Market Center

The market center has expanded considerably from the original forty-eight stone shophouses. Besides a new central market for fresh produce and cooked food, with a total of twenty-eight stallholders, four blocks of wooden shops have been added, as well as a dozen or so other semipermanent wooden shops and stalls. Six additional businesses are located in the new village. The market area boasts a total of ninety-three separate businesses in seventy-four shophouses, many of the larger stone shops being divided into two or more sections. Of the stone shophouses, only one is empty and one not used for business. Twelve wooden shophouses are used as residences only, but most of these are in a new section of shops built in 1965 in anticipation of expansion; at present only six of those sixteen shops house businesses. In addition to these commercial and service firms, there is a sawmill, a private rubber-processing factory employing two workers, a rubber smokehouse owned jointly by two of the three rubber dealers, and a large area set aside as a bus station. Sanchun is the junction point where two north-south bus routes connect, each operated by a different company, so all passengers except those on long-distance nonstop express buses must change vehicles in Sanchun. The town also has two licensed long-distance taxis and, to my knowledge, two illegal "pirate" (unlicensed) taxis. One family owns three timber lorries and contracts to haul timber.

Until 1965, when a bypass was built, Sanchun lay astride the main north-south trunk road. The new road was strongly opposed by local businessmen, and the council sent a series of memoranda to appropriate state authorities. One or two businesses closed at that time, but the market center is busy and reasonably prosperous today, despite the rerouting of the highway.

About two-thirds of the commercial enterprises are run by Chinese, who own sixty-seven of the ninety-two businesses in shophouses and twenty-two of the thirty-six stall licenses. Chinese clearly predominate in several specialties, notably sundry shops, or *zahuodian:* shops selling staple foods such as rice, flour, eggs, and canned goods, plus a good sampling of almost all regularly needed items, ranging from radio batteries and soap to cooking utensils, brooms, and Chinese spirit money and incense. Chinese also predominate in rubber dealing, bicycle shops, tailoring, and a number of lesser categories, while Indians are particularly prominent as owners of restaurants and general drygoods stores (cloth, ready-made clothing, housewares). A general idea of the services available in Sanchun and the ethnic identities of their purveyors is given in table 3. Some shops cannot appropriately be placed in only one category (for example, two of the three Chinese pharmacists devote half of their shop space to dishes and housewares) and are listed twice, in order to indicate the range of choice that the consumers have in each of the types of services or goods they may seek.

Formal businesses are supplemented by vendors offering less regular services. Stalls on the edges of the market include a Malay fishmonger and three more noodle stalls, one Malay, one Indian, and one Chinese. During the various fruit seasons Malays often bring in large quantities of fruit from the *kampongs* and sell them by the roadside in the market area. Itinerant merchants, operating out of small vans and selling cloth, clothing, and housewares, periodically arrive and set up shop in the open square for a day or an evening, usually timed to correspond with the semimonthly paydays of the surrounding estates. Service specialists include a traditional Chinese dentist, a government dentist who comes once a week to the government health clinic, two motor repair shops, and one government-licensed lottery office. In the village itself, a handful of housewives have small businesses in their homes, selling biscuits and candy to neighborhood children.

The market, most shops, and one of the restaurants close on Sundays, but being closed is merely relative. Most shopkeepers live above or behind their shops. At all times except late at night, a few of the wooden slats used to close up the broad open front of the shop are left to one side, providing access to the living quarters. Active business hours are generally from dawn to dusk, but merchants or family members are usually available to make small sales at all hours seven days a week.

Also located in the market section, in stone shophouses, are two political party offices and the Chinese Recreation Club, the gambling center. The offices of the Malaysian Chinese Association, above the club, consist of a large meeting room and two small guest rooms, one of which is occupied by the nonpartisan local council secretary during the working week (he returns to his paternal home in a larger town twenty miles to the north on weekends). The Democratic Action Party has a placard above half of a shop on the main road, but at present the space is rented to an Indian lawyer. (The UMNO has an office in a nearby Malay *kampong*.) Two Chinese native-place associations have headquarters in the village. Both are large houses; the main rooms are used to store the benches and tables that members may use for weddings and funerals, while the smaller rooms are

TABLE 3. Business ownership by ethnic group

	Chinese	Indian	Malay
Shops			
Sundry shops	17	3	3
Coffee shops	4	—	—
Restaurants	2	4	1
Bicycle shops	6	—	—
Rubber dealers	4[a]	—	—
Goldsmiths	2	—	—
Pawnshop (government-licensed monopoly)	1	—	—
General drygoods stores	7	6	2
Tailors	7	—	1
Barbershops	1	2	1
Beauty shops	3	—	—
Petrol dealers	2	—	—
Newspaper dealers	3	1	—
Electric shops	2	—	—
Tinsmiths	3	—	—
Furniture shops	3	—	—
Book seller and stationer	1	—	—
Chinese pharmacies	3	—	—
Market stalls			
Fish	5	—	—
Pork	4	—	—
Vegetables	3	1	1
Iced refreshments	2	—	1
Fruits	1	—	1
Biscuits, toys, etc.	1	—	1
Noodles (cooked food)	3	—	—
Beef	—	—	1
Tea	—	—	1
Goat meat	—	1	—
Cakes and goodies	1	—	—

a. Two of the firms dealing in rubber are owned by the same family.

rented out as residences to families, not necessarily members of the associations.

Family and Household

Among ethnic overseas Chinese, where landholding has been the exception rather than the rule, kinship patterns traditionally based on landed family (*jia*) estates (see Cohen 1976) are in a process of flux. When shops are large and sons few, the traditional structures of extended family relationships and forms of inheritance may obtain, but in most cases some sons, and now daughters as well, leave home to find employment. Most do not sever their ties, however, even in the absence of a paternal estate to inherit.

A landed *jia* estate is uncommon among Sanchun Chinese. Only 32.1 percent of the 184 families interviewed owned nonresidential land, and an additional 9.8 percent had the use of such land, under various arrangements.[2] While 122, or 67.2 percent, owned their own residences, only 23, or 12.4 percent, all in the street section, had permanent title to the land on which those residences were built. A large portion of the agricultural land of Malaysia is reserved for Malay ownership, and in populated areas there is a scarcity of other arable land because much of it is held by estates and planted either in rubber or in oil palm. Residential land is even more of a problem, particularly in the new villages, which during the last twenty years have grown in population but not in area. Despite original government promises of houselot ownership, all land in new villages was in 1972 still held under TOL (temporary occupation license), renewable yearly at the state government's discretion. If the land is to continue to be used as residential land, the current holder of the TOL has first option at renewal each year. Most people seem to feel secure, and some build relatively luxurious and expensive houses on their lots. A shift from TOLs to permanent land titles has been one of the chief demands of the Chinese political parties in recent years. Most of the nonresidential land held by Sanchun people is in rubber smallholdings, but over the last two decades rubber has dropped so much in the world market that five or ten acres of rubber is not a very valuable estate. Land used but not owned by the users is generally planted in small vegetable crops for home consumption, although in a few cases the vegetables are grown for market. It includes land owned by relatives or friends, illegally used state land, and recently replanted rubber

2. In autumn 1971 I found 358 Chinese households in Sanchun, from which I drew a random sample of 184 households for in-depth interviewing covering aspects of family occupational and educational history, kinship structure, income and expenditures, and attitudes toward local leaders. These data were supplemented with observations, interviews with key informants, and friendly discussions throughout my stay in Sanchun.

land on which vegetables are grown between the rows of immature rubber trees. Most families are dependent at least in part on wage income. The *jia* estate as such does not play a major role in a family's self-definition, nor does the concept of *fenjia* (formal family division at a given point in the family cycle), so important in traditional China.

Kinship patterns of solidarity seem to retain great strength in Sanchun, despite the dispersion of families resulting in part from the lack of compact *jia* estates. Many families are supported largely or in part by nonresident members. Often these are young men who work as wage laborers in construction, tin mining, or logging, and return home to the village only occasionally, the frequency depending on how distant their work is. In a number of cases these men have wives and children living virilocally in households that often include not only the husband's parents but also younger siblings and sometimes brothers and their wives.

Some absent family members send no remittances but are still unequivocally included in the family. These are frequently young men or women, unmarried, who have only recently left home. Some have not yet found a job; others are excused from sending money because they earn too little or are saving for a special expenditure such as a wedding or a motorbike. Job mobility in this category is exceptionally high. The extreme cases are young men who work in construction or logging in various parts of the country or abroad; they are absent for long periods and often send little money back. Such a man might eventually return to the village for marriage or bring back a bride; he deposits her with his parents while he goes off to work again and thereafter sends money dutifully for the support of the whole family. Some sons, married and living elsewhere with wife and children, are more clearly cut off from the family and send only token amounts, often specifically designated as a gift for the mother on the occasion of her birthday or a special holiday.

Absentee members of the community may play a more important role locally than might at first be imagined. A number of these young men are employed in logging, a skilled, fairly dangerous, and therefore extremely lucrative field, particularly for those who manage to obtain skilled positions with American and Japanese timber companies in Sumatra and Borneo. These men and their friends and families sometimes claimed that earnings could be as high as M$20,000 or more a year. In 1972 the monthly wages of a rubber tapper, by contrast, usually fell between M$100 and M$150. Construction work can also be somewhat more lucrative than other strictly local jobs; again it requires mobility and often means that the workers spend much time away from home. These young men constitute an important source of support for political change in the community. They do not necessarily actively seek change or provoke it themselves, but when the organizational means of change were introduced by an outside agency — the MCA task force — they proved ready to take part.

Over 15 percent of the people who are closely connected with an economic *jia* unit located in Sanchun go elsewhere for periods of time to earn money (38 percent of Sanchun's work force). Absentee workers are noted in other Chinese village studies as well — for example, in Gallin's work in Taiwan. Gallin states that during slack agricultural periods possibly as many as 15 percent of the registered residents of Hsin Hsing go to the city to find work, but they return to work their own land during planting and harvesting seasons (1966: 35). In Sanchun, however, people who own land are usually engaged in relatively nonseasonal work on it, such as rubber tapping (which is discontinued for only about a month when the leaves are changing) or truck gardening, and are thus tied year round to the land. It is families with little or no land, unable to utilize their labor power fully in Sanchun, who must rely on the support provided by one or more members working outside the village. More than 40 percent of the families interviewed include absentee members. Moreover, more than one-quarter of the households include one or more persons whose spouses work and spend long periods elsewhere, but who are obviously still intimately connected to Sanchun through their conjugal ties. In only 105 households (57.1 percent) are the residential and economic units identical. The mean size of the concentrated residential *jia* group is 6.7, while the dispersed but economically related *jia* group mean size is somewhat larger, 7.3.

Education

Primary education is now nearly universal in Sanchun; it is free but not compulsory. A few families have difficulty paying for school supplies and game fees, but with scholarships available, most children can complete primary school (six years) if they choose. Of 395 children aged six to fifteen, 361, over 90 percent, are in school. Just outside the village there is a lower secondary school (three years) that is attended by a number of pupils from Sanchun. Instruction in the three primary schools in the village is in Mandarin, Malay, and Tamil, respectively, while classes in the secondary school are taught in English; therefore one or two years of "removed" classes are necessary to provide adequate English background for the pupils who continue.[3] This extra work seems to discourage some, as do the

---

3. By 1978 the secondary school had added two more years of instruction, through Form V, preparing pupils for the Malaysian Certificate of Education (MCE), and all classes are now taught in Malay.

moderate school fees required, so even minimal secondary education is far from universal. Leaving the town for continued secondary education is somewhat more expensive and thus fairly rare. Fewer than two dozen San-chun youths were attending upper secondary school when I was in the village in 1972. About ten or so commuted daily by bus to a town eight miles to the north, and a handful of young people, mostly from wealthier families, attended schools in Ipoh, Kuala Lumpur, or Penang, boarding at school or with relatives or friends. One local boy, the son of the council chairman, was attending a university overseas.

Census data and personal surveys on adult education levels show evidence of the predictable effects both of differential educational opportunities provided traditionally for boys and girls, and of trends in recent times toward egalitarianism and greater overall opportunity. Most people of both sexes under thirty-five have had some schooling and are able to read and write. But while most men over forty-five had received at least some primary education, few women in the same age group had. The contrast is even more striking in the figures on literacy. While a large majority of men up through the age of seventy-five are literate, illiterates in the female population aged thirty-six to forty-five slightly outnumber literates, and among still older women illiteracy is very nearly universal.

Until a few years ago, the educational services provided by the government-aided schools were supplemented by a small private English primary school and an elderly Chinese scholar (now dead) who offered tutorial instruction in classical Cantonese. The private school closed when a government English primary opened in afternoon sessions in the Tamil school classrooms, but the language of instruction in that program, in accordance with national policy, is now gradually being converted from English to Malay. According to the government census, 79 percent of the Chinese population over twelve years of age claim to be able to speak Mandarin; 70 percent, Malay (the national language); and 13 percent, English.

Most Cantonese in Sanchun speak no southern Chinese languages other than Cantonese, unless there are family members of another speech group, but almost all non-Cantonese speak Cantonese in addition to their native language, as a minimum. Some children of minority speech groups admit that although they understand their parents or grandparents when the elders use the minority language, they themselves speak almost exclusively Cantonese, not only with their peers, but also in response to their elders. It is possible that minority languages may fall into disuse and nearly die out in regions where the number of speakers is extremely small. Since the different home languages predominate in different communities in Malaysia, however, none of these is likely to gain national priority. Mandarin is probably the language that offers most hope for eventual linguistic unity among Malaysian Chinese. It is still being used in Chinese primary schools while

English primary schools are being converted to Malay; thus enrollments in Chinese primary schools throughout the country are increasing as Chinese children are transferred from English to Mandarin schools. Malay is spoken by many Chinese, but in a rudimentary market form that ignores grammatical rules and is considered inferior by educated Malays.

Subethnic Groups

The 1970 Malaysian census asked respondents to designate membership in one of nine separate Chinese speech groups. All nine are represented in Sanchun, and the only group to be added is Hunanese. My surveys yield the data shown in table 4.

Speech groups have appeared to be salient social groupings in the research done in urban overseas Chinese communities (see, for example, Freedman 1957, 1960; Skinner 1957, 1958; Crissman 1967; Willmott 1967). The only previous systematic rural studies were conducted in villages dominated by one speech group (Newell 1962; Maeda 1967). Thus Sanchun presents an important case study of relative heterogeneity, providing a test of the role speech-group cleavages might play in social and political affiliation.

Speech-group membership in Sanchun, while clearly recognized and an important aspect of identification of individuals and families by themselves and others, is increasingly unimportant in social interaction. In observing friendship groups and inquiring about business and job connections and

TABLE 4. Speech-group distribution

	Persons		Household heads	
	No.	*%*	*No.*	*%*
Cantonese	623	44.8	81	44.0
Hakka	378	27.2	48	26.1
Hokkien	156	11.2	26	14.1
Teochiu	141	10.1	15	8.2
Kwongsai	48	3.5	7	3.8
Hokchiu	14	1.0	2	1.1
Hainanese	13	0.9	2	1.1
Hokchia	7	0.5	1	0.5
Hunanese	7	0.5	1	0.5
Henghwa	1	0.1	1	0.5
Total	1,388		184	

marriages, it became clear to me that in this rural setting speech-group membership retained only a modicum of the salience it once held, when immigrants indeed relied upon people with whom they shared their single spoken language for assistance, friendship, and marriage partners. Speech-group membership has no discernible bearing on political groupings today, nor on support given or withheld from local leaders. Contemporary cliques, both those clearly defined and those somewhat more nebulous, cannot be related to the speech groups of their members. Cooperation in businesses and introduction to jobs seem in most cases similarly unconnected to speech-group membership. Job connections, particularly among younger men, are based on kinship ties, school ties, and prior work together, ties that occasionally coincide with speech group but not to such a degree that speech group per se can be considered of great importance. Speech groups thus provide convenient categories for labeling and identification rather than forming important social groupings as such.[4]

Occupations and Incomes

Tables 5 and 6 provide information on occupational distribution, the first covering all persons, the second limited to the gainfully employed. In table 5, the category "not working" includes persons sixteen to fifty-five years of age who were neither students nor looking for work nor particularly involved in housework. Those "between jobs" were unemployed at the time of the interview, had worked before and were then seeking work, although most had no clear idea of what the next job might be or when it might be found. Several persons who had been consistently active for some time in a particular line of work organized on a contract system happened to be between contracts at the time of the interview, but were confident they could again find work in the same line before long. I classified these either as self-employed or wage laborers, as appropriate. The unemployed figure reflects the difficulty young people have in findings jobs once they leave school, before they have acquired skills, experience, and a network of *neihang* (coworker) connections.

In addition to their main source of income, most households could count on income from one or more secondary sources. Data were collected on the most important secondary source, if any (see table 7). Clearly, diversification of household enterprise is the rule rather than the exception. Only sixty-five (35.3 percent) of the households relied solely on income from within a single category. In eleven households (6.0 percent) the main

4. See Strauch 1981 for a more detailed and analytical discussion of Chinese subethnicity and its historical modification in the Malaysian context.

TABLE 5.   Occupational status

	No.	*%*
Self-employed/head of family enterprise	113	8.1
Wage laborer	324	23.4
Worker in family enterprise	111	8.0
Houseworker	96	6.9
Student	361	26.0
Child at home	258	18.6
Adult not working	49	3.5
Worker between jobs	12	0.9
Retired person	59	4.2
No information	7	0.5
Total	1,390	100.0

TABLE 6.   Cross-tabulation of occupational sector with occupational status (gainfully employed only)

Occupational sector	*Occupational status*				
	Worker in family enterprise	*Wage laborer*	*Self-employed*	*Total*	
				No.	*%*
Commerce	52	43	80	175	31.8
Rubber	21	60	24	105	19.1
Manufacture, construction	5	60	1	66	12.0
Logging, timber	3	49	—	52	9.5
Other agriculture	12	33	3	48	8.7
Services, transport	11	32	4	47	8.5
Tin	5	27	2	34	6.2
Professional	3	16	—	19	3.5
Investment, land	3	—	—	3	0.5
Total no.	115	320	114	549	
Total %	20.8	58.3	21.0		100.0

TABLE 7. Cross-tabulation of occupational sector with main and secondary income sources

Occupational Sector	Household's main income source		Household's chief secondary income source	
	No.	%	No.	%
Commerce	53	28	16	14
Rubber	25	14	52	43
Manufacture, construction	17	9	12	10
Logging, timber	37	20	4	2
Other agriculture	9	5	12	10
Services, transport	10	6	11	9
Tin	20	11	6	5
Professional	11	6	3	2
Investment, land	2	1	5	4
Total	184	100	119	100

source of income accounted for less than half of the total income; in sixty-three (34.2 percent), between one-half and three-quarters of the total; and in forty-five (24.4 percent), over three-quarters.

The range and variety of employment in this small town stand in contradiction to both the traditional rice-growing village of south China and the stereotypical picture of ethnic overseas Chinese as the shopkeepers of Southeast Asia. The economic life of Sanchun is essentially atomized, fragmented into numerous personalized activities that require little long-term or systematic cooperation or integration. An understanding of the economic base of the community forms an important backdrop to the study of its politics.

Commerce accounts for nearly a third of the employment and provides the main income for almost the same proportion of households, indicating the importance of Sanchun as a market center. In addition to the shop owners and their employees, a number of people are engaged in petty commerce. A few peddlers come through the village daily selling iced drinks and cakes from stalls constructed on bicycles. One man who owns a motorbike sells ice cream in the Malay kampongs several miles beyond the town. A few of the families interviewed received sporadic income by going to kampongs to pick up jungle fruits collected by the Malays and then bringing them in to sell to market stallholders. Two backyards have large ovens for pig roasting; they provide whole pigs for wedding feasts and smaller quantities for sale through the market pork stalls.

The second most important occupational category in Sanchun involves rubber. Rubber is a common community concern, and its price is a frequent topic of conversation. Nonetheless, only twenty-five families derive their main income from producing, processing, or dealing in rubber; fifty-two families earn secondary income from it. Fifty families own rubber land, but only thirty-seven were tapping it in 1972. Since rubber has declined in value, some rubber-owning families derive their primary income from wage labor, their own land providing merely a secondary income. But since a high proportion of the land in the Sanchun area is planted in rubber, large numbers of wives, daughters, and daughters-in-law supplement the main income of the family by tapping for either smallholders or estates. The price of rubber was so low in 1972 that old trees, which give little latex, or trees too distant or deep in the jungle were not considered worth tapping.

Some families had recently replanted all or part of their rubber acreage, often with the help of government grants, and were waiting out the seven-year period between planting and the onset of tapping. For the first four years, before the tree's root system is fully developed, vegetables, dry *padi* (rice), or combinations of these are planted between the rows of trees. Usually this is just for household consumption, but some of the truck farmers also make use of such land, paying the owner in kind and marketing the rest of the crop.

The single most common specific occupation of all categories is rubber tapping. Tappers may work on family holdings, for a nearby estate on a salary-plus-piece-rate basis, or for a smallholder under agreements that usually fall between a 50-50 and a 40-60 (tapper-owner) split of the profits once the processed rubber is taken to the rubber dealer. Before daylight, usually between four and five o'clock, tappers are off on their bicycles with large tin containers for transporting latex strapped on the back. Estate workers tap, go back to the trees a few hours later to collect the latex, and then turn it in to the estate factory for processing, usually returning home by two or three in the afternoon. Smallholders bring the latex home for processing, or to a neighbor's or relative's house if they lack the necessary equipment. After the latex is sieved to extract twigs and dirt, small amounts of acid are added to speed the congealing, and the latex is poured into rectangular pans, about 12" × 18" × 5". Within about half an hour it is ready to be removed from the pans and stamped into large flat sheets by barefoot women. The sheets are then put through two sets of rollers, a system very similar to an old hand-cranked clothes wringer. Going through the second roller the rubber sheets, now about 3' × 5', are impressed with an identification mark to minimize vulnerability to theft. After hanging outside for one day to dry, the sheets can be taken to the dealer, but usually people accumulate sheets for up to a week before transporting them to the dealer's shop. Much of the locally produced rubber then goes to a small smokehouse just outside of town that is jointly owned by two rubber dealers and operated by a family who lives on the premises. The sheets are placed on racks, smoked slowly for several days, and then baled and sent on to larger dealers for sale to processors and manufacturers.[5]

A number of families buy piglets and then sell the matured and fattened animals. Pig raising is often combined with vegetable farming, as the manure can be used as fertilizer and the vegetable stalks and leaves can be fed to the pigs. Pigs may also be raised on a larger scale in conjunction with fish: a square fish pond is surrounded by long pig sties that are slanted slightly so that the manure can be washed into the pond, where chemical reactions produce algae on which the fish can feed. One villager has such a pig farm about three miles from the village. In the same location he raises fruit trees, chiefly mango and *pomelo*, a large citrus fruit frequently used by Chinese as offerings to the gods. Other agricultural products grown by Sanchun people include hot chilies, which require fertilizer but much less intensive care than green leafy vegetables, tobacco, and *attap*, used in thatched roofs.

Miscellaneous unskilled labor is termed *zagong* (odd jobs). This phrase covers weeding and clearing on rubber estates and in the federal land development schemes, as well as all sorts of unskilled labor in the logging, construction, and tin mining industries. A number of Sanchun men term themselves labor contractors, undertaking to bring together a team of workers for such jobs as clearing tracts of land (unskilled) or building construction (skilled). Most "contractors," however, are themselves skilled workers who are occasionally approached to assemble a team for a job. Just as often another worker is the "contractor" for a given job, and there may be many layers of "contractors" and "subcontractors." One logging contractor, who in the past had organized work teams in which he participated, gave up boss status for a better-paying job working in Indonesia under a Singapore contractor. The labor contractors who organize the supply of local workers for the nearby federal land development schemes and private estates are outsiders, many from Kuala Lumpur, who disdain manual labor themselves. One Sanchun man is a contractor in this sense, but he has been nortoriously unsuccessful in recent years; he is frequently late in paying workers and is thus unable to keep enough workers to complete jobs on schedule.

Thirty-four of the families interviewed (18.5 percent) employ others. Most of these are shopkeepers with no grown sons and smallholders with

5. In 1978 many smallholders were no longer processing their latex at home, but were selling it through a local dealer to a government collection agency. Rubber prices were higher than in 1972, and the 8 to 10 percent increment in daily income that could be earned by selling sheet rubber instead of latex did not seem, to many smallholders, enough to compensate for two or three extra hours of labor.

more land than family members can tap, or whose adult family members are earning more as wage laborers elsewhere than they could in their own rubber gardens. Five families (2.7 percent) employ domestic help such as cooks or general amahs. In addition to the few local people employed in family service, one person works as a cook for a nearby labor *kongsi* (workers' quarters), and several others take in laundry or sewing at home. There are also teachers, bus drivers, four spirit mediums, including the temple caretaker, a few secretaries and clerks (in the council office, the school office, and three or four businesses), gambling club employees, and three organizers of rotating credit societies.

The wide diversity of occupations and the individual nature of most of them present a striking contrast to situations usually described in the literature on Chinese villages. There is no hiring out of water buffalo and owner for plowing, no labor exchange groups to cooperate at harvest time, no organization to coordinate irrigation, and in general very little dependence of one family on another for economic assistance of any sort. Since a strong land base and genealogical depth are both lacking, it is hardly surprising that there is also no significant agnatic kinship organization, no predominance of a few surname groups over others.

Because of this occupational diversity and the variable nature of much of Sanchun's employment, it is difficult to draw a sharp picture of the community's socioeconomic structure. For the most part, people willingly gave estimates of their earnings, but the estimates were often so vague as to be of questionable value for my purposes. Only salaried workers and shopkeepers, who maintain careful records for tax purposes, could provide reliable figures. Although the incomes of people involved in wage labor, petty commerce, or agriculture might be fairly regular over the long run, short-term variation introduces considerable uncertainty into attempts to portray accurately income distribution in Sanchun. Certain types of work are paid on a piece-rate or a day-rate basis. The number of days worked each month in such occupations as tapping, logging, and mining depends on the rains, which vary seasonally; thus a monthly wage is difficult to determine. Moreover, a number of people work fewer than twelve months per year — for example, loggers, who usually return home for a month or two at the Chinese New Year. In a number of cases, informants expressed a general idea of their household monthly income or expenditures (many explicitly equated the two — "We bring in just enough to eat up"), but could offer few details regarding individual incomes within the unit.

Nonetheless, a rough picture of income distribution is better than no picture at all; tables 8 through 10 show the distribution of estimated monthly incomes for individuals and for the residentially concentrated *jia* (including only remittances from absent workers, not their full earnings), controlled for household size. The sample size in these tables is limited by

TABLE 8.   Approximate monthly income per gainfully employed person

Amount (in M$)	No.	%
< 50	30	8.8
50 — 80	58	17.1
80 — 100	30	8.8
100 — 150	74	21.8
150 — 200	32	9.4
200 — 300	41	12.1
300 — 500	44	13.0
500 +	30	8.8
Total	339	100.0

the above considerations; only cases for which reasonably reliable estimates were given or could be constructed are included.

It is clear from tables 9 and 10 and figure 1 that in terms of income San-chun is a fairly homogeneous community. There are a few rather poor families and a few rather well-to-do families, but the majority fall into a middle or lower-middle income range. Table 10 documents the tendency for higher income to be associated with larger household size. The exceptions that appear clearly in table 9, families with two to five members and incomes over M$500, are for the most part produced by combinations of elements of modernization. They are cases of "modern" elementary or nuclear families coupled with higher earning power achieved through education: families of school teachers and office clerks.

Eight households have per capita indexes (income divided by family size) over 200, and another twenty-seven have indexes between 100 and 200 — considerably higher than the majority of households, as shown in figure 1.[6] There is a clear recognition within the community of some disparity in standard of living, but few people seem to resent this, except perhaps some of the very poor. For one thing, conspicuous consumption is not prevalent, particularly among the long-established families. For another, very few households make a portion of their income from land rents or investments, as shown in table 7; the vast majority in the community work for a living. Inevitably some are more successful than others, but there is no leisured

6. The index is unfortunately vague because of the necessity for grouping estimated income in sliding intervals, as informants showed a strong preference for dealing in very round numbers. Quantitative monetary data provided in rural studies is often presented in such a manner that it gives an impression of great precision and accuracy. My own field research in two different rural settings has convinced me that such precision may in many cases be illusory, and I reiterate my earlier statements about the approximate nature of this data because I wish to avoid creating any such illusions here.

TABLE 9. Approximate monthly income by size of household

Amount	Number in household																	Total	
	1	2	3	4	5	6	7	8	9	10	11	12	13	14	15	16	21	No.	%
<100	4	2	4	2	—	1	—	—	—	—	—	—	—	—	—	—	—	13	7
100— 200	1	3	6	4	4	7	4	6	4	—	—	—	—	—	—	—	—	39	21
200— 300	—	—	4	8	4	7	8	6	4	4	1	—	—	—	—	—	—	46	25
300— 500	—	—	2	7	7	6	3	5	6	2	2	—	1	1	—	1	—	43	23
500— 750	—	2	2	1	3	—	4	7	2	—	1	—	—	—	2	1	—	25	14
750— 1,000	—	—	—	—	2	—	—	—	—	2	1	—	—	—	1	—	1	7	4
1,000—1,500	—	—	—	—	—	—	1	1	3	—	—	—	—	—	—	—	—	5	3
1,500+	—	—	—	—	—	—	—	—	—	—	—	—	—	—	1	—	1	2	1
Total	5	7	18	22	20	21	20	25	19	8	5	—	1	1	4	2	2	180	100

TABLE 10. Approximate monthly income by size of household, with data grouped

| | Number in household | | | | | | | | | | | | Total |
| | 1 | | 2-3 | | 4-6 | | 7-9 | | 10-13 | | 14-21 | | |
Amount (in M$)	No.	%	No.	%	No.	%	No.	%	No.	%	No.	%	No.
<100	4	80	6	24	3	5	—	—	—	—	—	—	13
100— 300	1	20	13	52	34	54	32	50	5	36	—	—	85
300— 750	—	—	6	24	24	38	27	42	6	43	5	56	68
750—1,500	—	—	—	—	2	3	5	8	3	21	2	22	12
1,500+	—	—	—	—	—	—	—	—	—	—	2	22	2
Total	5	100	25	100	63	100	64	100	14	100	9	100	180

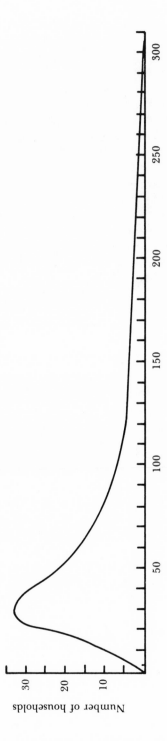

Figure 1. An approximate distribution of per capita income

elite. Even wealthy shopkeepers spend long hours managing their businesses, but most still find time to participate in community activities such as the temple festival, weddings, and, invariably, funerals. They eat somewhat better food than poorer families, send their children to the city for secondary education and occasionally overseas for advanced training, and they own motor vehicles of some sort. They do not dress differently from other townspeople, however, and their homes are not noticeably superior in quality to those of the local middle class.[7] Some lend money or extend credit on nonluxury items such as food or building supplies, but at little or no interest. Although there are some lines of distinction, they tend to be less pronounced than in larger towns. By and large, people in Sanchun share a sense of belonging to a coherent social community having equal value for all its members. The wealthy fill most leadership roles and provide essential services in aiding those less well educated and less sophisticated in their dealings with the government. Face-to-face contact on a frequent basis among all members of the community, in the marketplace and at social gatherings, prevents the development of extreme social distance between groups of unequal economic standing.

Organizations

Although Sanchun lacks extended kin groups and farmers' associations, other forms of formal organization do exist. None, however, is either broad in the scope of its activity or fully comprehensive in its membership. The largest are the mutual-aid societies and the native-place associations. There are two mutual-aid societies whose primary function is to provide assistance — money and manpower — with funerals. Each time someone in a member's family dies, members pay M$2 to help the bereaved family with expenses. Tables, benches, and a canvas canopy to cover the all-night wake are also supplied and set up by the organization. Members assist the family at the cemetery, carrying and lowering the coffin. Membership in the two organizations overlaps, since socially minded people who are not poverty stricken (as few families are in Sanchun) will readily contribute to such causes. Nonetheless, the mutual-aid society operating under the auspices of the MCA has had to reorganize and start from scratch twice in the last

7. By 1978 the wealthy and the middle class were widening the gap between themselves and the poor. In 1972, television sets and refrigerators were quite rare in the village, and there was only one flush toilet in all of Sanchun. By 1978 all of these amenities were becoming relatively common; people estimated that perhaps 30 to 40 percent of the villagers had built improved sanitary facilities, and a much higher percentage had acquired television sets. Nonetheless, there was still a small minority of poor families whose lives had shown little improvement over the years.

ten years because members whose elderly parents had died began to default in payment. The current membership list includes 241 names, but it is doubtful that all participate fully. The records of the second association, organized by one of the village elders, were not open to scrutiny, but its head claimed to have about 200 members and some of the same problems. A few years earlier one of the collectors of the contributions for this second group absconded. Almost half of the families interviewed, 83 (46.4 percent), said they were members of a mutual-aid society of this sort.

There are two Cantonese native-place associations in Sanchun, the Gugangzhou association and the Gaozhou association. The Gugangzhou association includes immigrants and their descendants from the four *xian* (counties) in Guangzhou *fu* (a former prefecture in Guangdong) making up the group commonly known as *sei yap* (Cantonese), as well as those from Chiqi *xian* and from Heshan *xian*. Members of the Gaozhou association trace their descent from Gaozhou *fu*, also a former prefecture in Guangdong. Both serve functions very similar to those of the mutual-aid societies, contributing financial aid for funerals and the use of tables and benches for both wakes and weddings. In addition, banquets are held twice yearly at the time of the spring and autumn cemetery offerings; some elders first visit the graves during the day, and in the evening representatives of all the member families join in the banquet. The Gugangzhou and Gaozhou associations have about fifty and thirty members, respectively. Only a dozen or so Sanchun families are members of the Hanjiang association, which has its headquarters in a larger town eight miles away. This association comprises people from Chaozhou *fu*, a former prefecture in northeastern Guangdong whose inhabitants are mostly Teochius and Hakkas. The local Hakka membership originates in Dabu *xian* and Jieyang *xian*, the latter almost all from the township of Hepo. The local Teochiu membership hails from several *xian*. Twenty or twenty-five local Hokkien families are members of the Hokkien (Fujian) association branch in the same nearby town and twice that number come together for the local banquets. These associations are not organized locally for mutual aid, but like the Gugangzhou and the Gaozhou associations they observe the spring and autumn rites. Since the two restaurants in town cannot accommodate the feasts of all these groups on one night, representatives of the associations agree in advance on different days for each group to observe the rites. In addition to providing funeral and other ritual assistance, native-place associations offer limited scholarship aid for school children. Although the local associations do not themselves offer scholarships, both the Hanjiang and the Gugangzhou are affiliated with associations in larger towns which do. Eighty-eight (48.4 percent) of the families interviewed said they were members of a native-place association, either locally or elsewhere.

Other local associations maintain lists of so-called committee members that are in fact lists of contributors and do not really indicate the scope of active cooperative participation. These are the Sanchun Chinese Recreation Club (73), the Chinese temple (115, including people from outside of Sanchun), the cemetery committee (37), and the Sanchun old people's home (30). The executive boards of these organizations are of greater interest than their membership lists, and will be referred to in the next chapter.

The board of managers of Chung Hwa Chinese Primary School is an executive board comprised of nine members, three each representing parents, alumni, and the general public. The government is now authorized to appoint three more but has never done so. Membership rotates yearly: one new member is elected in each of the three categories. The composition of the board has in fact changed little in past years; beyond the established community leaders there is little interest. The headmaster commented to me at the election meeting that some people avoid the position because new members are subject to investigation by the government. Furthermore, in his view, things run smoothly just as they are and a change would be undesirable. He was appointed by the board, so it is hardly surprising that he is satisfied with its present composition. Only twenty-five ballots were returned in the election, although all children had been given ballots to carry home to their parents. Most of the returned ballots came from school "subscribers" who contribute M$25 or more, the same group eligible for board membership.

Two government-organized committees exist in Sanchun, drawing members from the entire *mukim*. The Goodwill Committee, established after the 1969 disturbances, is composed of members of the three major ethnic groups. It meets only if an occasion calls specifically for interracial cooperation. The single meeting during my stay in Sanchun was held when tensions were high after a series of unsolved arsons. Even then it was an ad hoc committee formed by council leaders rather than the government committee that acted decisively, calling a general town meeting and organizing an interracial night-watch brigade to patrol the entire town for a few weeks, until all were convinced that the culprit had been caught. The second government committee, the Rubber Smallholders Association, formed recently and has as yet little significance for the community.

At the time of my initial field research, Sanchun had branch offices of only two political parties, the Malaysian Chinese Association (MCA) and the Democratic Action Party (DAP). Generally speaking, people held the view that politics is dirty, that it is better not to get involved. When I first inquired about party membership I was told that the MCA had about sixty members, and had not grown much nor changed composition significantly since it was formed to assist the relocated villagers in the early period of the Emergency. The DAP office, as noted above, is rented out. There are twelve members of the DAP in the Sanchun vicinity, but most of them are young men on the estates or in the tin mines. Only two Sanchun men acknowledge being members, both young shopkeepers who serve on the local executive committee. One, the son of a coffee shop owner, is rather nervous about belonging to the "wrong" party and is afraid it hurts his mother's business.

The club and the temple are the only organizations that serve in any real sense as focal points of community social activity. At the time of spring and autumn graveyard rites, after members of the cemetery committee have visited the old and new cemeteries and made offerings at the common grave in each (a tombstone dedicated to all Sanchun Chinese), an evening banquet, attended by a male representative from perhaps half of the families in the community, is held in the club. The front of the club building is given over to a newspaper reading room frequented almost entirely by adult men; in the back are the gambling tables, which are usually crowded till well past midnight and almost till dawn during the New Year holiday. It is chiefly men who gamble there; women play mahjong and card games in private homes.

The temple festival, held during the first nine days of the ninth lunar month to celebrate the birthdays of the *jiuhuangye* (the nine emperors) to whom the temple is dedicated, is the single fully communal activity of the year. Eighty or ninety percent of the families in the community make at least a token contribution of M$2 or so toward the festival expenses, which include the costs of an opera troupe giving two performances daily, large amounts of incense and paper money to be burned, and the special services of Buddhist priests and musicians brought in from nearby larger towns. The wealthy men who comprise the temple committee carry the burden of the expense, which is considerable. (In 1972 the opera troupe alone cost M$1,000 per day; by 1978 this had risen to M$1,400.)

At midnight on the last day of the eighth month, several hundred towns-people assemble by the river about a mile from the temple to await the descent of the gods, whose arrival is announced with music when the spirit medium goes into trance. Incense sticks, ready in every hand, are lighted, and paper spirit money is burned in offering. Two small sedan chairs carrying incense pots representing the gods lead the lively procession back to the temple, where offerings of fruit, cakes, and more incense and spirit money are made by a huge crowd that includes members of almost every family in the community. For the next nine days and nights throngs from all over the area gather to watch the operas, buying iced drinks, steamed peanuts, and other goodies from stands, which are located during festival time by the temple instead of in the market, and eating fried noodles and chicken-rice gruel at the outdoor restaurants set up for the occasion.

On the evening of the final day, *dabei*, a form of divination, is used to ask the gods whom they would like to have officiating during the next year's celebration and which Chinese language they would prefer for the opera performances. Two curved blocks of wood, flat on one side and rounded on the other, are thrown on the floor in front of the altar. If the sides match, either rounded or flat, the gods oppose the proposition put to them; if one block falls rounded side up and the other flat side up, the gods approve.

The men to serve throughout the next year as *luzhu*, keeper of the god's incense pot, his two assistants, the treasurer, and his two assistants are selected in this manner. The list of men contributing M$25 or more is read one by one, and the wooden blocks are thrown for each man until a negative reply is received. The man receiving the most successive affirmatives wins the first post, and the process is repeated for each of the remaining five positions. The *luzhu*, in addition to overseeing much of the ritual at the next festival, must burn incense in the temple on the first and fifteenth of each lunar month. Some men choose to make large donations to show their community spirit but withdraw their names from the *dabei*, not wishing to contribute so much time. This selection of the officials is very spirited, with people crowded around the current *luzhu* as he throws the blocks and cheering on any name that draws a series of affirmatives. At both festivals that I attended, the *luzhus* were young men whom I had not previously known, one from a nearby estate. Both were obviously pleased at the responsibility they had and at being in the center of attention, and were happy to be introduced to the foreigner taking notes and pictures. It was clearly a community duty that heightened their feelings of belonging, of sharing the strong sense of communal solidarity pervading the entire festival.

At midnight on the final night, a huge crowd again gathers to send off the gods, following the sedan chairs with lighted incense sticks. The incense pot is put in a floating box which serves as a boat for the next stage of the gods' journey. As the boat drifts out of sight down the river, colorful paper horses and a large and gaudy paper boat go up in a blaze, to serve as further conveyances in the spirit world, and the spirit medium comes out of the trance. The burning incense sticks are stuck in the ground, and people drift homeward in small groups.

The officials selected by divination have primarily ritual duties. The men who actually run the daily affairs of the temple, keep the regular books, pay the salary of the caretaker/spirit medium, and make decisions about matters such as which opera troupe to hire and whether to build a roof over the spectator area for protection in case of rain are the same men who are important in other areas of community leadership. During the rest of the year, the temple is a place of individual worship where people may come to ask the gods' advice on private matters or pray for personal good fortune. Only at this annual festival does it form a focus for community solidarity, and even then it is not exclusive. Outsiders may contribute to the temple, just as Sanchun people may contribute to temples dedicated to different gods in other places.

Sanchun has a clear notion of itself as a community, unambiguously defined by its administrative status and distinct territorial and social boundaries. The market center is the hub of the community and of a somewhat larger trading area. Within Sanchun, however, there is little integration. Each business is a self-contained unit, usually a family enterprise, but sometimes including clerks and shop assistants who take meals with the family. Each village household relies on its own members for income from individualized jobs such as rubber tapping or construction work, and sometimes, but less often, for their labor in a family enterprise such as a noodle stall or rubber production from their own smallholding. Vertical cleavages of subethnicity and language exist but are of little importance. Horizontal cleavages of socioeconomic status are only slightly more important. Networks of personal friendship are likely to link people at roughly the same income level while cutting across subethnic lines, with the income drawn from virtually any source: driving a taxi, tapping rubber, sweating over a hot *wok* in a restaurant, sitting behind the counter of a shop, or working as a salaried government clerk or teacher. Public occasions such as weddings and funerals, as well as yearly grave ceremonies and temple festivals, bring together representatives from families throughout the community.

Neither the economic nor the social organization patterns in Sanchun create solidarity groups above the level of the family. Larger kinship groupings are nonexistent. Occupational diversity precludes group vulnerability to the whims of nature, as in a fully agricultural community, or to the exploitation of "bosses," as on an estate or in a mining or factory town. If a worker has trouble with his employer, he usually changes jobs with little difficulty. Problems are individualized and often short-lived, and do not serve to coalesce groups that will take common action or have common interests. Family insularity predominates throughout.

But there is one factor common to the community that can and does serve as a crystallizing force for group identity and solidarity: ethnicity. Cantonese, Hakka, Hokkien, and the others—all are Chinese, and all are equally concerned about government policies regarding Chinese education, Chinese access to taxi or tin-washing licenses, and so forth. Ethnicity is meaningful only in terms of oppositions. Sanchun is Chinese only as it is conceptually juxtaposed against its non-Chinese surroundings, its Malay-dominated political environment. The discussions that follow—of the San-chun political leadership, of bureaucratic encapsulation of that leadership under the current system, and of political mobilization—will illuminate further the implications of ethnicity as a focus of political identity in a plural society.

5

The Configuration of Local Leadership

Patterns of local leadership in Sanchun have undergone marked changes over the years. The relationships binding the local unit to the political systems encapsulating it have altered, and the cast of characters participating in the local arena has been transformed in the natural course of events, as both the individuals who take part and the roles they play change and develop through the years. Within parameters set by changing political environments, individual actors have manipulated resources and capital of various sorts to win, or lose, places of prominence in Sanchun over the past half century.

Qualifications for leadership tend to correspond to the requirements of the position (see Skinner 1968). As the requirements fluctuate with the will and interests of the more powerful political center or with other modifications in the political environment, the character of leadership at the local level alters. During the Emergency, the wealth that had traditionally laid the foundation for a Sanchun headman's power became instead a liability. It was dangerous to be known as a "lackey of British imperialism" if one had logging and rubber interests that were vulnerable to the Communist guerrillas, so wealthy entrepreneurs voluntarily withdrew from positions of leadership. The prewar civil authorities had ruled indirectly through such successful men, but the military authorities of the Emergency administration needed and supported a different kind of leader, one who could not be intimidated by the "bandits" or forced to submit to their demands for food and money. The power that comes with external validation of a local leader thus passed into new hands. But tradition is important in a Chinese community. Once a man has achieved high status and prestige he is not easily pushed completely aside, though his power may wane and be replaced by influence.

It will be useful at the outset to define certain terms as they are used here. The distinction between *power* and *influence* is critical. Power is taken to mean the capacity for shaping or changing the life circumstances of other people, regardless of their wishes in the matter; influence refers to the ability to cause other people to share one's own views or wishes. Neither is a necessary concomitant of the other, although they are often associated. Either, depending on its primary source of origin or support, may be considered to be predominantly *political* or *economic* in nature. Moreover, either may be derived from sources either *external* or *internal* to the local system in which it is being wielded. Logically, we might also differentiate between external and internal spheres of application of such power and influence, but in fact this distinction is hardly relevant here. Persons at the most basic level of a centralized power hierarchy are unlikely to have power that is effective beyond their own local systems; nonetheless, they might have limited influence among external power holders where decisions specifically relevant to the local system are concerned.

The paramount leader at any given time holds a certain amount of power over members of the community, both the supporters within his own clique and the broader community as a whole. In a community such as Sanchun the power that is in this manner *public* in nature derives from the leader's external political support; he may also control *private* power (over individuals) by virtue of his control of economic resources, internal and external, and of course he may use his public power to private ends. Private power, however, cannot readily be used for public ends — that is, to affect the majority of the community — until it has been converted, either through external political legitimation or through use as influence over local actors who hold such politically legitimated power. Influence of a private sort, when it is among the ruling clique, thus approaches power. By contrast, influence among the broader public such as that held by respected mediators may have little relationship to power.

Contemporary friendships, alliances, and animosities in Sanchun have their roots in events of the past. The data to be presented are for the most part by nature nonquantifiable; they include anecdotes, observations, personal histories, and evaluations of character. Logical inference and speculation are necessary to fill in some of the gaps in important narratives. Such is the stuff of politics, and so must it be presented, spiced with some conjecture, postulation, and interpretation. The case study of Sanchun shows a pattern in which an individual's public power based on external legitimation gradually gives way, as leaders age and circumstances change, to be replaced by public influence based on the memory of power judiciously wielded in the past. Strong personalities have been able to make use of changes in the styles of center-periphery relations at crucial times to win power, manipulating new types of resources to establish and secure their positions: Lee Koi's rise to power in the 1950s is a case in point. External forces may at other times dominate the local scene, offering little recourse to the people who are themselves being manipulated: Chin Ta Hing in the 1970s has been confirmed and maintained almost against his will in a position of power, as the local system has served as a pawn in the power struggles going on at higher levels. Thus while individual inclination and strength of personality undeniably play a role in shaping local-level politics, an incontrovertibly larger role is played by the parameters that are set by external circumstances and conditions.

Traditional Patrons and Clients

The keystone of the ruling clique in the early 1970s was Lee Koi, an established patriarch born at the turn of the century.[1] He is still known to all as the *cunzhang*, the village head, a title that was rightfully his during the Emergency, though the office as such no longer exists. The creation of a formally elected *cunzhang* was the first of the modifications of traditional local leadership patterns that enabled Lee to rise to power. Had there been no Emergency, he might have remained the subordinate of a more powerful merchant headman.

Lee left China in about 1924. When he arrived in Malaya, he first spent two years in Ipoh, then came to Sanchun to join a paternal cousin who worked as a logger for Choong Hah. Lee also went to work for Choong; the two men got on well, and Lee became manager of Choong's logging enterprise when the latter decided to devote more of his own time to a new venture, tin mining. Choong, important also as a rice wholesaler, was wealthy, generous, and well informed in the law. He was generally recognized as a man of considerable stature, and his patronage was much sought after. Lee and Choong were both Hakkas, a bond that in the early days was of considerable importance, and according to some accounts the two eventually became sworn brothers (*jiebai xiongdi*) as well. Through Choong's patronage, Lee became manager of the Sanchun Recreation Club when it was formed in 1936. Not a rich man himself, Lee was nonetheless able to dispense patronage second-hand in the form of jobs in the logging and club operations that he managed, and he could act as an intermediary for people seeking aid directly from Choong himself.

Choong and Tan Tien Yu, another wealthy merchant, were the predominant local notables of the late 1930s and 1940s. Both fit the common mold of the overseas Chinese leader — wealthy, successful merchants whose

1. Many of the names mentioned in this chapter appear in a reference table in appendix B.

standing enabled them to deal effectively with outside authorities and who personally dispensed loans, favors, jobs, and aid of all sorts to less fortunate *huaqiao* brothers. Choong is credited with the reopening of the school after the war, and with the founding of the local MCA branch. Tan was chairman of several local organizations, including the maintenance committee under the Japanese. He was particularly renowned for his generosity; he granted loans or small gifts to almost anyone who approached him, and extended so much credit on goods sold in his sundry shop that his son estimates losses as high as M$50,000 on bad debts. Both Tan and Choong received formal recognition from the sultan for their contributions to community welfare through active service. Their large memorial plaques are kept by their eldest sons, each of whom has earned a plaque in his own name as well.

Lee Koi could never match Tan's financial generosity, but he was apparently able to build up a fair reputation of his own through service and brokerage within the local arena based on his relationship with Choong. It was through his willingness to serve during the Emergency period that he came into formal power in his own right. A number of informants concurred that Choong was the headman when the Emergency broke out, but that he had assiduously avoided taking on a formal leadership position which would in effect have put his head on the MCP block. His logging teams were too vulnerable to guerrilla attack for him to openly declare himself against the MCP by directly serving at the apex of the local British government organization. Tan was in a similar position, as a good part of his income derived from his sixty-odd acres of rubber, all well beyond the protection of the British. As a manager rather than an owner, Lee had, by contrast, little to lose materially. As an ambitious man seeking high position, he had much to gain, in fact, by coming forward voluntarily to serve as village head.

It seems that Choong and Tan, until their deaths in 1957 and 1968, respectively, retained a great deal of influence locally. Older villagers with long memories of the two assert that Choong and then Tan were the local headmen, Lee rising to that informal status only upon Tan's death. Through the early 1960s, at least, Tan was the man whom people approached with personal problems, whether they were asking for a loan, for assistance in resolving a dispute with a neighbor, or for help in making a recalcitrant son see reason. As village head during the Emergency, Lee built a firm power base through his connections with the British government, but it seems that only gradually was that power translated into local influence of the sort wielded by Choong and Tan.

The manner in which power and influence are associated at the local level in overseas Chinese society is not as straightforward, then, as one might assume. Choong and Tan built their positions first through wealth and success in broadly based economic enterprises at a time when political control external to the local system was minimal. Resources drawn from the larger capitalist system under the laissez faire indirect colonial rule formed the basis of both men's local power. Wealth enabled them to dispense patronage—jobs, loans, and related economic favors. The recipients of these favors repaid not in kind but in respect and support, thus forming a local political base that in turn won recognition from external authorities. With recognition came a measure of influence in external politics that might be used both to broaden economic enterprises in external arenas and to strengthen local political power. Through time, power used wisely became generalized into great local influence, effective in both political and personal matters. Then, in the Emergency, Lee came to control extralocal political influence, and through it, local power. The older men gradually slipped into somewhat less powerful but highly influential roles of community elders (*laobeiren*).

Lee talks proudly of his role in the Emergency. He boasts that he alone was uncowed by terrorists on either side of the fence. The assistant resettlement officer, Lee says, was afraid to move about freely even within the village without Lee by his side. Lee recounts in great detail his own narrow escapes from assassination attempts. Although other villagers also recall his bravery, they more often tell of times when he was able to give them or others they knew very concrete assistance based on his influence with the authorities. Lee could often obtain the release of suspected communists and communist sympathizers on his recognizance. As village head and chairman of the village committee, he directed allocation of relief funds to families whose breadwinners had been detained or deported. Some say he could also help certain people to obtain the more desirable houselots, but he denies this. A few specific cases are also cited from that period of Tan's largess, providing from his own pocket for a roof for a poor resettled family, or giving food and supplies from his shop to people unable to pay. Under military rule, however, life and freedom were more important than money alone, and Lee's connections with military and police officials provided the services most valued to the most harassed and frightened of the new settlers, and, as we shall see below, to some established merchants as well.

New Rules and New Resources during the Emergency

The institution of elections during the Emergency provided a new format for local rivalry. Records are spotty; Lee's oral account of the 1951 village committee election (see chapter 3) is followed by council records of the

1954 election, then yearly records from 1957 to 1962, apparently the last local election held. The scant and formal reports raise and leave unanswered tantalizing questions about precisely how the new process was used by local actors intent on achieving or consolidating power. Informants provided only slightly more information on the elections, but certain other events were better remembered and were freely discussed in detail. A picture emerges of a heated rivalry between Lee Koi and Tan Siew Hing, the son of Tan Tien Yu. The two men employed quite different sorts of ammunition in succeeding battles in a continuing contest, won decisively in the end by Lee Koi.

In Sanchun's first formal election in 1954, Tan Siew Hing, at the relatively young age of thirty, entered the political arena. He received four nominating votes to his father's one, and got fifty-three votes in the final ballot. He placed ninth and thus became one of the eleven councillors elected, while his father, Tan Tien Yu, received only twenty-six votes and did not place. It would be extremely unusual anywhere, and particularly among Chinese, for a son to compete against his father; it must be assumed both that the elder Tan chose to pass his support to his son and that the son was highly ambitious. Siew Hing explains that during those years his father was often out of town on business, and other informants concur that he sometimes spent as much as two or three weeks out of a month away from Sanchun. He may have been looking after business affairs elsewhere that took precedence over his rural rubber interests, or hoping that his absences would diminish attention that his estates might otherwise attract from the guerrillas. He may have had a second family elsewhere—that was a common practice among the wealthy, and his wife in Sanchun had borne him no sons, although two had been adopted.[2] In any event, Siew Hing took charge of local business interests, and local community responsibilities as well, as his father's representative. He was apparently extremely capable, and both father and son shared considerable local stature.

In 1956 Sanchun became a formally constituted local council area, and

2. It is considered improper to discuss the dead, so detailed information on Tan Tien Yu was difficult to come by. My speculation about the possibility of a second wife is based on a number of factors. Wealthy Chinese took second wives fairly often (and sometimes still do today, though less often), and would be particularly likely to do so if the first wife bore no children. Tan Siew Hing has two wives, although the first, who was brought into the family as a child in what Wolf terms a "minor marriage," has borne several children. In Wolf's studies of this form of marriage among Hokkiens in Taiwan, in which parents adopt a little girl, often an infant, and raise her with the intention of eventually marrying her to one of their sons, he has found a high incidence of apparent sexual dissatisfaction among both men and women involved in such marriages, as indicated in rates of divorce, fertility, taking of second wives, and involvement in illicit liaisons (Wolf 1966). The Tans are Hokkien, and the choice of a "little daughter-in-law" for his son might indicate that Tan Tien Yu was repeating a familiar family pattern—that is, that his own wife had similarly been a "little daughter-in-law."

in early 1957 the recently elected (most were in fact reelected) councillors cast votes to choose their officers. Lee Koi received seven of a possible eleven votes for chairman; Tan Siew Hing received nine for the position of vice-chairman. But Lee, the record reports simply and enigmatically, resigned the chairmanship immediately. Tan was unanimously elected to replace him, and Lee then accepted the number two position.

Given Lee's ambitious character, this straightforward statement begs for explication. Lee says that he resigned as an act of protest to the government over what he saw as an insult from the district officer in an unrelated incident. The DO had called a meeting to congratulate new villages that had recently been declared white areas, and Lee was invited, though Sanchun was still black. Lee was offended but attended the meeting, and once there he angrily accused the DO of insulting him, causing him loss of face by leaving his village, Sanchun, under a cloud of suspicion. Lingering anger over that incident, Lee says now, was behind his refusal of the chairmanship.

Another element of mystery, however, is introduced by what the record does *not* say about the resignation. The same secretary was responsible for council minutes from 1956 to 1968, and on other occasions he laboriously details attempts made by councillors to persuade members to reconsider resignations, whether from specific posts or from the council itself. In this case, however, no comment on the resignation was recorded.

Given Lee's pride and temperament, it is not beyond likelihood that he would be moved by simple pique to refuse the chairmanship. But it is possible that the pique, rather than being caused by the DO, was directed at Lee's fellow councillors, who were less than unanimous in supporting his continued chairmanship. His resignation may have been merely a challenge, and he may have been greatly disappointed to find that he was not considered indispensable as chairman. If that is the case, he was apparently misjudging the mood of the assembled councillors and their tradition-based views of the prerequisites of leadership. It was true that he had served for six years as head of the village committee, but now the committee was being advanced to the status of local council, and the Emergency and its special conditions were presumed to be on the way out. It was high time, the "towkays" (wealthy merchants) who numerically dominated the meeting might have thought, to return paramount authority to one of their own, which Tan Siew Hing certainly was, and which Lee was not. Those unwilling to break the conventions of a consensus-based society by casting a vote against the incumbent chairman on the first round may have been quite happy at being given an opportunity to reconsider. It is clear that Tan Siew Hing's support in the council — nine votes at first, then a unanimous eleven — was more solid than Lee Koi's.

Tan Siew Hing held the first chairmanship of the new council a scant four months before what he now calls his "misfortune" befell him. Lee's role in the misfortune is disputed, but the advantage he gained through the affair is clear, and, by inference at least, he had ample motive for the acts imputed to him by Tan and his friends. In 1957 arrests in Sanchun, still a black area, were numerous, and many resulted in long imprisonment. Tan Siew Hing and two other notables, Chin Ta Hing and Lung Sooi, were arrested and charged with contributing money and goods to the Communists. Lee, as vice-chairman, replaced Tan as head of the council.

That there was personal animosity between Tan and Lee is clear, but both its roots and its magnitude remain obscure. They were openly at odds on numerous occasions even in Tan's four short months as chairman. For example, as councillor for public works, Lee was authorized to implement small projects without first consulting the full council, but he infuriated Tan when he proceeded to rewire the council hall at a cost four or five times the maximum amount stipulated for "small" projects requiring no joint decision. Tan questioned not the wiring job but Lee's impertinence in refusing to follow proper procedures, and a heated argument ensued. Such displays of anger are frowned on, and the council ended the matter by voting approval, after the fact, with no formal comment on the procedure.

The animosity between the two men might have been based in part in subethnic differences, though none of my informants offered views along these lines. Nonetheless, it is quite reasonable to speculate that Lee Koi and Choong Hah, as fellow Hakkas, may have frequently found themselves in opposition to the elder Tan, leader of the Hokkien community, a group that was proportionately larger and more important locally before the founding of the village than after. If so, strained feelings may have been transferred to the son.

When the arrests occurred, Lee recalls, he did everything he could to help all three men. He went to each of them separately and advised that the best course of action would be to confess, guilty or not, pleading that they had been forced and had had no choice but to comply, and, averring repentance, promising not to err again. Lee assured them that he would use his personal influence in their support. He points out that Chin and Lung, following his advice, were released with an admonition to be loyal in the future, while Tan, who was afraid that his confession would result in deportation, staunchly maintained that he was innocent and eventually spent three years in prison. Telling the story Lee shakes his head, saying sadly that Tan has only his own stubborness to blame, for all would have been well had he only trusted in Lee as the others did.

Tan viewed the situation differently, according to his friends, and suspected that Lee was behind the whole affair. Of the three men arrested, Tan did in fact have the most to fear. Lung was already over fifty and was less likely to be deported than a younger man. Chin was about Tan's age, but he could pass the blame to his recently deceased father; thus he was confessing someone else's crimes. Moreover, Tan no doubt felt, possibly with reason, that he would get less than an enthusiastic character reference from his rival Lee, no matter what assurances the older man might offer. So Tan went to prison, and Lee took over as council chairman.

For several years after Tan's release and return to Sanchun he was barred by the government from any political activity. Although by the early 1970s he had rejoined the MCA, he took no part in party and council affairs, confining his community activities to the temple, school, and club committees. He kept himself aloof, mixing little with the men who, from his point of view, had failed him by not working energetically enough to secure his release. When both Tan and Lee were present at school and club committee meetings, they seldom spoke directly to each other or even looked at one another.

To what extent Lee might actually have been responsible for the arrests cannot be known. In any case, once they had occurred, he astutely made effective use of his influence with higher military authorities to consolidate his local power. The demonstration was, no doubt, lost on no one. Lee had been actively proving his worth to both officials and villagers for some six years. In this event he cashed in some of his chips with the authorities, and saw one rival banished from the political arena and two other members of the political elite incur considerable debts of gratitude to him for his successful intervention on their behalf. These debts, and those of other members of the local community, he would continue to call in for the next two decades and more. The priority of external political resources over internal economic ones was indisputably proven, as influence in high places accomplished, or at least was given credit for accomplishing, what private capital could not have — and credit, in politics, is what counts.

The Leadership Elite in 1972

During my initial residence in Sanchun, the necessary leadership functions were carried out by a cohesive clique with a core of six or eight activists, supported by another dozen or so more passive followers who provided legitimacy to the core as well as financial support to community projects. From their number are drawn nearly all the members of local groups such as the council, the school board of managers, the temple and cemetery committees, and the MCA branch. The partnership that dominated council and community affairs was that of Lee Koi and Chin Ta Hing.

Chin Ta Hing, current chairman of the local council, first stood for election in 1954 at the relatively young age of twenty-eight. He was defeated, and thereafter rejected nomination twice, but was eventually elected to the council in 1959. In 1962, Chin, a Cantonese, became deputy chairman under Tan Tien Yu (who had succeeded Lee Koi as chairman in 1961). From 1963 on, Tan was frequently absent, leaving the chair to Chin. Upon Tan's death in 1968, Chin served as acting chairman and subsequently was elected chairman unanimously.

Chin's family had never shown political interests. His father, a wealthy businessman with investments in rubber, land, and the local sawmill as well as his sundry business, had a reputation for being stingy. He was never a council member, nor was he particularly active in any other groups. Chin was born in Sanchun; he completed Chinese middle school in Ipoh and taught in the local primary school following the war. He apparently followed his father's path by and large, even after he joined the council. His friends say he was not very active socially or politically for many years. Like his father, he was considered tight-fisted; his numerous additions to the family holdings in the 1960s lend credence to that view. The four Chin brothers (two of whom are not resident in Sanchun and are partially separated from the family economically) own eighty acres of rubber, the local rubber-processing factory, three town shop lots (in partnership with Lee Koi and with Chin's wife's brothers), two pawnshops elsewhere, sizable deposits in other pawnshops, and interest in the sawmill, in addition to the shophouse two of them occupy. Chin is the sole agent locally for a major soft drink company, the major newsagent and liquor dealer and one of two petrol dealers. He is known, probably accurately, as one of the richest men in town. According to informants, it was only after the 1969 racial disturbances in the capital that Chin began to participate more actively in local politics and welfare organizations, making significant financial donations to school funds, funeral societies, and various other organizations, and showing somewhat more enthusiasm in his role as council chairman.

Chin's power in 1972 was largely formal in nature, inherent in the many roles he filled: local council chairman, MCA branch chairman, MCA district committee member, treasurer of the school board, assistant treasurer of the temple committee, secretary of the mutual-aid society, vice-chairman of the club executive committee, chairman of the local Gugangzhou Association, and member of almost every other committee in Sanchun. In any of these roles, Chin could give orders and expect them to be carried out. Furthermore, through his council and party roles, he had (and still has) some influence at higher levels. As an official, Chin can make appeals to the state party apparatus or the civil service on behalf of the bodies he represents or on behalf of a single person within his sphere of responsibility.

Chin is a gentle, mild-mannered man, a fluent public speaker, but somewhat quiet and shy, almost self-effacing. Though he states his views clearly, he never speaks forcefully, raises his voice, loses his temper, or displays any other strong emotion. He laughs frequently, but it is sometimes a laugh which may express embarrassment or polite evasion of an issue as he skillfully changes the subject. His efficiency and thoroughness contribute greatly to the smooth functioning of the community, as he capably fulfills his numerous and varied responsibilities.

Despite the apparent ease with which he plays the role of council chairman, however, Chin maintains that it is not a job to be sought after. Chin speaks in general terms of difficulties he has with friends who expect favors and are displeased if they are not forthcoming. He concurs with an acquaintance, chairman of another local council, who says that with every passing year he makes a few more enemies. Several Sanchun informants agree that Chin has repeatedly tried to withdraw from the position, seeking in vain for someone willing to relieve him. He remains chairman only at the urging of his friends, who feel that there is no one else so capable of managing both the council affairs and the council personalities involved. A commonly expressed view was that Chin's most ticklish problem was not friends' demands but the challenge of keeping Lee Koi placated, showing him adequate but not excessive deference, while still maintaining the esteem of others.

Lee Koi's personal style stands in marked contrast to that of Chin Ta Hing. Lee is a proud man, no doubt with justification. He has indeed had a successful career, rising far from the immigrant laborer he once was. He is well aware of his accomplishments and is not hesitant to boast of them. He speaks thoughtfully, but volubly, and usually at great length on any subject. A leader of unquestioned stature over a long duration, Lee is accustomed to being listened to and agreed with, and will raise his voice if necessary to remind others of his expectations. He is also sociable, a genial host, a man who enjoys drinking games at banquets, consuming good quantities of Hennesy brandy straight, drunk from a water tumbler. In his seventies, he retains a healthy vigor about all he does, showing his age perhaps most clearly in his propensity to talk about his own past exploits rather than about hopes for the future.

For his service as village head, Lee has received recognition from the sultan. He is the only man in Sanchun able to place on proud display the letters P.J.K. (Pingat Jasa Kebaktian) after his name, a title given for long or honorable service to the government. A measure of Lee's popularity and the high esteem in which he is held may be seen in attendance at his family celebrations. He boasts, for example, of sixty tables (about six hundred people) at his second son's wedding. Many of the guests appeared without invitation, but bringing, of course, the traditional cash gift in a "red packet," and the government officials from district and state capitals filled three tables alone.

Honor and prestige are Lee's only rewards for years of community service, for he is no more a rich man now than he was thirty years ago. He is a partner in the sawmill and in a pork roasting and selling partnership, but he estimates average monthly income from the two to be less than M$300. Lee speaks of other income, specifying some commission as a go-between on land sales, and it is likely that there is some "tea money" also in this category, but this is not discussed. Lee presides over a household of sixteen people, including his fourth son and his wife, plus wives and children of two other sons. The absent sons send money monthly; some of it is pocket money for their families, and some goes into a common fund for purchase of food shared by all. On occasion, Lee has benefited personally from his power and position—for example, he has extended his house beyond the normally prescribed limits—but he has not been avaricious, as evidenced by his moderate standard of living and minimal estate. The moderation he has shown is one of the touches that retain the respect and affection of the villagers.

Lee Koi is undoubtedly still among the most influential men in Sanchun, but like the aging leaders he once replaced, he now holds influence, for the most part, rather than power. People still do his bidding, and he is called on to help settle family and neighborhood squabbles. Many villagers I talked with thought of Lee's position as *cunzhang* as a formal office, and those who differentiated between his role and that of council chairman tended to see the village head's job as concerned with village matters such as street lighting, roads, and drains—duties that fell under Lee's jurisdiction as councillor for public works. But they correctly perceived the council chairman as the intermediary responsible for dealings with the government, for indeed it is Chin Ta Hing who now controls the local links to external political resources.

Chin frequently travels to district and state capitals on both public and private business. When the MCA task force organizers arrived in Sanchun in 1971, it was Chin and other younger men whom they approached first and consulted with most often. Lee, in fact, showed little interest in their program, as it had no effect on the strictly local spheres that had come to form his chief interests, the club and the council. Party leaders and government officials alike stop by casually in Chin's shop on the main road when they happen to be passing through en route to and from larger centers. Lee seems increasingly to participate less in informal exchanges of that sort, although he is still present at slightly more formally convened meetings and casual but regular evening gatherings. Simply by virtue of his formal offices and the access to external authorities that they entail, Chin, despite his own reluctance, has been gaining the shifting balance of power for some time. Malaysia, like most developing countries, is staffed with young men rather than old, in civil service and in the police, and to some extent in political organizations. A high proportion of civil servants in the district are young Malays who, like the Chinese political organizers, tend to regard

Lee Koi as an aging patriarch to be respected and Chin Ta Hing as the man more able to get things done.

In 1972, Lee Koi and Chin Ta Hing stood at the center of an unchallenged leadership clique comprising all of their fellow councillors and a few other activists who participated in other local committees. They received passive support from a more peripheral group of wealthy men who attended some meetings, contributed money, and accepted their decisions. A few respected men, such as Tan Siew Hing, stood aloof, and some grumbled privately about Lee's domineering character and refused to serve on committees because of his presence, but no one openly opposed him or the clique he headed. To round out the picture of Sanchun's political elite I will provide a few more brief sketches of members of the dominant group, as well as descriptions of men who have some political standing but bear somewhat ambiguous relationships to the central clique. Sons of two members of the core are noticeable on its fringe, but, interestingly, the sons of the early leaders Choong Hah and Tan Tien Yu both fall in the latter ambiguous category.

Lung Sooi, a Cantonese shopkeeper in his mid-sixties in 1972, served as treasurer of the council, of which he has been a member since 1954, and of the MCA branch. He was chairman of the school board and of the recreation club, and was active on most other local committees as well. Lung is a sundry dealer, well known personally to most local people as generous, fair, and kind. He extends credit freely and gives interest-free loans readily. Most of the pig farmers, whose income is seasonal rather than regular like tappers or wage earners, buy their provisions exclusively from him on credit; other villagers mention having borrowed from him for house repairs or extensions. Thus he is not only powerful in leadership circles but has a loyal following in the community as well.

Chong Kit is another Cantonese councillor and active member of most other local committees. His rather stately demeanor makes him appear older than he is—in his early fifties. Since the war he has had a vegetable stall in the market, and more recently he took over the selling of chips as a member of the club gambling farm, thus spending long hours at the club each night. In 1975 he opened a noodle shop in his home on the edge of A section, where his wife, eldest son, and a couple of daughters do most of the work. He is the organizer of the private funeral association mentioned in chapter 3. Through these enterprises he has scores of acquaintances and is widely respected among both villagers and the elite.

Lee Koi, Lung Sooi, and Chong Kit are the men most commonly thought of as the elders (*laobeiren*), called upon as mediators of disputes between neighbors or within families, trusted to be wise as well as just. Chong and Lee are close personal friends. They are neighbors, and one of Lee's sons married one of Chong's daughters. Lung was at one time also close to Lee, but now their relationship is little more than civil. Lee's propensity to act without consulting others offended Tan Siew Hing as council chairman in 1957, and it has offended Lung more recently in incidents involving both the school board and the club. In 1965, Lee, then school manager, decided that the school needed a new office and staff room, so he extracted promises of financial support from four wealthy men and went ahead with the construction, not bothering to convene the board to discuss the project or to consult Lung as chairman. On another occasion, Lung found that Lee, as club manager, had instructed the caretaker to open the guest room only with Lee's personal approval, and chairman Lung had to get that approval before the caretaker would unlock the door for a friend of Lung's.

It is not without some reason, it appears, that Lee is accused by his detractors of being dictatorial, tyrannical, and high-handed in his dealings with other people. Lung might privately agree with such an assessment, but, like his friend Chin, he owes a debt of gratitude to Lee for his quick release during the Emergency when he was charged with providing material support to the enemy. Moreover, in light of the still earlier incident when Lung was forced through torture to betray Lee to the Japanese, Lee's intervention with the British authorities no doubt left Lung doubly grateful, and enhanced Lee's reputation as a noble and just man who bears no grudges. It is noteworthy that even though some of Lee's peers may find his one-man decision-making style impertinent, he has no trouble with the lower-level functionaries who are called on to act on his orders. Power, when judiciously applied, breeds more power, as Lee's example proves time and again, and even once on the wane its memory strongly undergirds a position of high prestige and influence.

Lee Koi, Chin Ta Hing, Lung Sooi, and Chong Kit are the four most important men in council and community affairs. They get together casually, in varying combinations, to discuss issues and to decide on agendas for the larger assemblies. The yearly council proposal for capital works to be submitted to the district office is worked out in committee, so to speak, and when a community response was needed after a sudden spate of arsons, it was this group who planned a night patrol and called a general town meeting for its organization.

Most matters brought up at council and committee meetings are routine, however, and pre-assembly consultations tend to be very informal and may include other members of the clique's support group. Many of the men drop by Chin's shop in the morning to pick up their newspapers and pass some time chatting casually. In the evening they meet in coffee shops for drinks, noodles, and gossip. In such casual conversations, opinions may be voiced about someone's illegally erected garage or storage shed, for example, or whether market stall holders are keeping the market clean enough, or the relative merits of new lighting for the basketball court or new equipment for the badminton court.

One man who played a focal role in such casual, mundane local politics in 1972 was Liew Kam Ming, a Hakka born in Perak, then forty-one. He was at that time the single local councillor living in the heart of the new village (a second was appointed in 1974). Like his father and elder brother, Liew had been a logger, but both he and his brother have been far more successful than most in that trade. The elder brother, now living in Ipoh, has become a wealthy tin mine owner and hobnobs with the sultan of Perak. Liew Kam Ming is involved in numerous investments, including 30 acres of rubber of his own and partnerships in a logging tract, 66 acres of tin mining land, and 174 acres of oil palm. In 1972 he also owned a 10-acre pig, fish, and fruit farm where he managed much of the work himself, but he sold it in order to have time to spend on the oil-palm estate when the land was cleared for planting. Liew is the epitome of the stereotypical Hakka: brash, almost aggressive, extremely hard working, full of zest for life, and rich in warmth and humor — but slightly boorish withal. Until the events surrounding the MCA task force and its dissolution, Liew was well regarded by both leaders and villagers, though like his brother he is known to be occasionally unscrupulous. An ambitious man, he ran for the local council several times when still in his twenties but was consistently defeated. He was eventually appointed to the council in 1964 and is now an active member in most other local committees as well. Liew talks more freely than most people about politics and power in Malaysia. Cynicism mixes with pragmatism as he jokes about converting to Islam and taking a Malay name, but sends his sons to English-medium schools and plans ultimately to send them overseas for a "better life." Nonetheless, Liew has more contacts among Malays than most of the other men, and he defends some of his Malay friends as individuals when other Chinese are spouting standard stereotyped prejudices about "all Malays." His position in the community has undergone radical change in recent years, and will be discussed at length in chapter 7.

Another young councilman, in his late thirties in 1972, is Loh Kow, a Hunanese dentist, trained in his craft by his father. Loh came to Sanchun from a nearby town in 1960 and was appointed to the council in 1964. His standing within the community as a whole is perhaps less notable than those already mentioned, due, no doubt, in part to his youth and his relatively short residence. Within the governing clique, however, he is well respected. Loh is present at most meetings, and is a particularly close friend of Chin's, visiting his shop each morning to read newspapers and pass the time of day. In his student days in Penang, Loh was enamored of the Socialist Front, a leftist party since disbanded. He is progressive in his thought and, like Liew, pragmatically tolerant of some of the government's solutions to its more sticky communal problems.

Also of some importance in 1972, though not yet serving as councillors and still carefully showing proper filial reserve, were two men of the second generation in Sanchun leadership circles. The third of Lee Koi's five sons, Lee Wan Chun, was thirty-five and a teacher in the Chinese primary school, and was quietly in evidence at many committee meetings, as was Lung Sooi's elder son Lung Teng Yu, forty-one. Lee Wan Chun was secretary of the MCA-sponsored mutual-aid association, while Lung Teng Yu was its treasurer. Wan Chun, who lives separately from his father although the family has not yet formally divided, feels somewhat constrained politically by his position as a government employee, but in recent years he has accepted appointment to the council. Teng Yu, who lives with his father and handles much of the shop business, has also become more prominent recently since his father's health has caused him to withdraw a bit. In 1972, both Lee Wan Chun and Lung Teng Yu, in contrast to Tan Siew Hing in earlier years, very carefully and respectfully remained in the background while their fathers played more prominent roles, but their quiet and capable presence lent an air of stability and continuity to the leadership circles of Sanchun.

Liew Kam Ming, Loh Kow, Lee Wan Chun, and Lung Teng Yu all acted as informal liaison between the elders of the community and the younger generation, particularly when the youth-oriented MCA task force was initiated. They attended the meetings regularly, and joined coffee shop groups of younger workers afterward to offer and hear opinions on both local and national issues. They had equally free access to casual encounters with the older men, and generally attended meetings of most committees they did not serve on officially as well as of those they did. Liew and Loh, not inhibited by the propriety of showing deference to a father, freely made their views known in all settings. All four of these men could be said to hold a certain amount of influence within the central clique. Liew, as we will see below, was also conscious of the value of influence in external places, to be used both for private ends and eventually in a bid for public power as well.

A few other men are near the inner circles and probably are not without some influence either as friends or functionaries. The council secretary, for example, tends to be consulted on many matters, in part because he is usually the one to implement decisions, issuing reminders to people late in paying their house rates or in complying with a council request that they tear down a shed or clean up the offensive smell of latex and acid which neighbors are complaining of. He is close to Lee, very deferent to him, and spends a good bit of time at Lee's house, situated just behind the council office. Another councillor, Wong Ching Chee, is employed as a manager in the club, and is frequently seen managing many other things as well— organizing helpers at a funeral, directing preparations for the temple festival, ordering tea for the councillors or committee members at almost any meeting. He, like the secretary, is privy to the inner workings of the clique, but cannot quite be said to be a full-fledged member.

There is a larger circle of more peripheral support, men who contribute funds and thus sit on committees but seldom influence the course of events in any way; they frequently remain completely silent throughout the course of a meeting. This group includes a number of wealthy and elderly shopkeepers, men whose money is needed but who lack the forceful personality or perhaps the inclination needed for active involvement. They enjoy the periodic social gatherings and banquets but do little more than lend passive support to decisions made by others. A few younger men such as Chin Ta Hing's brothers-in-law and two or three villagers similarly offered acquiescent support. They regularly showed enough interest in public affairs to join coffee shop groups after public meetings, thereby lending support in numbers and tacitly accepting the decisions and actions taken in the more formal gatherings, as they were rehashed over tea and late-night snacks. These men, too junior to find a place in traditional community institutions, were among those attracted to the task force, and through it they gained experience in leadership and community activity.

Prominent Men on the Periphery

The central leadership clique had no active opponents in 1972, but there were nonetheless several men of high standing in the community who withheld their support from the clique simply by abstaining from formal politics. Most prominent among these was Tan Siew Hing. Though he continued to eschew party and council activities, he retained the chairmanship of the temple committee, participated in the school and club committees, and was the acknowledged leader of the Hokkien community in the spring and autumn rites. At important public functions, such as the visit of a federal minister, or the urgent meeting convened at the time of the arsons, Tan inevitably took his place with Lee, Chin, and Lung at the head table. Moreover, he was instrumental in obtaining a large grant for the construction of new teachers' quarters at the Chinese school from an outside philanthropic foundation. Tan's business enterprises include one of the largest sundry shops, two rubber dealerships, sizable rubber holdings, and partnership in the rubber smokehouse, enterprises that employ a dozen or more people. Three of his former shop employees have been successful enough with him to be able to open their own shops in Sanchun, all leaving Tan's employ on very amiable terms. The personal support he enjoys in the community is thus based on a combination of his community service and his material support of a number of individuals, as well as a measure of positive affect and esteem adhering to the memory of his father.

Choong Hah's elder son, Choong Kwan Foh, who was forty-one in 1972, has made an attempt, like Tan, to follow in his father's footsteps, but without much success. He suffers in part from a fall in the family's fortunes, which he blames on his father's tin speculation, but which others blame on his own ineptitude as a contractor. Choong Kwan Foh formerly served as a local councillor; some say he resigned because of financial difficulties, but he maintains that he refused to kowtow to "tyrannical" Lee, who should (but does not, Kwan Foh implies) treat his old patron's son with respect. Kwan Foh has been involved in shady land deals and purportedly accepts "tea money" for bureaucratic favors which he then may neglect to deliver. Moreover, he drinks heavily, a habit that, although not necessarily severely censured, is a rarity in Chinese society, where drinking occurs chiefly at banquets. His drinking affects his status at least to the extent that it affects his public oratory, a skill important to those wishing to build reputations. Kwan Foh too often arrives at a meeting slightly drunk, tries to speak passionately on some subject, and is humorously jeered and shouted down when he becomes too repetitive and meandering in his speech. Though still an officeholder in some local organizations, Choong Kwan Foh is gradually sliding further away from any chance of achieving the power his father once held. Nonetheless, he is genial and sociable and on amiable terms with both Chin Ta Hing and Tan Siew Hing, as well as others on the periphery.

Woo Lee Sen is a prominent Teochiu sundry dealer, forty-two years of age in 1972, who came from northern Perak to Sanchun in 1951. He worked for Tan Tien Yu as a shop assistant until he was able to go into business for himself in 1965. He is a hardheaded businessman, and in 1972 was treasurer of the cemetery committee, auditor of both the temple committee and the MCA mutual-aid society, and officeholder in the MCA branch, though fairly inactive in the party. He has been asked to join the local council, but he is an ally of Tan Siew Hing and Choong Kwan Foh and considers Lee Koi a dictatorial tyrant; he will not serve as long as Lee remains in power. Social drinking and evening excursions to nearby larger towns are favorite pastimes of Woo's, but he does not carry drinking to excess. Woo's elder brother is a rubber dealer in Sanchun, but it is Woo Lee Sen who shares with Tan Siew Hing the credit for obtaining a sizable grant for the school from one of the large and philanthropic Chinese-Malaysian rubber companies, the company that buys most of Tan's and the elder Woo's rubber.

The Sanchun man who was in some respects most nearly the image of a small-town politician, Yap Hoi Fatt, at thirty-nine had never joined a party. Yap's family has lived in Sanchun for some twenty years, and his father was the founder of the sawmill. Yap, a Hakka, was educated first in Mandarin through primary school and then in English secondary schools. Following a teacher-training course, he began teaching in the Chinese primary school in 1961, and he is now assistant headmaster. He is completely fluent in English, Mandarin, and Malay, a combination of skills that makes him unique in Sanchun and gives him a decided advantage over his peers. But as a teacher, like Lee Wan Chun, he feels somewhat constrained by the government's power to transfer him at will should he become too political for its liking. For many years he stayed off the council and out of the party, confining his public service to personal assistance given freely to the many who come to him to sort out complex government forms and legal papers. Only after the MCA task force had been operating for several months, obviously winning support in the community, did Yap finally decide to join and become politically active. When questioned about national and state difficulties within the party, factional disputes, and so forth, Yap proves to be a skilled fence-sitter. But as he is quick to point out himself, Yap is eminently qualified for a local leadership role. As he puts it, he is well established in the community, has no skeletons in his closet, and would be willing to serve the people to the best of his ability.

Yap Hoi Fatt, Woo Lee Sen, and Choong Kwan Foh, along with a few even less politically inclined friends, are to be found nearly every night socializing in the coffee shops, frequently joined by Loh Kow and, before the party split, Liew Kam Ming, and more occasionally by Tan Siew Hing or Chin Ta Hing. In 1972, the development of a rival faction headed by either Tan Siew Hing or Yap Hoi Fatt would have been quite readily conceivable, as each had some support of his own and either would have received strong backing from Woo and Choong. But neither openings nor incentives for rival factional activity existed. The bureaucratic and party structures in operation monopolize access to power, restricting it to their own limited channels, and at the same time deprive local power holders of the perquisites and prerogatives that would make their positions attractive enough to invite risk by rivals intent on unseating them. Structural constraints imposed by the broader political environment in Sanchun thus act to minimize political activity within the local system and thereby strengthen whatever status quo obtains. Moreover, each of the two men in Sanchun who seem most likely to be capable of successfully mobilizing a rival faction have personal reasons for maintaining a low political profile: the individual's vulnerability to the will of higher powers was brought home to Tan quite convincingly in his own past experience, and is a condition written into Yap's employment contract.

Over the past half-century Sanchun has found itself in three sharply contrasted situations of encapsulation.[3] The relative freedom enjoyed by the local system under colonial indirect rule was replaced by the restrictions of a military government during the Emergency. The current situation under the Malay-dominated bureaucratic state system is by no means as harsh as during the Emergency, but there are still severe constraints on local autonomy.

If these changes in external form are traced from the viewpoint of the political actors operating within them, however, it is striking to note the remarkable degree of continuity and consistency to be seen in the processes within the structures. In each situation it is access to externally based resources that enables a local-level leader to establish and maintain his position. In one period the resources required are more clearly economic, and in the next, political, but in neither case is the paramount leader's resource base coterminous with the system in which he is operating. Tan Tien Yu and Choong Hah were not landlords controlling peasants' access to the means of subsistence, but entrepreneurs involved in an international capitalist economy, providing jobs to a rural proletariat. Lee Koi did not head a private warlord army, but through his influential contacts with the lower-level functionaries of what was essentially an occupying or encapsulating army (the British Military Administration), he wielded power over the freedom and livelihoods of the people of Sanchun. In the following chapter I shall describe in greater detail the bureaucratic framework within which Chin Ta Hing operates, which serves less to provide resources to local actors than to discourage local action, thereby strongly biasing the system toward a static status quo. While the administrative system appears motionless, the drama of the early 1970s is provided in the sphere of party politics—the rise and fall of the MCA task force. When a split occurs in the national Chinese leadership, Chin Ta Hing and Liew Kam Ming find themselves the leaders of two opposing factions in Sanchun. In all of these examples, however, leaders' "legitimacy" comes not from below but from above.

Another interesting consistency that appears within the overall variation is the tendency toward a bifurcation of leadership roles. Although Lee Koi held power in the 1950s, the elders, Choong Hah and Tan Tien Yu, appeared to be more highly esteemed, regarded with greater affection, and

---

3. I am leaving aside, of course, the brief and rather aberrant period of the Japanese occupation.

perhaps even more highly trusted. Choong and Tan filled important roles as mediators, even arbiters of justice, while Lee served as intermediary with the state. Today, though the state in question has changed and the center-periphery relations are markedly different in form, the internal differentiation has reproduced itself. Chin Ta Hing is the new intermediary, an educated part-time bureaucrat linking his local system to the lowest rung of the superimposed state hierarchy, and Lee Koi now smoothly fits into the mold of the esteemed patriarch.

Overall, the pattern of local leaders relying on externally derived resources for a start toward local power and prestige is strikingly similar to that noted in chapter 2 at the national level, in which Chinese politicians first establish their connections with Malay leaders in the encapsulating political system, and then parlay the political capital of their acceptability to Malay leaders into positions of power and influence within the Chinese party and then the broader Chinese community. Encapsulation effectively structures all lower-level, circumscribed processes, regardless of their distance from the power center. The system itself determines the first cut of the deck, so to speak, and the individuals within it may then carry on with the play.

6

The Formal Structures of Administration and Politics

To attain leadership status, local political actors must be able to manipulate external connections and resources. A closer look at bureaucracy and party, two of the prime channels to such external resources, will show that both serve to constrain local initiative rather than to facilitate it. As two arms of the ruling government, both bureaucracy and party are essentially conservative, supporting the maintenance of a stable status quo. They undermine the development of strong and independent local leadership and local government both actively, through policy decisions, and passively, through inefficiency. The administrative functions of the local council are limited not only by their narrow definition, but also by specific controls and checks allotted to the higher levels, primarily the district office and the state land office. The MCA, the single Chinese government party in 1972, offered nonbureaucratic links to external power and resources that were essential to the local activist, but an effective monopoly allowed the party to provide little more than token benefits through those links. The politically ambitious in Sanchun could do nothing without bureaucratic and party connections — and not much more with them.

Bureaucracy and party are the two direct links between Sanchun and its encapsulating environment that have played active roles in minimizing local political activity (the MCA task force being the notable exception). Two additional elements, the economy and the traditional value system, contribute more passively to the conservative nature of the community. The economic base of the community provides adequate sustenance to most people so that felt needs are basically satisfied, undercutting a possible source of agitation and efforts toward change. But local economic resources do not constitute so much of a prize that people are willing to take heavy risks in struggling to win control over them. Moreover, the economic structure of the community is highly fragmented; it is distinctly lacking in the kind of interdependent web of economic relations that might lead to reliance on important patron-client ties which could restrict individual or familial political independence. Finally, the values and traditions of the Chinese peasant and worker have never favored active political participation or agitation for change, either of specific leaders or of the broader political system. The Sanchun focus on family interests rather than community involvement is in keeping with a long-standing cultural orientation that has received further validation in the context of Chinese experience in Malaysia. All of these elements, in 1971, combined to foster a relatively static "balanced equilibrium" in local political life.

The Local Council: Bottom Rung of the Bureaucracy

Local government in Malaysia, modeled on the British system, provides for locally elected bodies with varying degrees of autonomy, ranging from municipal councils through town and rural boards to local councils, first established in 1952. Local council areas are in effect administrative islands within larger rural areas, *mukims*. These are controlled more directly by the state governments through district officers and *penghulus*, who were once traditional Malay leaders but are now appointed civil servants.

The aim of local government, according to a ministry report, is "self-government through the medium of popularly elected councils with a large measure of freedom of action and financial independence" (Ministry of Technology, Research, and Local Government, n.d.: 2). In fact, councils are neither popularly elected nor particularly independent. Since the suspension of local elections in 1964 during the Indonesian Confrontation, council seats left vacant by retirement or death have been filled by appointment. As to freedom of action and financial independence, district officers have comprehensive advisory duties in relation to local councils within their jurisdiction, and have the power to approve or reject budgets prepared by the councils. The councils operate a simple form of local taxation on buildings, receive remuneration for services such as the removal of garbage and night soil, and collect fees from petty traders, but a considerable measure of grant-in-aid is received from the state government to meet capital requirements.

A review of Sanchun monthly council statements indicates that the sums the council deals with are small. Receipts collected by the council include house assessments, conservancy (night soil removal) fees, license fees, receipts from the sale of license plates on peddlers' carts, abattoir fees, and receipts from the rental of the community hall, from lighting of the bad-minton court, and from the telephone coin box. Expenditures include administrative costs such as staff salaries, payments to the government-run employees' providential fund, office and hall lighting, travel and trans-port, stationery, telephone, water, and incidentals, as well as a stipulated payment to the conservancy contractor, salaries and providential-fund payments for garbage collectors and a lorry driver, maintenance and up-keep of vehicle and tools, maintenance of the market, the abattoir, open spaces, buildings, roads, drains, and wells, provision of street lighting, and purchase of conservancy buckets and dust bins. Of the items listed, only incidental administrative expenses could lend itself readily to padding, but in accounts covering several years this item was large, over M$300, only once; in most months it was under M$10. The only consistently large items were salaries. The council keeps its own accounts and audits them inter-nally, but they are also subject to unscheduled periodic audit by the district office.

Total yearly budgets between 1960 and 1972 ranged between M$10,000 and M$40,000, including balancing grants from the state equal to 25 per-cent or less of the total. Capital expenditures have been for such things as constructing drains and roads, building a badminton court, erecting lights on the basketball court, and remodeling the community hall. Such capital works must be outlined in detail in the yearly budget, and funds approved for one project or item must be returned to the DO if not exhausted in the stipulated use.

Councils are required to obtain specific prior district office approval be-fore spending any sum over M$200, even from local reserves. Moreover, the district office controls all tenders for capital works over the M$200 limit. Thus the jobs that the Sanchun council can hand out directly are only minor ones, and kickbacks are small or nonexistent. Most bigger con-tracts for work in Sanchun are won by contractors from larger towns nearby, men who, along with the people in the district office, participate in a stratum of economic and social interaction somewhat above that of a small local council area such as Sanchun.

Apart from financial transactions, numerous administrative actions taken or suggested by the local council are similarly subject to review or approval by district-level offices, a process that generally means a sacrifice in efficiency as well as a loss of autonomy. Council buildings and *kongsis* occupied by council laborers, for example, are the property not of the council but of the district department of public works, and repairs or im-provements of these buildings must be approved by that department, which has led to delays of several months. Council membership is subject to control from above, and resignations are not official until the district office recognizes them. One man formally on the council roll in 1972 had not attended a meeting for over a year. Three unexplained absences justify removal from office, according to district regulations, but repeated requests directed to the DO for a clarification of this man's status received no response for several years, and the matter was not settled until the entire council was reorganized in 1975.

Certain affairs, such as land titles and citizenship papers, require the common man to deal directly with higher levels of government, giving the local council no formal intermediary role. Nonetheless, councillors and council staff are often approached for assistance with filling in forms and filing them with the appropriate authorities. Instances of well-connected councillors turning a profit by providing assistance of a more substantial sort are of course not unknown, but are nevertheless few. Gossip attributes responsibility to two local councillors for shady land deals negotiated in 1971 in which several villagers paid a few hundred dollars in "tea money" for help in obtaining temporary occupation licenses for houselots on land outside the council boundary that was not zoned for housing. One of these men, it is alleged, was further involved in 1975 in opening up railway reserve land to occupation by some thirty or so families, which was in fact illegal squatting. More commonly, however, a literate man such as the council clerk or secretary or the assistant headmaster Yap Hoi Fatt simply gives assistance in preparing routine forms—for TOL yearly renewal, for example, or for transfer of a TOL from a deceased head of household to a son—and may (or may not) receive tea money of a few dollars as a token of thanks.

Applications for identity cards and work permits are handled routinely by a team of clerks who come twice monthly from Papar to the Sanchun council office. At the age of twelve, children must register for citizenship papers and identity cards. Most applications are relatively uncomplicated, but there are still many cases in which lost documents or spelling errors in the romanization of Chinese names cause serious difficulty; then people seek help from a knowledgeable and influential person such as Lee Koi, Chin Ta Hing, or Lung Sooi, who can sometimes facilitate such matters.

The most crucial power held at higher bureaucratic and political levels is, of course, the appointment of local councillors to office. After local elections were "temporarily" suspended in 1964, new vacancies were filled by appointment within the party branch that had previously held the seat, subject to approval first from the state party committee and then from the state government. In 1975, the central government began making plans for a complete reorganization of local government, and local councils were appointed for one year terms, renewable pending their ultimate incorporation into new district councils under the Local Government Act of 1976. By 1978 this reorganization had been effected only in a few places in Penang. In Perak, local council seats were allocated to the various component parties of the Barisan Nasional in proportions worked out in negotiations among the state party committees and the *Menteri Besar* (chief minister). Local branches then submitted nominations for the seats they were allotted, to be approved by their own state committees, the state BN, the DO, and the *Menteri Besar*. In Sanchun, of the nine Chinese councillors who were in frequent attendance in 1972, only four had once been elected by popular vote. The ten Chinese councillors appointed in 1975 and reappointed in 1976 included only two who had originally been elected.

Inefficiencies and Obstructions in Bureaucratic Channels

The above descriptions of the structure of bureaucracy at the lowest levels in Malaysia indicate the weakness of local bodies and their formally inferior status in relation to functionaries closer to the center. It is also instructive to study the actual working relationship that exists between the local council and the higher levels of government and bureaucracy. Numerous examples demonstrate that the district office maintains and affirms hierarchical subordination of the local council by its *non*-action as well as by its action.

The district officer, or a person representing him, should be present at every council meeting, but of the fourteen meetings I attended in 1971-1972, an ADO was present only twice, the district health inspector once, and the district police chief once. In the minutes available for nineteen meetings in 1969 and 1970, a single visit from a Chinese-affairs officer (CAO) was the only instance of a representative from the district office being present. District office personnel argue that meetings should be held during the day, rather than in the evening, as is usual in Sanchun. Attending a meeting in a town fifteen miles distant is part of their job as full-time bureaucrats, but they feel such meetings should take place only during office hours. For the councillors, who receive no pay for council participation and have other full-time work to occupy them during what is usually longer than an eight-hour workday, evening is the most logical time for meetings.[1]

Difficulties in bureaucratic communication are exacerbated by the government's frequent rotation of civil servants. During my fourteen-month stay in Sanchun, the DO, the district officer in charge of police, and the two ADOs were all transferred and replaced at one time or another. The

1. This practice varies with the size of the council. I have learned of a local council in Negri Sembilan in a town of about seven thousand where councillors do receive minimal remuneration (Dr. Lawrence Seow, personal communication).

CAO was transferred in late 1971 to a region in northern Perak where, in a campaign against Communist guerrillas known as Operation Loyalty, four Chinese new villages were refenced and a curfew was established throughout the area. CAOs were sent there in force both to elicit information and to restore confidence in the government. By 1976 Papar was still awaiting the appointment of a new CAO. The single district official in frequent contact with Sanchun who was not transferred during my stay was the health inspector.

Chin Ta Hing felt that both personnel changes such as these and the infrequent attendance of district office staff at council meetings seriously hindered the smooth functioning of the council. During the Emergency the central government had shown greater interest in local activities, since the military goals that predominated at that time required active compliance and commitment at all levels of the system. Now, however, the higher governmental strata take relatively little interest in Chinese local systems, except perhaps at election time, or when order goals come once again to the fore as they did in the Operation Loyalty area.

But issues arise continually that require consultation with or confirmation by the district office. In the minutes of virtually every meeting there are items of council business that have been either referred from previous meetings or postponed till a later time, pending action or approval by the district office. Many of the items reappearing month after month could be disposed of rapidly if a district office representative were in fact present. A case in point was a request for the DO's approval of a council plan for levying charges against the two bus companies for the maintenance of the area they use as a bus station, since the council had no funds for this purpose. It was a reasonable plan and no objections were raised, but three months passed before approval was received. A similar case was a council request for permission either to demolish or to put to use a building which had been the home guard headquarters during the Emergency but which had been sealed for some years. After four months permission was granted to demolish it.

Some issues have been delayed not simply by inefficiency, but because other, more powerful interests conflict with those of the local community. For example, in January 1959 an item began appearing monthly in the minutes noting that an application the council had placed for a thousand acres of state land for cultivation was still under consideration by the DO. In August 1959 the matter was referred to two state councillors, one Chinese and one Indian. Minutes for the next three years are missing, but in January 1963 items appeared noting continuation of applications for land for new burial grounds and for two hundred acres for cultivation. In March of that year the DO sent a message saying that land for cultivation was difficult to obtain because of conflicting applications for tin and logging tracts. He advised the local council to leave such problems to the district rural committee, and the application in question was eventually withdrawn. By April 1964, however, the issue of the burial grounds had still not been resolved, and a delegation was sent from Sanchun to confer with the DO. In November the issue was mentioned in the minutes again, with the explanation that it was a difficult question because the land was also under consideration as a mining site. In August 1965, a decision was finally reached to allot five acres for a Chinese burial ground and ten acres for an Indian burial ground.

A similar issue was the council's application to expand the local council area in order to have a slightly larger tax base and include the low-cost housing units and other nearby houses whose residents take advantage of Sanchun's facilities. The matter was first broached in March 1970, when letters and plans were sent to the DO, the Perak state government secretary, and the town planning board in Ipoh. In June the council secretary was sent to the CAO in Papar, as no response had been forthcoming. The CAO commended the council for following the correct procedures, and informed them that the final approval could come only from the state legislative assembly. In April 1971 the council received a counter proposal from the town planning board, but after discussion decided to continue to push for the acceptance of their own proposal. In May, representatives, including the MCA federal parliament member from the district, were sent to Ipoh to call on the town planning officer regarding the matter. They had neglected to make an appointment, however, and upon arriving in Ipoh found that the man they wished to see was on leave, so nothing could be accomplished at that time. In September, the state assemblyman, a PPP member, attended the council meeting. His support was secured, and the council resubmitted the original application for expansion to the same offices. By late 1972 the matter had been brought up again with an ADO who visited Sanchun, and it was mentioned periodically throughout the year at council meetings. After six years of bureaucratic lethargy, the matter has finally been settled, at least in principle, by the Local Government Act of 1976, which calls for the eventual incorporation of local authorities under expanded district councils. By 1978 there was as yet no sign of actual reorganization, however, and the local council, having given up its expansion plea, continued to function as usual.

Examples of effective cooperation between the district office and the council are not, of course, entirely lacking. As a result of repeated requests some years ago by the council for notification of pending changes in TOLs, the DO now writes to the council to inform it of both new applications and transfers of existing TOLs, soliciting remarks or recommendations and verification that no taxes are outstanding in the name of the previous holder. A problem had arisen originally when the land office gave a hawker a TOL for a small piece of land on which to set up a permanent stall. The council, however, felt that a stall in that location would obstruct traffic, and repeatedly refused the application for a building permit. Prior notification now precludes such a situation arising.

When enforcement of council or government rulings is difficult within the context of the social harmony of a small, face-to-face community, the council can pass responsibility upward by referring cases to the district office. This occurs routinely with public health matters. If the council receives complaints about garbage in someone's yard, smelly ducks or rubber latex, a coffee shop or restaurant with low standards of cleanliness, or a shophouse falling into a hazardous state of ill repair, the secretary is usually charged with delivering a first warning to the offenders. If that fails to bring a response, as is frequently the case, the minutes record that the health inspector should be asked to look into the matter on his next visit. The collection of overdue rates is similarly referred to the DO. Once a year the council is requested to supply the names of those in arrears; thereafter responsibility for exerting further pressure in the form of official reminders and occasionally threats of prosecution rests with the district office. There have been no cases of actual prosecution.

The Inquiry into Local Government

In 1965, during the Indonesian Confrontation and the suspension of local elections, a royal commission of inquiry was established to probe the value and desirability of retaining local government and renewing local-level elections. The commission solicited comments from local government bodies; the Sanchun local council prepared a memorandum, dated October 27, 1965, offering an expression of strong support for the continuation of elected councils, and a request for broadened powers and privileges for council members.

In advocating the continuation of local councils, the memorandum notes four advantages offered by the system as it was then: (1) local councils are the essence of democracy, for they can truly represent the will and wishes of the people; (2) local councils provide a significant convenience for the public, by obviating the need for people to go to distant offices to deal with routine matters such as paying rates; (3) local councils can render invaluable advice to the public in matters of government policy; and (4) the existence of local councils instills in the villagers the pride of being able to govern themselves.

The request for expanded powers and privileges to accrue to the council includes five items: (1) broader administrative powers in such matters as renewal and issue of TOLs, leasing of land, and allocation of land under the Rural Development Program; (2) the power to call for and accept tenders for capital works; (3) more administrative powers to deal with internal problems; (4) allowances for councillors for attending meetings and traveling on council business; and (5) medical benefits in the form of free medical treatment for councillors and their families, and admittance to the first-class ward if a councillor or family member is hospitalized.

The commissioner's report was published in December 1968, but it was not released until December 1971 after three years of study by the government. The recommendations of the commission unequivocally favor the retention of elected local governments, as well as political party activity at all levels in elections. On the day following the release of the report, however, the government issued statements clearly implying that the report would not be acted on in the forseeable future. The government was critical of the report because it was already out of date and included no reference to developments since the 1969 riots, such as the New Economic Policy and the government's commitment to the "restructuring" of the society. The minister of technology, research, and local government announced that the government would not consider any local elections until the state governments had restructured local authorities (*Straits Times*, December 11, 1971).

The fate of local councils, uncertain for over ten years, was sealed with the promulgation of the Local Government Act of 1976, though by late 1978 implementation of the act had hardly begun, and lame duck councils continued to sit. Local government in Malaysia is hardly true independent self-government in the sense once envisioned. Bodies once intended to be elected are now tied instead to the appointive civil service bureaucracy, sharing many responsibilities with it and frequently subordinate to it. Local autonomy is thus strictly circumscribed. Moreover, the uncertainty that has so long prevailed as to the future of local government has no doubt served to weaken what little authority and independence local bodies might once have had.

The Uses of Local Power

In their 1965 memorandum the Sanchun councillors made clear their view that the role of the council and the status of its members should be upgraded. They saw themselves — correctly, I believe — as impotent, constrained by the external bureaucratic structure in their attempts to serve the community. And they felt they received too few benefits for their troubles.

Nonetheless, councillors were not completely bereft of power and influence that sometimes enabled them to protect personal interests more effectively than they might have done as private citizens. For example, Chin Ta Hing and Lee Koi jointly own a town lot on which they intend to erect shops. In the fire of October 1971, a row of three wooden shops on an adjacent string of lots was burned to the ground. The owner of one, a man no longer resident in Sanchun, rebuilt the shop before the plans he submitted had been passed by the council. It was discovered that due to a ten-foot extension in the rear the new shop encroached on the fire lane separating it from the lot owned by Chin and Lee. Buildings were often completed before the plans were approved, and many were slightly overextended. But in this case two important leaders were threatened by the action, for if they later erected a building themselves, the regulation width of the fire lane would have to be maintained. The issue was discussed widely in coffee shops, along with another dispute that grew out of the fire, and with public opinion on their side, Chin and Lee made a point of informing the district office of the matter. When the ADO came to Sanchun on other business he was taken to view the offending extension. The public record is clear: should Chin or Lee choose to build in the future, they will have grounds for demanding that the other shop extension be demolished.

According to the record, Chin Ta Hing was able at one point to get the council to agree to lower the assessed rates on several houses he owns in the town area. Chin also used the forum of the council to complain about the offensive smell of his neighbor's latrine. Applications for government-subsidized low-cost housing units opened in 1969 were processed at higher levels with recommendations of the local council, and one councillor was allotted a unit despite the fact that he already owned adequate housing.

On the other hand, councillors in Sanchun seldom use their powers arbitrarily in a negative or threatening manner against others. Spheres of control in which petty corruption might thrive but seems to be absent include the issuing of trading licenses and building permits. Licenses and permits to carry on small business are normally issued as requested, although they are occasionally refused for apparently good reason—if the proposed stall would block traffic, for example. None of the hawkers I knew had any complaints about the licensing system and two commented spontaneously that tea money was not accepted for renewing licenses.

The most common council problem seems to be the construction of new houses, or the renovating of old, before the council has had time to approve the plans. This is in large part a function of timing rather than intent, as people often make a decision and proceed with construction before the next monthly council meeting rolls around.[2] On one occasion, accord-

---

2. The construction of a new house suitable for the tropical climate requires only a few weeks of work; waiting for a council decision could mean the loss of the chosen craftsmen to another contract.

ing to minutes of past years, the visiting health inspector suggested prosecuting someone who had built a house without prior approval, but the councillors rejected the suggestion, noting that although the plans when finally submitted described an existing house rather than a proposed one, they were after all quite acceptable. This seems to be the predominant attitude toward offenses of any kind. If a person can be made to change his ways, even if only after several months and repeated warnings, no need is seen to punish him. There were numerous cases that could have been subject to prosecution — shops in dangerously tumbledown condition, blockage of public drains through dumping of private garbage, arrears in payments of rates — but I was told that there had been only one actual prosecution, several years earlier.

That service on the council is hardly seen as a real prize is indicated by the difficulty the council has had over the years in maintaining a full contingent. Throughout 1969 and 1970 only nine councillors were listed in the minutes, including one Indian and one Malay, and meetings were usually held with only four or five members present. One Chinese councillor and the Malay were absent almost without fail. In 1971 three new councillors were added, one Malay and two Chinese; the Malay named never appeared at a meeting. According to the minutes, fifteen was the number then permitted, and the three Alliance Party local branches (MCA, MIC, UMNO) were each invited to submit one more name, after which an additional Malay became fairly regular in attendance. Membership noted in the minutes during 1971 and 1972 was twelve, though attendance was usually between six and nine.

Several peripheral leaders told of being approached to serve on the council, but refusing, and several councillors told of attempts to resign, remaining only because of pressure from friends. In 1965 Loh Kow served as head of the committee for assessments and evaluations, a job that led to his temporary resignation from the council. He found himself in open conflict with Liew Kam Ming's elder brother when he raised the rates on the elder Liew's house subsequent to the completion of major improvements on the building. Other councillors supported the decision (Kam Ming's stand is unknown), it held, and the brother eventually moved to Ipoh, transferring the house to Kam Ming's name. Loh, however, was apparently somewhat shaken by the furor of the attack leveled at him by the elder Liew. Being the center of attention in an unmannerly and lengthy dispute was not to his taste, and he resigned, despite attempts by his friends to change his mind. Wong Ching Chee, according to the minutes, resigned shortly after, though I do not know if there was any connection. In 1971, despite objections from his wife and father, Loh found himself persuaded to rejoin the council, as did Wong. Loh sees service on the council as an almost onerous duty: townspeople malign councillors for alleged graft and personal gain, but ignore the real difficulties inherent in the job, and do not appreciate the councillors' efforts and sacrifices.

It is clear, contrary to "common wisdom," that although opportunities for personal gain do exist for councilmen and local leaders, they are in Sanchun both relatively minimal and seldom utilized. Lee Koi, the councillor who is among the least wealthy and has through the years been the most powerful, appears to be a basically honest man who has profited materially only in small degree through his position, gaining instead high status and respect. These obviously have intrinsic value for him, and he has apparently not been tempted to jeopardize his prestige, so laboriously achieved, by misusing it for flagrant personal gain. Tan Tien Yu and his son and Chin Ta Hing have achieved far greater material success in business than they could hope to through political manipulation in an arena so well policed by external powers. None of these men have been noticeably disposed toward graft or corruption, and the administrative system within which they must operate in any case strictly circumscribes opportunity for such impropriety. Men outside the circles of power see few material benefits within those circles worth fighting over.

The Party Prior to 1971

Since by 1971 there had been no local elections in nearly a decade, newly formed opposition parties had had no opportunity to get a foothold in small rural towns, and the Alliance—in effect, the MCA—was firmly in control in Sanchun. In 1969 the state legislative seat for the district was won by a PPP man, then in opposition, who was reelected in 1974 as a member of the expanded Barisan coalition, but the PPP had never had an organization or much active support in Sanchun. The Gerakan and the DAP, which emerged in 1969 as major opposition forces, had only embryonic support outside the urban centers that formed their bases.

Party politics were not of major significance in Sanchun. Examples of past conflicts and petty squabbles within the community indicate that membership in or affiliation with the central clique tended to be more salient than party membership per se, though clique members happened also to be MCA members. Nonetheless, the common view among those who did not support the party was that they were more often subject to council harassment than were MCA men. The single case of court litigation on record in Sanchun involved a shopkeeper known to be consistently anti-MCA. He had erected a garage without obtaining proper permits. After issuing repeated warnings demanding that he demolish the structure, the council finally took the case to court and won. The shopkeeper was particularly bitter because a similar illegal structure had been built only a block away, but its owner was a councillor, a business partner of Tan Tien Yu, and a core member of the ruling clique at that time, and his shed somehow never came to the attention of the council.

Other cases of unauthorized building involving party members outside the central clique were treated as petty annoyances but were not prosecuted. In the early years of the new village, councillor Liew Kam Ming's father erected a shed with neither a TOL for the land nor a building permit from the council. He ignored repeated council warnings, but when he eventually was granted the necessary TOL by the land office, the council agreed to certify the structure as soon as building plans were formally submitted. Woo Lee Sen and his brother were cited frequently in 1970 and 1971 council minutes — Woo for an unauthorized garage, his brother for smelly and unclean conditions around his rubber shop. In these three cases party membership was not sufficient protection against what might be construed as minor harassment, an indication that personal rather than party ties have primary significance.

Nonetheless, a number of informants are firmly of the view that opposition to the MCA can be bad for business. The two young DAP branch organizers have said as much, as has the son of the late business partner of Tan Tien Yu referred to above, who expresses interest in opposition ideas but will join no political party. When the MCA carried out a voter registration program before elections, people known to oppose the MCA, according to their own report, were systematically excluded.

While negative effects of nonsupport may be disputed, there is little doubt that party affiliation does on occasion bring positive rewards from outside the local arena to party stalwarts at the local level. In 1969, thirty-two units of government-subsidized housing were completed just outside the Sanchun local council area. They are now occupied by eleven Chinese, eleven Malay, and ten Indian families. All are Alliance Party members. They include the local chairman of the Indian Alliance partner, the MIC, Lee Koi's son Lee Wan Chun, councillor Loh Kow, and several others who are very active in the MCA. Councillor Liew Kam Ming and Choong Kwan Foh were members in a multiracial logging partnership that in 1972 began work on a timber tract allotted by the government, according to Choong, as a reward for active party work in the 1969 election.

Chin Ta Hing, as chairman of the council, has repeatedly expressed the view that party channels are essential to the workings of local government. The Chinese members of the government coalitions, first the MCA and now both the MCA and the Gerakan, provide extrabureaucratic links to the more central and more powerful members of the government and bureaucracy. The problems existing in lower-level bureaucratic communication have been detailed above. Chin and other councillors often call on high-ranking Chinese party officials to intercede with Malay bureaucrats of similar rank on matters that the lower levels of the bureaucracy are slow in treating. A local leader without access to these party channels would be at a serious disadvantage in necessary dealings with the center.

The MCA in Sanchun has been little different in composition from the other leadership groups, simply offering one more formal and visible validation of the already proven hegemony of the dominant clique. Party leaders have invariably been community leaders. The party has, in the past, firmly maintained its monopoly over external channels to power, providing no opportunity for new faces to come into prominence, no openings for competition or opposition to the entrenched leadership. In late 1971 the introduction of the MCA task force by a group of cadres from the state MCA working committee provided such alternative channels for the first time, and did in fact bring to the fore individuals previously inactive in the political scene. Until this innovation, however, the party, like the administrative structure, passively upheld a rather torpid status quo.

Additional Conservative Elements

Systemic elements contribute passively to the maintenance of the status quo that is the more active goal of center-periphery policy. The internal economic makeup of Sanchun and its place in the broader national economic system both serve the same ends.

In socioeconomic terms Sanchun is reasonably homogeneous despite the diversity and atomization of economic activity. Both exceptionally rich and exceptionally poor families are few in number, and the range of lifestyles and standards of living is fairly narrow. Sanchun lacks the gross inequities of sustenance and opportunity so often found in urban areas of all nations. Even the poorest families in Sanchun have adequate housing, sufficient food, and just enough job opportunity to allow them to continue hoping that things might take a turn for the better. Most people are able to maintain themselves fairly comfortably and independently, and are unlikely to be forced by economic necessity to forfeit that independence by becoming pawns to be bought and sold in leaders' maneuvers for political support. Economic need is not likely to provide motivation for the common person to join in a political fray.

While the Sanchun economy provides enough to satisfy basic needs, it does not offer spoils great enough to interest a big-time operator. In recent years there have been cases of men whose success has expanded their interests far beyond the confines of the local system of Sanchun. One of these is Liew Kam Ming's brother, mentioned above, whose skillful investment in tin mining tracts has enabled him to move into a higher socioeconomic stratum than Sanchun could offer. While in the village, he proved on at least one occasion — in his quarrel with Loh Kow — to be a source of disruption. But with his departure, he left his younger brother free to move into a role of prominence.

A second man whose successes drew him out of Sanchun was another Hakka, a good friend and business partner of Liew Kam Ming. This man is a logging contractor, heading among other things the logging partnership that includes Liew and Choong. He has not totally cut his roots in Sanchun, as he has opened a lumberyard there, but he is now living in a town eight miles north of Sanchun and about four times its size, which has a broader range of business contacts than Sanchun. By removing himself from physical residence in Sanchun, he has severely limited any local leadership role he might have had there. He is on good terms with many Sanchun leaders, and, for example, attended a school board banquet as a contributor to school funds, but he has effectively chosen to trade any political power he might have had as a big fish in a small pond for the economic advantages of a larger pond.

In light of such cases, we might postulate a given economic threshold below which certain types of economic competition are not profitable, with the effect that certain personalities opt out of the political competitions they might win easily in order to engage elsewhere in more interesting economic contests. Sanchun as an economic community falls below such a threshold, and the more avaricious or economically ambitious individuals, as we have seen throughout Sanchun's history, are likely to seek richer pastures elsewhere rather than play for the small stakes Sanchun has to offer. This self-selection of political personnel, influenced by the overall economic environment, is no doubt a factor of some importance in determining the nature of Sanchun internal politics.

A second conservative element lies in the traditional value system of the Chinese, particularly of the overseas immigrants. In relation to political issues of the larger arenas, the Chinese of Southeast Asia have often been dismissed as largely apolitical, concerned only with their money and their businesses. Wang Gungwu goes beyond this overly broad generalization to provide a more trenchant analysis of Chinese politics in Malaya, but still defines a large middle group in terms that could understandably be called apolitical:

> Group B consists of the hard-headed and realistic majority of the Chinese who are more concerned with the low-posture and indirect politics of trade and community associations. They are also the most modest in their aims and frequently give the impression of being non-political. This arises from the fact that they seldom openly engage in issues of national or international power and rarely express themselves on questions of political ideals and long-term political goals. They are usually content to work through established hierarchies and calculate

matters of influence and power *within* such hierarchies, whether they be Chinese, Malay, or British. (1970: 5)

This low posture is generally considered to be characteristic of peasant China as well, a functional survival tactic in a situation of gross power imbalance. The Malaysian new villagers have found themselves in a particularly clear situation of power imbalance, experiencing fences, curfews, and physical coercion. They have seen threats of violence carried out and their neighbors deported and imprisoned. In Sanchun, as elsewhere, the experience of the common person has shown the safest course to be a low posture, little or no involvement with persons or organizations that are openly political in goals or methods. These lessons did not end with the Japanese occupation or the Emergency. In the early 1960s people witnessed the attempted deportation of a Sanchun secret society leader—when neither Taiwan nor the People's Republic of China would accept him, he was sent instead to prison in Kuala Lumpur, where he remains today. Most recently, as an aftermath of the MCA task force movement, there have been expulsions from the party at state and local levels, further validating the lesson that total noninvolvement is the best way to avoid trouble.

The Chinese value harmony and peace, and they generally believe they can best serve these values by staying out of politics altogether. In a town such as Sanchun, economic problems of family sustenance are relatively atomized, depending on flexible networks of contacts. If accepting favors from one quarter threatens to involve a man in unpleasant demands for political support, he can usually find alternative means of satisfying his needs. Minding one's own business is quite possible and is in fact the chosen path of the majority. Most members of the community show little interest in either local or higher-level politics, preferring to share their opinions quietly with friends and neighbors rather than openly entering the political arena. Social leadership is seen as necessary, and men come forward to fill the required roles, but the common folk concern themselves little with who those men might be as long as the roles are filled. The villagers who remain outside the leadership circles can hardly be seen to constitute a volatile group that is ready and eager to actively assist men who would engage in rivalry for power.

Some change is evident among the younger generation. These men, slightly better educated, have grown up in a country proclaiming itself a parliamentary democracy and a model of racial harmony and equality. Moreover, as noted above, many of the younger generation are involved in construction or logging work that takes them outside the quiet local arena and exposes them to larger arenas and more politically active groups of Chinese. These young people formed the core of the support drawn by the task force program. By and large, however, the people of Sanchun, through their passivity, contribute to the perpetuation of the local hegemony of the dominant leadership clique within a placid political arena.

The elements that jointly determine the nature and level of political activity in Sanchun can thus be seen uniformly to favor the status quo. Some specifically suppress the development of catalysts for change; others merely foster existing tendencies toward a general conservatism. But in combination all act to support the system in its present form, with its present personnel.

Channels for dissent, or for effective action of any kind beyond the basic minimum necessary for maintenance of the system, are narrow at best. Response from the upper levels to initiative shown by the lower levels is slow in coming, and often negative. Power for meaningful action is siphoned off by encapsulating systems holding a firm monopoly beyond the immediate grasp of local actors, who are left playing largely symbolic roles of leadership. The net effect is to reduce political activism to a minimum. Potential competitors for positions of power and influence at the local level have thus been deterred because the prize seems to have little real value and the risk may be high. In Sanchun in 1971 the current leadership was firmly entrenched, and the prize, such as it was, could not easily be won, so the competition itself seemed hardly worth the trouble. Just as external forces provided the critical constraints that maintained a placid political atmosphere, however, it was also an external impetus, the MCA task force, that sparked the upheaval Sanchun experienced over the next few years.

7

The Rise and Fall of the MCA Task Force in Perak

[handwritten annotation: "Retribably" ... minority like PRc]

The Malaysian Chinese Association, in the context of communal politics in Malaysia, functions essentially as an ethnic pressure group within the government. Since the inception of the Alliance formula in the early 1950s, it has been the role of the MCA to represent Chinese communal interests within the government. By the 1960s the MCA's electoral record indicated that it did not have the support of the Chinese. It was instead caught in a downward spiral, its support within the community declining as it became more dependent on government (UMNO) indulgence and thus less able to act aggressively in the Chinese interest, and its position within the government growing ever weaker as its lack of broader backing grew increasingly evident. The 1969 electoral losses were serious for the MCA; a new effort at revitalization of the party and unification of the Chinese community had to be attempted.

In early 1971, almost two years after the riots of May 1969, parliament was convened and the moratorium on political life was lifted. A group of young reformist politicians emerged intent on organizing a Chinese unity movement that would cross party lines. The political infighting that developed all too quickly among its leaders, as well as problems it encountered with the new sedition law, led to its rapid demise (see, for example, Von Vorys 1975: 426). Some of its leaders then turned their energies to a grassroots political experiment in Perak, approved and funded by the MCA central leadership. By the closing months of 1971 the MCA task force (*ganxunban*), as the movement was known, was fully operational in nearly fifty of Perak's new villages, but a year later, in November 1972, the MCA center ordered the task force dissolved. Nonetheless, the factional fragmentation that ensued is still a force in Chinese politics today.

The rise and fall of the task force was ostensibly a Chinese affair, in fact an MCA affair, a conflict of interests within the party. When viewed in this way, the internal repercussions that were felt in Sanchun can be seen to be a direct result of the power of the encapsulation of local- and state-level Chinese politics by national-level Chinese politics. The course of events was determined by vertical relationships within the Chinese community, as middle-level leaders built up enthusiastic backing for their program among the masses but were eventually deprived of legitimacy by the central leaders. Temporary confusion and then realignment of loyalties resulted, bringing about some shifts in power at the local level.

Chinese political affairs, however, are themselves constrained by the political environment dominated by the UMNO. The Malay-Chinese elite relationships, which are an ambiguous blend of horizontal and vertical ties, came into play in the MCA party crisis in 1973 just as they had in 1959 (see chapter 2). Final sanction as to who may play the game and by what rules rests ultimately with the center. The parameters thus established may nonetheless allow for sufficient maneuverability to permit the development of some very interesting new trends whose long-range implications cannot readily be predicted.

The Perak MCA Task Force

In the summer of 1971 a struggle developed within the Perak MCA, in part as an outgrowth of differences of opinion regarding the abortive Chinese unity movement. The younger, reformist faction that eventually took control was headed by Dr. Lim Keng Yaik. He and two others, Dato Teh Siew Eng and Paul Leong Khee Seong, were the prime organizers of the task force program, which had the full backing of Tun Tan Siew Sin, national MCA president. In backing a program run by the "young turks" of the Perak MCA, Tun Tan was undoubtedly taking a risk. His likely motivations for doing so were complex, involving an attempt to balance rivalries within the party as well as to respond to the open challenge from the opposition in the 1969 elections. Tan promised the pilot program an initial three years' funding, and agreed that if it proved successful in Perak it should be replicated in other states.

By the time the program was operational, Dr. Lim was being drawn into federal politics, where he was about to head a federal ministry newly created to deal with new-village problems. The acknowledged leader of the task force, then, was Dato Teh, a wealthy tin magnate of considerable standing in Perak political circles. Teh brought together a large corps of young, enthusiastic cadres to do organizational work in new villages throughout the state. Within the first year, in August 1972, Teh claimed seven thousand members in forty-nine villages, with sixty to seventy salaried cadres (*ganbu*). Cadres and state leaders met every week at the Ipoh headquarters, so that issues arising in the village work could receive immediate attention. I attended one such meeting when the program was only two months old, at which eighty to a hundred people were present. The majority were young people under thirty, many under twenty-five, but those in charge were somewhat older. The young cadres, however, even the women among them, took full part in the discussion, raising questions, offering suggestions, and entering into dispute occasionally with some of the organizers. A sense of equal participation and a strongly felt *esprit de corps* were evident.

The aim of the task force was to build a strong base of MCA support among the young adults of the new villages, and from among them to pick and train new leaders. Although the task force concentrated its appeal on the eighteen to twenty-five age group, care was taken to avoid generational conflicts within villages wherever possible. Teh and Leong recognized the existence of traditional village leaders whose status was based on ability proven by wealth and success, but they felt that these men had little understanding of the broader political and economic situation in Malaysian society, and, lacking perspective and foresight, could not provide progressive leadership. Teh argued further that the traditional strength of the Chinese family acted to inhibit the formation of other social groupings that might better represent Chinese interests to the society at large. The task force was intended to raise group consciousness in the villages, and through working with the youth to foment a "revolution in thinking" (*sixiang geming*), focusing people's orientation beyond the family and the village to the broader Chinese community.

The organizational work of the task force in Sanchun was impressive. Four cadres, two men and two women, who lived in the new village of Batu Hitam, sixteen miles to the south, worked in teams in four villages in the area. In Sanchun political lectures and seminars were held weekly on Thursdays, singing lessons on Wednesdays, and classes in *boqiquan* and *taijiquan* (Chinese martial arts and exercises) on Tuesdays.

The lecturer and leader of the seminars was a young returned student named Cheah with a degree in political science from Taiwan University. His coworker in Sanchun, Miss Ao, was only twenty, with three years of secondary education (Lower Certificate of Education). She had been working for the MCA near Ipoh for a year or two assisting people in filling out citizenship and registration forms, and was asked to work in the task force when it was formed. It was clear as she talked with me about her work that she enjoyed meeting people and helping them, but she expressed no strong political commitment or awareness. Cheah and another of the four, Robert Ong, who came to Sanchun only irregularly, were more clearly political in their orientation. Ong had studied prelaw and law for six years in

Australia, and had been drawn back to Malaysia by his interest in the Chinese unity movement and the new hope he felt it offered his ethnic community. Ong felt strongly that the Chinese and Indians must put real pressure on the government to "come to its senses" and ameliorate its pro-Malay policies. Like virtually all Chinese I talked with, both professional political organizers and common people, Ong viewed the Chinese-Malaysian community as essentially apolitical, interested only in business and in the well-being of the family unit. He felt this insularity should be broken down not only for the good of the Chinese, but in the best interests of the country as a whole, and he believed the task force program had a good chance to accomplish these ends.

At the opening meetings in Sanchun, Cheah assured his listeners that the MCA factionalist split in Perak had healed, and that despite past failings the MCA was now determined to correct its errors, to listen not only to old-guard leadership but to dedicated and dynamic young members who wished to have a voice in the direction of the party. He reminded them that only the MCA had the national strength and the governmental influence to enable them to serve the interests of the Chinese community effectively. He affirmed a staunch anti-communist stand, explained in pragmatic economic terms.

These themes were present in every meeting, but the main content of the early lectures was considerably more theoretical, dealing with basic concepts of political science and government. The lecture topics, on which prepared notes were distributed, covered various political ideologies such as nationalism, fascism, communism, democracy, and capitalism, historical events such as the industrial revolution and the French and Russian revolutions, and theories of Plato, Marx, Hobbes, and Rousseau. Cheah worked hard at holding his audience, a difficult task given the weight of the material and the lack of sophistication of most of his listeners.

After two or three months, the lectures were replaced by seminars. Members were encouraged to voice their own opinions on government matters that affected them personally and the Chinese community generally. By the end of the second month a *banzhang*, or group monitor, had been selected by Cheah, and activity leaders had been chosen for various sections (badminton, ping-pong, and so on) by nomination from the floor, followed by unanimous acclamation. Late in December, when the task force was a month old, Dr. Lim Keng Yaik came to Sanchun for a highly successful public meeting attended by the MCA chairman and task force members from Batu Hitam and by the district member of parliament, as well as a large crowd of Sanchun people. Dato Teh appeared at a regular task force meeting in March, and other lesser task force officials came from Ipoh every two or three weeks. Locally organized activities included joint meetings with nearby task force branches, a cleanup campaign in a nearby village, picnics, and a one-day trip to visit the capital and meet federal officials.

Initially the task force was described as an organization for all Chinese, members of any party or the politically unaffiliated, with special encouragement for young people. It was clearly an MCA organ, however, and people attending meetings were urged before long to apply for MCA membership. As the Sanchun group became more formalized in structure, task force members wore T-shirts identifying themselves as such at all task force functions. The Sanchun branch of the MCA Youth, an inactive subgroup of the MCA made up of men in their thirties and forties, offered no resistance to the establishment of the task force, unlike some youth branches in larger towns. Instead, those members who were politically interested themselves joined the task force, which in Sanchun quickly came to be the most active of the party organs. But it nonetheless remained carefully compatible with the senior branch membership.

Sanchun's Response to the Task Force

One assumption that underlay the choice of new villages as targets for the initial task force mobilization, according to the organizers, was that villagers had less to fill their evening hours than people in larger towns and cities—fewer social activities and less access to entertainment such as movies and nightclubs. This was certainly true in Sanchun, and no doubt it contributed to the immediate success of the task force in drawing fairly large attendance, regularly reaching fifty or sixty by the end of the first month. Most of the people I talked with then said they went to the meetings for social reasons, urged on by friends, or simply to fill the time. They cared little about the state MCA's factional infighting, and most admitted that they were little concerned with politics at any level. Nonetheless, all had evening leisure hours that were usually spent in the gambling club or in coffee shops; a new diversion was welcome.

The street section and the village were about equally represented in attendance, as were young men under thirty and older men in their thirties and forties; few men above fifty attended. Lee Koi, for example, went to meetings only very rarely, although he met with task force cadres informally, occasionally inviting them to his house for lunch or dinner. Despite Miss Ao's encouragement, only six or eight women came to the political sessions; more attended picnics and singing lessons. Those who participated were all unmarried, between eighteen and twenty-five, and only one or two ever expressed any understanding of or interest in the political discussions that they quietly sat through week after week. The *boqi* lessons in traditional Chinese martial arts, given throughout the district by Yim Lee

Sen, lifetime devotee and a skilled and qualified teacher, were extremely popular with the young men, and eventually several young women overcame their shyness and joined in the training. Yim and his wife, a professional singer, were also in charge of the community singing sessions, teaching Chinese folk songs and ballads as well as rousing political songs, all of which had first been submitted to the police special branch for approval.

As the program took root, changes became evident. Many of the young men who had considered the initial political theory lectures dull became more involved as the discussions opened up to include specific state and federal policies and actions affecting Chinese. After the meetings, groups of men adjourned to the coffee shops to continue the debates. Liew Kam Ming was one of the active catalysts, regularly raising questions and asking that the MCA look into matters and attempt to effect favorable policies. Cadres cited the creation of Dr. Lim's ministry as one concrete example of the MCA's effectiveness, and continually referred to that achievement and other less specific good works at the federal level, but Liew, Loh Kow, and a few others kept more locally relevant matters to the fore. In a nearby village the state government threatened to plow under a few acres of chilies raised by Chinese on unused state land (possibly in response, some thought, to an undiplomatic remark Dr. Lim had made about the state land office's inefficiency). Liew demanded that the MCA intervene. A villager called for an increase in licenses for tin washing (panning in streams near mines). Loh complained that the council office had received no application forms for federal land development schemes; they were available only through the Malay *penghulu*'s office, but Chinese requesting forms there had been turned away empty-handed. When a young Sanchun man died as a result of internal injuries sustained in a motorcycle accident, though he had been examined after the accident and pronounced healthy by a government doctor, the task force members rallied behind a demand to investigate the doctor and government health services.

The issues of land — permanent titles to replace TOLs and more agricultural land — and education surfaced regularly, and the task force could claim some minor successes in these matters. After much pressure from the MCA, the Perak state government announced a decision in late 1971 to begin changing TOLs to thirty-year leases, purchase of the leases being mandatory (*Straits Times*, September 30, 1971). This was in fact a questionable victory for the MCA, however. Thirty years was a rather brief term, hardly encouraging great security, and the quitrents on the houselots were to be based on current land values. In the case of the new villages appended to urban areas the land values were inflated by the development potential of land, a potential quite irrelevant to people who wished to live quietly in their small homes. According to Robert Ong, this policy would in some cases result in quitrents up to five hundred times the cost of the

TOLs they were replacing, quite beyond the means of the villagers. Further MCA pressure was instrumental in getting some modification of this scheme. The government announced in March 1972 that villagers would be classified as original settlers or immigrants, and only the latter would be required to pay rates based on current market value. Those to be classed as immigrants, however, included all whose TOLs did not originate before 1960. People who may have been original settlers in a different village or the descendants of settlers, who had moved to a new house due to lack of space, were nonetheless classified as immigrants. The MCA and the DAP both argued against this classification, pointing out that most new villages provided substandard living at best, and most residents lived in them only through lack of alternatives due to poverty (*Straits Times*, March 10, 1972).[1] The issue is not yet fully resolved, and the permanent titles and land for cultivation are matters that are broached every time an outside official visits Sanchun.

In education, Cheah was able to cite more tangible victories. In five secondary schools attended primarily by Chinese in Ipoh and a nearby large town, the state education office initially refused permission to open Form IV classes, though in each case thirty or more pupils had passed the lower-certificate examination at the end of Form III. The education officer directed the students to other schools that already had higher classes in operation, although the students did not want the inconvenience of changing schools, and parents wanted more classrooms available to encourage children studying in lower-secondary forms. Cheah told his listeners that because the MCA symbolized the collective strength of the Chinese community it was able to exert pressure successfully and cause the ruling to be changed in four of the five cases. Moreover, the new blood of the MCA took credit for pressuring the government into recognizing Chinese-medium senior middle-school education as equivalent to the Cambridge School Certificate, claiming that Dr. Lim was the only cabinet member to actively support the measure, while two other MCA ministers remained silent.

When I arrived in Sanchun in August 1971 the membership of the MCA branch stood at about 60, little changed from the time of its founding. In August 1972, after a door-to-door membership drive in which cadres and local men explained the goals and achievements to date of the task force, the rolls listed 406 names. Yim Lee Sen, the martial arts instructor, had himself not been a party member until the reorganization and the institution of the task force. He believed that many of the other new members

1. The DAP was as active as the MCA in arguing publicly for Chinese interests, but it lacked local organization in rural areas. See Strauch 1978 for a comparison of the two parties in rural Perak.

had formerly shared his feelings that MCA leaders, like all politicians, were interested only in their own personal gains, could not be trusted, and cared little for the common man and his problems. He was convinced that the task force organizers were more public-spirited and sincerely wanted to reorganize the party in such a way as to wrest control from powerful self-seekers and give it to leaders from the ranks representing a united Chinese community. It appeared from the membership figures and from conversations with many young Sanchun men that such faith in the task force movement was widespread at the grassroots level.

Though of course not all 406 members were active, a gradual shift in the composition of social and political groupings became apparent. At the task force meetings, Liew and Loh were the most vocal of the leadership clique; Chin attended only occasionally and the elders not at all. But it was not only Liew and Loh who spoke out. Many young men from the village, loggers and construction workers, began to ask questions, about both political theory and its application in Malaysia. Older men spoke up less frequently, perhaps being more embarrassed about public speaking, particularly as Mandarin was encouraged, though not used exclusively.

In summer 1972, the mutual-aid society formerly under the auspices of the MCA Youth was reorganized under the task force, with a logger returned from several years' work in Indonesia and a village carpenter, both about thirty-five, and two young women about twenty-five on the committee, and assistant headmaster Yap Hoi Fatt as chairman. Chin Ta Hing was treasurer, and Lee Wan Chun secretary, and several others of the regular leadership, including Liew Kam Ming, Loh Kow, and Wong Ching Chee, appeared at the meetings. These meetings, unlike most gatherings of earlier months, began on time. Even more striking, Mandarin was used almost without fail for the first hour or so, after which people began to lapse back into the more familiar and comfortable Cantonese. As a result of the responsibility the task force now accepted for mutual aid and community social welfare, the number of young people turning out for village wakes and funerals grew markedly.

The task force cadres in Sanchun were successful in their attempts to draw out new young leadership without alienating the old. Lee Koi seemed little interested in the new group, whose major concerns were national and did not immediately impinge on his local domain. The cadres, who saw Lee as a basically honest and socially responsible leader by no means deserving of attack, treated him with respect. Two of Lee's sons attended the task force meetings regularly, and Lee Wan Chun was often called on to assume responsible duties. Lung Sooi, Chong Kit, and Tan Siew Hing themselves displayed no interest in the group, though sons of each attended meetings at least occasionally. Lung Teng Yu was the only person from the three families to take real interest.

It was Chin Ta Hing's wife's younger brother, Lim Tien Ho, who was selected by the cadres as group monitor, although Cheah later regretted the choice. Liew Kam Ming had been considered, showing himself from the outset to be a natural leader, but was dismissed as a bit too old, Lee Wan Chun had seemed too reserved, and Lim, serious, hardworking, and Chin's brother-in-law, had seemed to be the best choice at the time. It became apparent, however, that although he was well liked he lacked the natural dynamic qualities needed for real leadership. Although Lim was introduced as *banzhang* early in January, and formally elected to the position by a hand vote (called at his own request) late in the month, he was at first given only simple tasks of organization between meetings. Not until April did Lim rather than Cheah lead the group in opening the meeting with the task force song.

Nonetheless, the reform movement could not completely avoid being caught between the imperfections of the powers that be and the new young idealism it sought to create. Some villagers had built homes on land not zoned for housing, trusting, so the rumors went, the assurances of Liew Kam Ming and Choong Kwan Foh, who had allegedly obtained their "irregular" TOLs for them, for a consideration. When the state threatened the villagers with demolition, a young sundry dealer called Ah Ming tried to help them; he took the case to Robert Ong and Miss Ao, complaining that the unsophisticated villagers had been exploited unscrupulously by the councillors and were now likely to lose their homes. He was told he would receive a confidential reply once they had looked into the matter. When nothing further happened, Ah Ming tried to speak to Dr. Lim personally when he visited Sanchun, but, he says, Choong Kwan Foh prevented him from doing so. When I queried Ong later on the matter, he admitted knowing of the case, but he was of the opinion that some "minor irregularities" were unavoidable. Though Liew was being watched carefully before being trusted with responsibilities, Ong said, it was deemed best to let the matter lie. Ong's pragmatism spared Liew embarrassment, but it also cost the task force the support of Ah Ming and doubtless some of his friends, for he became understandably cynical toward the reform and reorganization movement.

Crisis within the Party

Within its first six months of operation, it was clear that the task force was achieving success in many of its local-level goals. MCA membership had more than quadrupled in Sanchun and had tripled in two nearby towns. According to the cadres, all the target towns and villages evidenced similar support. Beyond the impressive numbers, the task force stirred active participation and provided opportunities and training for new young leaders who were emerging. Large numbers of Chinese who had in 1969 rejected the MCA wholeheartedly were now joining the reorganized MCA in the belief that grassroots strength could not only better the party's bargaining position with the UMNO but could effect new directions within the party itself.

Task force cadres repeated often that only by joining the party and thereby increasing the reformist votes at the grassroots level could the average Chinese hope to affect the course of political events. They promised that local votes would count in national MCA party elections, and task force members or leaders imbued with *xinsixiang* (new thought) could replace the corrupt and inefficient old guard. As it became clear that this was the element of the task force program that attracted many heretofore apolitical people, the party center showed signs of nervousness about the new grassroots strength that was building in Perak.

The first real crisis, which occurred in April 1972, centered around the national Alliance decision to form a coalition government with the People's Progressive Party in Perak, a decision purportedly made without consulting or informing the Perak MCA or its acting secretary, Paul Leong. In mobilizing new support, Leong and other task force leaders had made much of the MCA as the only viable Chinese pressure group available within the government, arguing that Chinese unity within the MCA was essential to the advancement of Chinese interests. Now they were presented with a coalition that offered the man in the street a different option: he could support a strong Chinese-oriented "opposition" party which was free of the Uncle Tom image of the MCA old guard but which was now also represented in the government and so presumably had new powers to make its voice heard. The task force program, which did its best to present an anti-Uncle Tom image but was nevertheless still part of the MCA, felt threatened. Leong and another high-ranking state officer, T. C. Choong, criticized the coalition and the manner in which it was formed in a press release, and both were subsequently expelled from the party.

The task force branches were irate at the summary expulsion of Leong and Choong, and prepared press releases for regional Chinese newspapers attacking the party's actions both in the forming of the coalition and in the expulsion of state leaders. Shortly thereafter the MCA acting national chairman, Lee San Choon, came to Sanchun for a party meeting convened to publicize a new MCA Youth program, but he was no doubt intent on a general pacification of the grassroots as well. After a long silence followed his speech, he was informed that people wished to ask questions on other matters. The hall was filled, and task force members had turned out in force, wearing their T-shirts. Liew Kam Ming was the first to speak. He strongly criticized the actions of the party executive committee, demanded explanation, and charged that the MCA national leadership had once again, as always, completely ignored the views of the branch membership. His speech met with long applause. Choong Kwan Foh spoke next, unfortunately lacking Liew's eloquence; then a local party man launched a personal attack on Tan Siew Sin, calling him a big snake who was unfit for party leadership because he didn't even speak any Chinese dialect. Lee San Choon responded to all attacks as a careful politician. He stressed the need for party discipline, emphasized Tan's good points, and promised party support for the task force and greater communication with the branch membership in the future.

The April crisis had the effect of drawing even greater support for the task force at local levels. In Sanchun both membership and attendance increased, and task force and party issues were the prime subjects of discussion in the coffee shops and on the streets. In May, Yap Hoi Fatt joined the party and the task force and began teaching Malay language classes for task force members. The visibility of the group increased over the next few months as they organized to paint the old people's home, cooperated with Alliance partners in the National Day celebration and in a big picnic at a nearby waterfall, and held a hugely successful community party for the Chinese moon-cake festival in September, always wearing task force T-shirts.

Though the first storm was weathered successfully, others followed. A clash occurred between task force leaders and the MCA Youth in a large town to the north, and between an old-guard party chairman and the task force group in Batu Hitam to the south; in both cases police were called in. UMNO members and MCA leaders alike began accusing the task force and Dato Teh of being too chauvinist, too radical, and possibly under communist influence. Tan Siew Sin withdrew the MCA's financial support, but funds were then collected privately, cadres willingly accepted salary cuts of fifty percent, and the task force continued to grow. The central party membership committee delayed the processing of thousands of new applications, depriving the reform movement of voting power, and eventually called for a review of some existing branch memberships. In September, Tan Siew Sin removed Dr. Lim from his position as head of the Perak state liaison committee and took over Lim's duties personally, whereupon a number of subcommittee heads loyal to Lim resigned. Lines were being clearly drawn as the conflict deepened.

The task force showed considerable resilience due both to the excellent groundwork that had been done in the villages and the continuing commitment of the cadres, and to the crucial fact that a task force leader held a national position from which he could not easily be removed: Dr. Lim

Keng Yaik retained his position in the federal cabinet, and the MCA center could not persuade him to resign. Thus, unless the prime minister chose to enter what was essentially an internal MCA squabble and request his resignation, Lim held an unassailable position from which to continue to rally the support of the newly mobilized Chinese rural proletariat, who had for years seen the old-guard MCA as a party representing not them but the wealthy Chinese business elite.

In late November 1972 the MCA central committee ordered the task force disbanded immediately. The action was taken, spokesmen said, in the interests of party discipline, but it was also stated that the decision followed discussions with "others" concerned (*Nanyang Siang Pau,* Nov. 24), implying UMNO or government interest in the decision. Nonetheless the task force would not die easily, and in February 1973 the MCA headquarters had to disavow publicly any connection with the organization that had circulated a newsletter to all Perak branches under the name of the Perak task force (*Nanyang Siang Pau,* Feb. 27). Throughout the spring of 1973 Lim Keng Yaik was active not only in Perak but also in Johore and Selangor, and the Chinese press was replete with statements issued by all levels of the party both praising and reviling him. By the end of May, however, he decided his position within the MCA was no longer tenable and resigned his cabinet post; he was then immediately expelled from the party. A series of mass expulsions continued throughout the summer as the MCA central committee tried to eliminate any possible opposition delegates from the August national party annual meeting. Two full divisions with seven and nine branches, respectively, and fifteen additional branches in Perak, and another division and nine additional branches in two other states (Selangor and Johore) were summarily dissolved prior to the national meeting. Individual expulsions in Perak were listed by the MCA as 158. In addition, hundreds, perhaps thousands, of new applications made through task force branches were never accepted.

In subsequent months the leaders of the now-defunct Perak task force found themselves courted by other Chinese-oriented parties, both the opposition and new members of the expanded government coalition. Factional splits within the task force leadership itself came to the surface. Dr. Lim and a number of other popular leaders chose to join the Gerakan and were followed by a good proportion of the grassroots membership, while another faction headed by Dato Teh went to a minor opposition party, and still others simply withdrew from formal politics in disillusionment or disgust. A fair proportion — perhaps a third — of the grassroots membership elected to stay with the MCA. Exact figures are difficult to determine, as the Chinese press throughout 1973 and 1974 is full of boasts and counterboasts, charges and countercharges, about new membership applications and defections on all sides.

The Fall and the Aftermath in Sanchun

Like nearly all the grassroots task force branches, the Sanchun task force actively supported its leadership throughout the months of turmoil, giving out periodic press releases and continuing local activities. By the spring of 1973 (several months after the task force had been officially disbanded by the center), the *banzhang* position had passed to a respected young construction worker, Wong Mau Sang. When Dr. Lim Keng Yaik returned to his home base of Ipoh early in June, following his resignation from the cabinet and expulsion from the party, he was met at the airport by several thousand supporters mobilized on twenty-four hours' notice, including two busloads from Sanchun, brought on buses chartered with MCA branch funds.[2] Chin Ta Hing termed this a truly extraordinary event; it aroused new spirit even among members who had formerly been passive in supporting the reformation movement. The new spirit carried Sanchun through a tumultuous summer of meetings and demonstrations, and culminated in the displays of large banners "mourning the death of MCA's democracy" and denouncing Tan Siew Sin as a "traitor against the MCA" (*Ma Hua zuiren*) and finally in the burning of Tan in effigy.

The Sanchun branch had not desired such turmoil, and it is likely that many of the thirty to forty task force-controlled branches shared its feelings. Before Lim's expulsion, the new acting state MCA chairman had visited Sanchun, and Chin Ta Hing and other local leaders voiced strong sentiments in favor of some kind of compromise between the factions, and a cooling-off period. But when the open split came, loyalty to Lim remained strong. By July, when local branches were submitting their nominations for delegates to the August national convention, rumor spread that nominees from task force-controlled branches would be expelled from the party. Six names were put forth in Sanchun, including Chin Ta Hing as MCA chairman, Wong Mau Sang as task force *banzhang*, Lee Koi's son Lee Wan Chun, Liew Kam Ming, another councillor, and a tin mine worker. The task force held a general meeting and agreed to withdraw en masse if there were any expulsions. Chin and Wong were expelled shortly thereafter, and a week later the Sanchun MCA branch was declared dissolved by the state MCA liaison committee.

In the ensuing weeks Lim Keng Yaik, Paul Leong, and other leaders of the reformist faction visited their grassroots supporters to sound out their sentiments before deciding which of two primary options to take. They were being courted concurrently by the Gerakan, now a government coalition member, and Pekemas, a small opposition party. They found that the

---

2. Estimates range from four to ten thousand supporters, but the latter may be simply the use of the traditional Chinese figure, as in *wan sui!*— ten thousand years of life, or "long life!"

village task force members throughout the state overwhelmingly favored remaining within the government. Most were willing to join the Gerakan, though some clearly intended to stay with the MCA, but virtually none expressed willingness to go into opposition, thereby removing themselves from what government benefits they might retain in the Gerakan and moreover exposing themselves to the uncertainties of being opposition islands in a rural sea of Malay UMNO supporters. A general meeting of task force representatives was ultimately held at the Ipoh headquarters. When the majority vote favored joining Gerakan, a resolution considered binding on all members was passed and negotiations were begun with the Gerakan national chairman. As noted above, splits within the leadership surfaced in the fall, and similar, though not necessarily parallel, splits materialized in Sanchun and probably in other local groups as well.

During the summer months the beleaguered Sanchun branch had appeared to be fully united behind Lim Keng Yaik and Paul Leong. But after the MCA August general meeting was safely past, disbanded local branches received invitations to re-form, so broader options were once again open. Chin Ta Hing and Wong Mau Sang were among the many expelled individually who received personal invitations to reapply for MCA membership. Both assured me that they would not have left the MCA by choice in the first place, but, given the course of events, both felt righteously indignant toward the MCA and remained committed to the new direction they had taken. Others in Sanchun felt no such compunctions, however, and a new MCA branch was opened with Liew Kam Ming as its chairman and Yap Hoi Fatt as chairman of the subsidiary MCA Youth branch.

Since both Liew and Yap, and others who joined with them, had participated in meetings with Paul Leong and Dr. Lim and several had been present at the effigy burning (Yap Hoi Fatt claims to have been out of town that day), their return to the MCA was seen as sudden betrayal. Moreover, it was rumored that during the earlier months of conflict Liew Kam Ming had been observed in Kuala Lumpur conferring with MCA old-guard forces; his current actions could be construed as confirming suspicions that he had acted as a spy. According to all reports, the usually peaceful community of Sanchun saw no peace for several months. Tempers flared, heated arguments in coffee shops were commonplace, and strong and open criticism and accusations flew with an acrimony nearly unprecedented in Sanchun. The Gerakan branch was formed in due course, headed by Chin Ta Hing, with Wong Mau Sang and Chin's brother-in-law among the officeholders, and the majority of the former task force members joined them enthusiastically.

By the summer of 1974 tempers had cooled, and the two parties, so they say, cooperated as fellow Barison Nasional members in the fall general elections. In summer 1975 the government reorganized the local council, now known as the local government office, making it fully appointive; that too apparently went smoothly. The MCA received five seats, the Gerakan four, the PPP one, the UMNO two, and the MIC one, as a result of bargaining among the Barisan Nasional parties at the state level. Branch nominations were sent to the state parties for consideration, and passed with little apparent change to the *Menteri Besar*, who also considered recommendations advanced by the DO and the CAO. Appointments were made originally for one year but have been renewed yearly since then. The council chairman was appointed directly by the *Menteri Besar*; other officers were to be elected by secret ballot of the council itself. Chin Ta Hing was retained as chairman, and Liew Kam Ming was elected vice-chairman.

The Divided "Family"

In the seven years that I have known Sanchun, changes in the community have been considerable. Formal structures, informal processes, social alignments, and personalities all show some alteration, and by no means entirely in directions that might have once been predicted. The social rift that accompanied the party split follows an uncertain course, crosscutting lines of friendship, kinship, and political commitment, forming new alliances and enmities that would have seemed highly improbable a few years ago.

Most people seem disturbed by the breach, so much so that many insist there is no breach. "Friendship is friendship and politics is politics," I was told more times than I can remember. The public value placed on solidarity and harmony is strong in Sanchun, and is mentioned in many contexts. Discussing costs of the upcoming festival at a 1978 temple committee meeting, Tan Siew Hing chided the group for stinginess, pointing out that "we are all Sanchun people" and the festival is for "our own people" (*zijiren*) — so why skimp on costs? The morning after the 1978 elections, in which the Sanchun constituency returned two Barisan Nasional (MCA) candidates, I approached a Gerakan friend who I knew had favored the opposition state assembly candidate and asked if he was satisfied with the election results. His earnest reply: "Of course! We're all BN members here; why shouldn't we be satisfied?" During the election campaign, virtually all of the people I queried regarding the extent of cooperation and coordination between the MCA and the Gerakan in sharing the campaign work responded initially with assurances that all was well. But some spoke almost sheepishly, well aware that they were fooling no one, and many gave more candid opinions as the conversations wore on.

Time does heal wounds, it appears. Men who called Lee Koi a tyrant in 1972 no longer begrudge him his honor and status in 1978, as it carries less power and he is mellowing with old age. Tan Siew Hing is amiable and pleasantly respectful in Lee's company now and is more at ease with other members of the fateful 1957 council as well, as they sit together at committee meetings and later adjourn to the coffee shop together, in 1978. Liew Kam Ming, who was by all accounts a social pariah in 1974, was still unwelcome in 1976 at a series of banquets that would once have included him. His absence, nonetheless, embarrassed people; one man commented sadly on the fact that "we can't even all sit down to a meal together anymore." But by 1978, though he was not yet fully reincorporated into the social group, he was no longer shunned: he could be observed stopping to chat casually with other leaders on the street or at a basketball game, and on one occasion after a meeting he hosted a coffee shop gathering that included a number of his former antagonists. The communal impulse toward social harmony is strong, and the strain toward its realization is seemingly unrelenting.

The communal myth of solidarity—"one big family"—notwithstanding, the line of division in Sanchun today is real and persistent. The internal cleavage today is not one of personalities, as it was, for example, between Lee Koi and Tan Siew Hing when I first arrived. Instead, as a direct result of higher-level rivalries and conflicts, it has a firm structural basis expressed in formal organizations, two parties that claim to be allies but are in fact rivals. The council meetings I attended in 1976 differed perceptibly from those of earlier years. Though informants admitted to no new problems in council procedures as a result of the new multiparty representation, there was an almost tangible tension in the air. And in 1976 I witnessed for the first time a public dispute-mediation session that nearly broke down in hopeless disorder as respected leaders shouted in irate voices at one another. The issue was the demolition of part of the old school building, and which of two carpenters had been given the demolition contract—like most other internal contracts in Sanchun, a verbal agreement. The carpenters were members of opposite parties, and the support shown for each of them followed party lines to a degree that seemed unlikely to be purely coincidental. As all sides of the complicated question of who had promised what to whom were aired, real anger erupted, and shouting matches spun off the subject to ad hominem insults having nothing to do with the carpenters or their questioned contracts. The combined authority of Lee Koi and Chin Ta Hing eventually triumphed and a compromise was reached, but personal feelings were far from soothed. The group broke up and went off in different directions, tacitly avoiding the traditional sharing of tea and snacks that should have sealed the dispute resolution.

The Sanchun Gerakan branch officers in 1978 were the same ones who had taken office when the party was founded four years earlier, but there had been changes in the MCA branch in that period. Liew Kam Ming had

been appointed chairman from above in 1974 and held the position unchallenged through late 1976, despite local dissatisfaction within MCA
ranks. Yap Hoi Fatt, who with strong support from MCA Youth would
have been the most likely rival, chose not to stand against him. Yap is
aware that as a government servant subject to transfer he is vulnerable to
an opponent with strong outside connections such as Liew's, and he has
family roots in Sanchun that he will not willingly sacrifice to the game of
politics. With no one contesting the chair, branch elections were not held
in 1975. When elections were held in 1976 Liew had decided to step down.
Yap too withdrew from his party office, due to high blood pressure and
related health problems. Councillor Wong Ching Chee was prevailed upon
to take the chairmanship, which no one seemed to want, but he is recognized by most to be a capable managerial type rather than a leader, and
Liew, now treasurer, still provides most of the party's dynamism.

My 1978 visit coincided with the general election campaign, when all
parties were actively mobilizing supporters in the effort to win votes. The
Gerakan branch appeared to have lost a little of its earlier momentum —
there were no longer regular Saturday night social gatherings in the party
hall, for example — but the activists turned out enthusiastically to campaign, driving some distances to work in the constituencies of Paul Leong
and Lim Keng Yaik as well as helping out in another Gerakan parliamentary constituency closer to home. Both state and parliamentary candidates
in Sanchun's constituency were MCA men, and the Sanchun MCA branch
provided eager workers in the home constituency. The fact that the two
"allies" campaigned separately reflected both local incompatibilities and,
more significant, serious infighting between the two parties at the national
level (see Strauch 1980 and Lee 1980).

At the outset, on nomination day, Sanchun Gerakan activists felt that
their party had been unfairly treated in the allocation of seats, as did many
Gerakan members everywhere. Specifically, there was bitterness because
high-level bargaining within the Barisan Nasional had given Lim Keng
Yaik's home parliamentary constituency to the MCA to contest, and Lim
received only a state seat. Throughout the intense two-week campaign
there were rumors of MCA supporters actively sabotaging Gerakan cam-
paigns throughout Perak and Penang, and of course counter-rumors leveled similar charges against the Gerakan. Some MCA men in Penang, disappointed when their chosen constituencies were given to the Gerakan,
stood as independents, openly challenging their Gerakan "allies." In Paul
Leong's Taiping constituency it was widely rumored that the MCA was giving substantial financial support to the opposition DAP candidate. Sanchun men, who were working in other constituencies and bringing home
fresh rumors regularly, concerned themselves personally with the battles
being fought by their leaders. Their identification with the Gerakan as a

national party besieged by its "partner" within the Barisan was exceedingly strong; it could not but affect the local MCA-Gerakan working relationship. Moreover, there was widespread dissatisfaction over certain of the MCA's candidates in southern Perak, including the state candidate in the Sanchun constituency. Sanchun people of all political persuasions expressed resentment that the man was Ipoh-based, a total stranger to them, and many openly favored his DAP opponent, who lived only fifteen miles away and was well known locally for his public service.[3] Although the MCA had no worries about the local parliamentary seat, the state seat was in doubt. The party understandably wanted to take no chances with campaign workers who might be less than enthusiastic in their support of the candidate, so they were very careful in their distribution of electioneering permits. Only the Gerakan men serving on the joint Barisan election committee received local permits, and the other Gerakan members eager to campaign were forced to turn elsewhere to offer their services.

The myth of community solidarity would not die easily, however. The responsible party leaders Chin Ta Hing, Liew Kam Ming, and Wong Ching Chee all tried to maintain face when I talked with them in the first days of the campaign, growing more candid only as the split grew to glaring proportions. Informants who were frank from the outset included Yap Hoi Fatt and Woo Lee Sen (MCA) and Loh Kow (Gerakan), all of whom opted to stay on the sidelines during the campaign (though their support of the DAP man was widely known). A telling observation by Yap on the first Barisan election committee meeting, which he attended, sums up the whole problem of the divided family. There was debate as to which of the two party offices should be used as election headquarters. Agreement could not be reached by the usual consensus procedures, so, much to Yap's disgust, a vote had to be called. "A vote!" he snorted; "if we can't agree on a simple thing like that, how can we agree on anything anymore!"

The Impact of National Politics on the Local System

The task force movement has clearly had important repercussions within the Sanchun community. The state and national MCA politics that encompassed the Sanchun party branch are themselves encompassed, or encapsulated, by the national political environment. The MCA is but one compo-

---

3. See Kessler 1978, chap. 8, for a discussion of Malay villagers' views of elections in 1969; strikingly similar concerns are expressed — dissatisfaction with "carpet-bagger" candidates, sad resignation regarding new splits and disharmonies within the rural community as a result of higher-level political party rivalries and machinations, and so forth.

nent member of the government, and a junior member at that, as real power lies more immediately in UMNO hands; thus MCA politics cannot be divorced from the government's internal politics. Elements within the national political system defined parameters for the action of the Perak MCA task force drama, which served as a middle-level mediator, in this case, between the political center and the local systems at the extreme periphery.

None of the district, state, or national Chinese politicians I talked with in 1976 imputed any major significance to government or UMNO views or actions regarding the MCA struggle. Nonetheless, my outside observer's model, which is more concerned with structures and processes than with isolated events, calls attention to two particular aspects of the broader political environment that had relevance for the intraparty conflict. The first highlights the role of the values of the dominant political culture; the second, the importance of the action not taken.

First, in their attack against the young turks, the old guard had recourse to a political myth that holds considerably currency in Malaysia but is more often used by Malays against Chinese than within the Chinese community itself. The task force was accused by both MCA leaders and low-ranking UMNO members (top UMNO men took no public position) of Chinese chauvinist extremism. In Malaysia, once Chinese chauvinism is charged in anger, if the anger turns to irrationality—as it does almost inevitably in factional fighting—the "communist" label is seldom far behind. When the MCA old guard called their opponents communist-inspired Chinese chauvinists they symbolically lined themselves up with democracy and honor and the government, against a clique now defined as antigovernment and subversive. They thereby legitimized their own position by labeling the opponent not just the Enemy but the Devil, and thereby probably rallied some conservative moral support in the ranks of both the MCA and the UMNO.

The second point is related to the first, and shows the way the rulemakers can put their own rules to use by not using them. The charge of communist influence was not made formally, but it certainly reached the highest attention. Had the government taken the charge at all seriously, or had it chosen to back its own allies within the ruling councils, the prime minister could have moved swiftly to undercut the task force's growing strength by removing Lim Keng Yaik from his cabinet. Instead, nine months passed after the onset of open confrontation (September 1972, when Tan Siew Sin relieved Lim of his duties as Perak MCA head) before the prime minister took action. Finally acquiescing to the MCA leadership's demands for higher validation of its authority within its own party, he requested Lim's resignation in May 1973. Politicking on both sides was frantic in those nine months, and the factional struggle ultimately reached proportions that severely damaged the party's national strength and viability as the "legiti-mate" representative of the Chinese community within the government. In the new Barisan Nasional government the MCA now finds itself forced to share the Chinese portion of government power with a "friendly" rival with whom it shares little friendship. The Gerakan was formed and is still headed by Dr. Lim Chong Eu, who had been drummed out of the MCA years before; and in 1974 he was joined by many of the politicians the MCA had expelled so recently with such animosity.

One UMNO leader, questioned on his party's position on the MCA crisis, observed simply that divide and rule is always a good policy. The UMNO did not need to take active part in the MCA strife in order to divide. On the contrary, its careful noninvolvement effectively projected the favorable image of Malay power holders democratically unwilling to meddle in inter-nal Chinese affairs, even to come to the aid of their allies. But the dilution of Chinese strength that resulted from protracted infighting is unlikely to be viewed with alarm or disfavor in Malay-dominated government circles.

Thus the MCA struggle was allowed to run its course unimpeded. The rival faction built such strength that not only the core leaders had to be ex-pelled, but the grassroots followers as well. Sanchun was not happy with such developments and made its feelings known to both factions early on, in the fall of 1972 and again a few months later. But competition and riv-alry grew to full-blown conflict, and the axe was felt in Sanchun as sharply as elsewhere. Subsequent realignment of leadership patterns in Sanchun have come about as a direct result of the wholly external conflict in which Sanchun people found themselves unwillingly but inextricably embroiled.

Chin Ta Hing and Liew Kam Ming present contrasting examples of the ways in which personal fortunes are molded by the external political envi-ronment. Chin, as we have seen, began his rise to power in Sanchun some-what reluctantly, first becoming chairman through the death of the in-cumbent and retaining the position only at the constant urging of his friends. In the task force crisis, Chin was swept along by circumstances be-yond his control, but the events of that period seem to have raised his con-sciousness and touched him personally in a way that has changed the char-acter of his leadership. Had the MCA not expelled him, he would probably have ridden the storm through and remained with the passively conserva-tive old guard. But once singled out, and seeing himself eagerly supported by the majority of the younger activists of the community, Chin felt he could not accept reinstatement without serious loss of face and abandon-ment of principle.

Liew Kam Ming, by contrast, has profited by his own conscious and cal-culated manipulation of external contacts, but his successes have under-mined his former local popularity. After winning appointment from above to the MCA branch chairmanship, Liew used his government and party connections, it is widely believed, to effect a series of corrupt land deals in 1974 and 1975, for which he is severely censured. He is not immune to local social pressures — no one living in a face-to-face community can be — and he seems in recent years, as he attempts to regain local respect, to have modified his exploitation of external resources.

Liew Kam Ming, through ambition and avarice, might well have alienated himself from his fellow councillors even without the party split. But the split did occur, and as a result not of local but of external rivalries and factional conflicts. In consequence, despite his personal ostracism, Liew found himself in a position of leadership, as chairman of the MCA branch and as vice-chairman of the council, though he later withdrew from the former role. Chin Ta Hing might have continued as council and party chairman and eventually, with Lee Koi's death, become nominal head of the community, or he might have been overshadowed by Tan Siew Hing. But now Chin has been steeled in trial by fire, so to speak, and has thus won a much stronger position of leadership in his own right based now on some mild-mannered charisma overlying the quiet technocratic competence he has always shown. This, too, is a consequence not of his own efforts and planning, but of developments in the course of a struggle between more powerful rivals. And perhaps the most important ramification for the Sanchun community at large is the establishment of a second party branch, enlarging the boundaries of the local stage and allowing for an expanded cast of political actors. Though in the central leadership cliques of Sanchun no totally new faces have appeared over the past seven years, the younger activists in the Gerakan and the MCA Youth are taking advantage of their party forums to test and develop their political and leadership skills, and the potential leadership pool has grown considerably since 1971.

Politics is an ongoing process; there can be no "final outcome" to a drama such as the one set in motion by the task force program. Nonetheless, the pattern emerges clearly. External forces were responsible for the local-level split that now defines local politics. External events and powers created it in 1973, maintained it through the structural stability of the parties involved, and in 1978 once again exacerbated it during the general election campaign. Throughout Sanchun's history, its leadership has been dependent for self-definition and shape on its relationship at any given time with the larger encapsulating system. The definition and shape may change, but the locus of definition remains essentially external.

8

Conclusion

Although the political and personal comings and goings of people in a town like Sanchun hold intrinsic interest, the real value of a case study lies in the way it illuminates existing theoretical statements. A study may provide corroborating evidence for propositions advanced in earlier works, or it may call into question assumptions or conclusions found either in scholarly literature or in the common wisdom. With the Sanchun material now fully elaborated, I will turn once again to some of the issues raised in the first two chapters.

Vincent, concluding her review of action theory in political anthropology, observes that is has moved "from the study of the manipulative strategies of a rather narrow range of political actors (i.e. the men in the middle) to a greater clarification of the particular circumstances within which they operate" (1978: 190). My analysis of the political life of Sanchun, placing the study of actors' strategies firmly within the context of the constraints and resources imposed and provided by the wider political environment in which they are located, demonstrates the value of such clarification. This broader perspective, complementing local-level analysis, is increasingly recognized as imperative in the anthropological study of political action.

The Framework for Local-Level Politics: Autonomy, Encapsulation, or Integration?

Political events in Sanchun, as the preceding chapters show, are powerfully shaped by events and relationships beyond the local system. Sanchun leaders have always relied on the manipulation of external resources to win and maintain their local positions. But the form of such resources and the ease with which a limited number of local actors could monopolize access to them have varied. In a period of an expanding economy, high mobility, and relatively open competition, early headmen relied on financial resources accumulated through participation in a larger economy to build political support groups among local people. Under the Japanese occupation local political processes were to some extent held in abeyance. Despite the severity of the period for health and livelihood, significant long-term changes in political personnel or style do not appear to have arisen out of that era. A major change occurred, however, under the Emergency administration that followed: the relevant external resources were no longer economic but political in nature. The same has remained largely true in the context of an independent bureaucratic state, although economic resources play an indirect consolidating role today much as they did in traditional times by affording the leader both leisure and capital to invest in local social obligations. Personal connections to important individuals or groups in the higher levels of the political system now constitute the resources most crucial for local political actors. Unlike economic assets in a boom period, such connections are by the nature of a centralized state system a limited good. Effective monopoly of such external links by a few constitutes effective monopoly of the highest local positions of power, although local influence and esteem may still be awarded to others on the basis of other criteria.

Looking at Sanchun, one is struck by the overriding importance of the encapsulating environment, the constraints it imposes and the resources it offers, in the molding of local political life. How is it, then, that so much of the earlier anthropological literature treating local-level politics concentrated so heavily on internal political processes, with little more than passing acknowledgment of a larger environment? Possibly the cases being studied were in fact quite different, special in some sense, and thus the generalizations drawn were unwittingly overextended.

A significant number of the anthropological studies that focus on politics in complex agrarian societies have dealt with South Asian cases, and I believe we find some clues there regarding the directions that local-level political analysis has taken. Even before independence in 1947, Indian political thinkers abhorred the idea of strong centralization; Gandhi, Roy, and Jayaprakash Narayan all strongly advocated government by true democracy in near-anarchist terms. There was considerable local agitation during the 1940s in support of their ideas, and in the 1950s and 1960s village councils were widely implemented. Tinker suggests that the pattern of the first five years of the councils "shows a substantial transfer of power into local hands, and the adaptation of the historic apparatus of district administration to some sort of partnership with local leaders" (1968: 224).

Gandhian teaching advocated selection of council members by consensus, but when the Congress Party sought to limit that to consensus within its own membership other groups objected, and "village elections turned into contests between economic and social power groups" (1968: 224). It is clear that there are critical contrasts between the Indian political system and the one that was established at independence in Malaysia and progressively modified through the years to intensify centralization of power.

Nicholas has written numerous articles on factions and group conflicts and rivalries in Indian villages, and he grants in a 1968 paper that until that time he as well as others had generally analyzed such villages as having a high degree of autonomy, integrity, and internal coherence. He offers a partial explanation: "[There is] a relatively small annual production per cultivator; thus, only a small proportion of each peasant's product is free for taxes, trade, and savings; and, thus, economically and politically integrated territories are of limited size . . . [This] takes us partway to understanding why the great majority of Indian villages have such a degree of autonomy in their political lives" (1968: 307). He goes on to treat examples of local groups making use of new national laws that affirm voting rights regardless of caste, and concludes that "if it was once possible to speak in a reasonably realistic way about the political integration of an Indian peasant village as if it were autonomous and integral, it is no longer so" (1968: 320).

A century ago Malaya too was made up of a number of small, loosely integrated sultanates in which low population and low productivity combined to limit the size of politically cohesive units. By the middle of this century, however, the country was already one of the most highly developed in the region, with an economy tied intimately into the world market in metals and raw materials. A rural proletariat made up largely of Chinese and Indians provided labor for the extractive primary industries, while Malays remained chiefly in the traditional agricultural sector. Rural market towns such as Sanchun even at independence were well integrated into the regional and national economy. There were crucial differences between such market centers and the more traditionally rooted Malay peasant villages, which I will return to below. Nonetheless, both were more coherently linked economically and politically as well to higher-level centers than similar rural communities appeared to be in the South Asian examples analyzed in the literature.

A recent study of structural change in the political system of a Sinhalese village, however, reaches some of the same conclusions in the South Asia context that I come to in the Malaysian case. Robinson (1975) discusses the breakdown of traditional village leadership patterns in the mid-1960s, which she argues grows directly out of national-level decisions and policies. For her, the political watershed is not independence per se but rather the aggressive implementation of centralized nation-building policies that in Sri Lanka came only later (1975: chap. 11). Local leadership in 1963 had depended on high personal standing in the community and on smoothly functioning channels of communication to the outside; by 1967 these rules were no longer universally held legitimate, but no new rules had emerged to replace them. Given certain changes in the state and political party system, exclusive control by a few men over external channels was no longer possible,[1] and a local leadership vacuum ensued, with political party factions arising to fill the breach. Local disputes are no longer merely local, and cannot be mediated locally because there are no effective leaders. The Village Committee is in fact made up of representatives from several villages, and they now follow party lines in voting. Moreover, Robinson contends that the concepts of village arena and encapsulating system as an independent variable are meaningless, for the village "is now largely an undifferentiated part of the bigger political field in which the old rules are competing against new rules which emphasize perception and eradication of present economic differentiation, political party allegiance, and the commitment to change through encounter and fight" (1975: 275).

In Robinson's description of her field site at the time of her first visit in 1963 there are parallels with the local systems discussed by such writers as Bailey, Nicholas, and Mayer — all are relatively autonomous, integral communities. But the system she sees evolving by 1967 has more in common with Sanchun as I have presented it above, at least insofar as both are dependent for the broad outlines of their political lives on the encompassing state systems in which they find themselves. Independence came ten years later to Malaysia than to the South Asian countries, but in Malaysia the new national leaders incorporated a strong, purposive nation-building ideology from the outset. Their motivation to do so may have come from recognition of the special difficulties entailed in binding together the various ethnic communities, as well as the special value that lay in minimizing expression of local antagonisms in order to maximize Malaysia's success as a commodity producer for the world market. Thus the critical process in which the center impinges strongly on the internal affairs of communities on the periphery, a process apparently becoming significant in some parts of the Third World (for example, South Asia) only in the mid-1960s, was well under way much earlier in other areas (for example, Malaysia). Moreover, the Sanchun case provides evidence that the intensification of the process continues.

---

1. Parties in Sanchun have, as I noted above, had the opposite effect, perhaps because organizational forms — whether parties, funeral associations, or temple committees — appear to be much more carefully structured in Chinese villages than in the village described in Sri Lanka.

Some important contrasts between the Sinhalese and the Malaysian cases remain, of course. Robinson opts in effect to discard the concept of encapsulation, though not because the Sinhalese local system is fully autonomous but because it is, or is rapidly becoming, virtually fully integrated into the larger system. I argue that the same is not happening in Sanchun, that although integration may in theory be the aim of national policy, ethnic differences intervene between the ideal and the real, and a form of attenuated encapsulation persists. This contrast is no doubt largely a function of the relative positions of the Sinhalese and the Chinese within their respective multiethnic states: the Sinhalese are the dominant majority, and Sinhalese villagers in Sri Lanka, like Malay villagers in Malaysia, may as Robinson contends experience full integration into an undifferentiated national political culture. Chinese villagers in Malaysia, however, are constrained by the relative encapsulation of their own ethnic Chinese national leaders within what remains a predominantly Malay political culture. Integration can come about only when communal lines lose the prime salience they retain today.

Groups, Leaders, and Middlemen

Another feature of local-level politics that commands attention in much of the literature is the interdependency of leaders and groups (see, for example, Barth 1959; Nicholas 1965, 1966; Mayer 1966; Bailey 1968, 1969). Bailey (1969) in particular seems to see leaders almost exclusively in the context of their followers, the groups of people who form bases of support for the decisions and actions taken by leaders. Leaders and groups take on a different cast in Sanchun, however.

When we shift attention away from "autonomous" to "encapsulated" systems, we are reminded that standard conceptions of legitimacy and support, given by subordinates to superordinates, are not adequate to explain the support and legitimacy of a local leader who is himself a subordinate within an extended hierarchy. In the early years in Sanchun local support was in fact important, though never to the total exclusion of external validation. But in later years support groups are seen to play a much smaller role in shaping the configuration of local leadership.

Lee Koi, the man who came to power in the Emergency, had begun his rise before the war by winning the favor of a powerful patron; he then translated that favor and its advantages into support at lower levels. But his steady move upward in power owed more to his good standing with the military authorities than to the few votes that were cast at the first village committee election. Thus, a middle-ranking activist moves into the top

164

rank by gaining higher validation first within the local system, then higher validation from beyond it.

Chin Ta Hing's history is similar. His acceptability to all as chairman of the local council apparently derived in no small part from the tacit stamp of approval he received from the powerful Lee Koi. When the party split came in 1973, the task force did indeed form an important support group, and it was its backing that induced Chin to reject the invitation to return to the MCA. But in reality the young men and women of the task force offered their support not to Chin himself but to state leaders such as Lim Keng Yaik, Paul Leong, and T. C. Choong. Chin happened to be conveniently placed as local intermediary between the grassroots activists and the higher, charismatic leaders of the reform movement and was himself a part of that grassroots support. He retains the esteem of the community and of the membership of the new party branch he heads, but his formal recognition, now more than ever before, comes from higher authorities outside the system: he holds the council chairmanship by appointment approved by his party's state committee, the *Menteri Besar*, and the district officer.

Chin's brother-in-law was somewhat retiring until he was chosen by the task force cadres, more because of his kinship connections than because of his personality, to be the group's leader. He has since then taken a more active political role and now serves as treasurer for the Gerakan branch. And Liew Kam Ming, who faced strong local antipathy after the task force's demise, was nonetheless appointed MCA branch chairman by the state party head. Opposition to him is still voiced more often than support, but his connections with the party hierarchy are known and respected, so he remains unchallenged in his chosen local roles — treasurer of the MCA branch and vice-chairman of the council.

The local leader in Sanchun, as in similar local communities in all centralized state systems, is something of a combination of a middleman and a chief. He heads a community, in the sense of holding high prestige, being called on to mediate disputes, being able in turn to call upon others for service of various sorts, either for his personal benefit or for the benefit of the community. At the same time, since his community is encompassed by a wider political environment, he inevitably acts at least in some contexts as a middleman bridging the gap between the community and the larger system. Bailey depicts a middleman as a self-serving individual, profiting in an almost underhanded manner from his ability to control information across that gap and allowing each side to have only that conception of the other that is to his advantage, so that both sides will continue to need and utilize his services (1969: 168). Certainly such middlemen exist, in Sanchun as elsewhere; but though a few such men may be counted among the ranks of the political elite (for example, Liew Kam Ming), such a characterization is not in my view applicable to any of the paramount leaders I have known there or have heard described at length by local people. The best counterexample is Chin Ta Hing, who, to the extent that he seeks position at all rather than simply being pushed into it, probably desires and enjoys a certain esteem in the eyes of his fellow townsmen, and finds to his dismay that holding high status in Sanchun is accompanied by fairly onerous middleman duties. Far from trying actively to deceive both sides, as Bailey would have it, Chin Ta Hing simply performs necessary functions linking the government to the people.

The Sanchun case, then, offers alternate perspectives on some of the central issues in political anthropology. Leaders commanding the allegiance of groups, and even groups with no leaders (action-sets and quasi-groups) are of course fascinating, but Sanchun provides convincing evidence that important alternative forms exist. Leaders legitimated from above must be understood as part of the whole phenomenon of local leadership. And while some middlemen are no doubt crafty, the Sanchun case demonstrates that the middleman notion can be more useful if it is more broadly conceived.

Malaysian Local Systems: Alternative Modes of Encapsulation

Sanchun, as an encapsulated local system on the political periphery of a centralized state, contrasts strikingly with the relatively autonomous local communities discussed above. An equally enlightening contrast can be drawn with local systems much closer at hand. In chapter 2 I argue that sharp differences may be seen in the encapsulation situations experienced by local systems of various ethnicities, depending on the proximity of the national leaders of each ethnic community to power at the national level. This proposition is strongly supported in the Malaysian case when Malay and Chinese communities are examined concurrently with respect to features of political life.

Malay village studies by Husin Ali (1975) and Rogers (1969, 1975, 1977) provide evidence of forms and patterns of Malay involvement with national political life that differ markedly from those of Sanchun. A direct comparison with Kessler's Malay village in Kelantan (1978) is more problematic, though his study, like this book, is specifically concerned with demonstrating the impact of higher level political forces on the local community. Kessler's Jelawat, however, is caught up in political rivalry between ruling UMNO and upstart challenger PAS, a party uniquely threatening to the UMNO precisely because of its striking success over the years in the east coast states, particularly Kelantan, where, as Kessler notes, the very small numbers of non-Malays rendered communal issues irrelevant, leaving room instead for intra-Malay conflict that he analyzes in terms of both class and power. By contrast, Sanchun and the villages studied by Husin Ali and Rogers are in the western part of the country, where the communal population balance is more complex. And although branches of opposition parties exist in some of these communities, in none of them is opposition support comparable to that found in Kelantan. Instead, these communities operate politically within the framework of the government Barisan Nasional parties. Political exhortations are directed at the faithful, to encourage them, to urge them on to greater support. Though there are, as we have seen in Sanchun, political cleavages and fights within the encompassing alliance, the nature of such conflict is quite different from that between formal power holders and outsider challengers who seek not just to gain a bigger share in joint control but to replace completely the currently entrenched power elite.

Even in villages less recalcitrant than Jelawat, however, ethnic commonality with national leaders in Malaysia does not appear to lead directly to the sort of integration into the national political culture that Robinson reports in Sri Lanka. In Husin Ali's analysis, Malay villages are "encapsulated," much as I have suggested in chapter 2. As he puts it, "A gap does exist to a certain extent between the three rural communities studied and the wider structures that 'encapsulate' them, but it is more in the nature of some divergence in their cultural values rather than their cultural base" (1975: 164). Malay peasant villagers, in contrast to urban people, are "still strongly dominated by tradition and religion," and are distinct even in terms of dress, housing, manners and family life. In Husin Ali's terms, the elements of Malay tradition and Islamic religion form the cultural *base* that is shared, while it is the domination of daily life by those elements that infuses the cultural *values* that distinguish Malay villagers from Malay urbanites.

Nonetheless, though very "urban" themselves, UMNO leaders find ways to make use of the strength of rural cultural values in building political support for the party and the government in rural areas. In the Johore Malay village studied by Rogers, "Local UMNO meetings reinforce the villagers' belief that religion and politics are inseparable. The assemblyman emphasizes UMNO's achievements for 'Our race!, Our religion!, Our homeland!' " Party meetings are sometimes held in the mosque, and men wear traditional Malay dress "usually reserved for religious services and weddings." Programs may include Koran readings and always close with a prayer by the community religious leader (Rogers 1975: 218-219). Thus, the religious values that are so important to Malay villagers are consciously incorporated as normative incentives to political participation in compliance with government aims.

Comparable use of the same incentives with Chinese would naturally be totally ineffective, yet any attempt to substitute similar *Chinese* cultural orientations in an overtly political context, as was seen for example in certain elements of the task force program, are decried as chauvinist. Thus politics for Malaysia's Chinese lacks an important normative/ideological dimension, and remains instead very instrumental in nature.

In both Malay and Chinese rural communities, a single office represents the link between the local system and the government: the functional equivalent of the Chinese local council chairman is the Malay *penghulu*.[2] But both the formal and the symbolic content vested in the two offices differ markedly. The local council chairman, as we have seen in Sanchun, is a private individual quite distinct from the bureaucratic hierarchy. In many cases, as in Sanchun, he receives no emolument from the government for his services. When the office originated, the local council chairman was meant to be a representative of the people and elected by them directly; although he is now appointed from above, his nomination is still made by his political party, an organization that theoretically grows out of a mass base and serves the people's interests.

The *penghulu*, who acts as head of a *mukim*, is by contrast a government servant, appointed as a member of the civil service, directly responsible to the district officer, salaried, and subject to transfer like any other civil servant. Husin Ali tells us that "it is often the case that the penghulu is also involved with party politics, particularly that of the ruling party" (1975: 165). The *penghulu*'s office, however, is much older in the minds of the people than political parties and civil service, and it has traditionally been held in high esteem and regarded as an important unifying factor for the rural community. In the past, although the *penghulu* was formally the representative of the ruler or chief, the people under him were generally all his kinsmen, so he was an integral member of the community as well (Husin Ali 1975: 128-129).

Thus through the direct incorporation of the office of *penghulu* into the government bureaucracy, contemporary national leaders are taking over an important traditional Malay leadership role with roots in the feudalistic past for use as symbolic legitimation for modern Malaysian political culture. For Chinese-Malaysians, by contrast, there is a clear differentiation today between the council chairman (*zhuxi*) and the more traditionally esteemed but unofficial role of village headman (*cunzhang*), and the symbolic link of traditional leadership and contemporary government is not attempted.

In the ideological realms represented by politics and leadership in Malay

2. In some places Malay communities are also organized under local councils; see Kessler's Kelantan study (1978).

communities, then, the government builds on traditionally strong symbolic elements of the shared cultural "base." At the same time it seeks actively to bridge the gap that exists between center and Malay periphery in terms of cultural "values" ("development orientation") through the inducements it offers in the economic sphere. Malay rural communities are the primary targets of many of the government development plans. They are bombarded with agricultural officers, health officers, and various other government specialists who teach them ways of improving their daily life and increasing their economic output. They are invited to participate in the highly publicized federal land resettlement programs as settlers, and offered easy loans for business or agricultural development. The studies by Husin Ali and Rogers are replete with examples of the government's apparent concern for the Malay rural communities, concern that without fail is expressed in most concrete terms at election time, when votes are needed. And, in the disbursement of monetary incentives to government support, the center again builds effectively on the strength of its traditional symbolic links with the peasantry. Rogers notes that "an important element of the government's rural assistance program has been its extensive support of Islam. This aid, which costs only a tiny fraction of the overall expenditure to assist Malays, has strengthened allegiance to UMNO and the Malay-led government" (1975: 222). State funding for mosques and prayer houses is thus as important as that for roads and schools, in political terms.

Chinese, by contrast, are offered not only a purely secular and rather insipid political culture, but a somewhat less extensive range of economic inducements as well. Passive compliance with essentially status quo goals is what the government requires of the Chinese rural market town, rather than active participation in centrally orchestrated change and development.

Chinese and Malay local systems exist today side by side within a highly centralized state system intent on fulfilling goals of nation-building and development. Both experience the powerful effects of the larger encapsulating polity as it provides the parameters shaping and limiting their internal political activities and forms. Though the fact of encapsulation is shared, however, the impact differs critically.

Malay local systems appear to be less than fully integrated into the centrally defined national political culture because of a relative lag in development orientation; it is the stated policy of the center to close that gap, by "restructuring society" to enable Malays to participate fully in every aspect of modern Malaysian life. Critics of the government charge that the economic restructuring of society should focus more directly on redistribution of wealth so that the poor of all groups would benefit. Their persuasive arguments that Malay peasants gain far less from government programs than official pronouncements would lead one to believe are supported by the recent peasant demonstrations in Kedah (see *Far Eastern Economic Review* 2/22/80: 28-30, 41-44). Though opinion may differ as to the sincerity or cynicism of the government's concern for the peasantry, however, it must be acknowledged that the enthusiastic involvement of rural Malays in development plans and programs is pursued unrelentingly, and inducements offered to secure Malay commitment include both material and highly symbolic incentives.

Chinese local systems, by contrast, fail to achieve full integration less because of their insufficient understanding of or participation in the "modern" aspects of national life and culture than because of an apparently more fundamental dissonance vis-à-vis the true political center, based not in orientation but in ethnicity. But while the center has a concerted "Malay policy" on orientation, it lacks an effective "Chinese policy" on ethnicity. Rural Malays might be induced to change their development orientations. But Chinese, who for the most part already identify themselves solidly as Malaysians, are unlikely to be induced to alter their ethnicity further, certainly not to the extent that they fear is being required of them today.[3] Enthusiasm for Malaysia's contemporary political culture is not easily rallied among Chinese-Malaysians; low-profile passivity apparently remains for the present the best response available to them other than outright opposition (a path that some, of course, do take).

Ethnicity appears the world over as a doggedly persistent characteristic of social life. Hence, though Malay local systems may gradually "modernize" and be brought into or join the mainstream, gaining larger shares of Malaysia's relative economic affluence, the ultimate integration of Chinese local systems into full membership in a Malaysian political culture may continue to be problematic. This will be particularly true if the definition of that political culture remains couched so clearly in terms that can be readily appreciated and valued by one group only, Malays. The Malaysian government's current stated policies are designed to effect a significant restructuring of society; yet they seek rectification of only one of the nation's major communal inequities, that of economic distribution and participation, and persist in neglecting the other, that of meaningful political participation.

Economic and political rectification are of course not unrelated. If economic redistribution among classes were more effective than it is at the present time, Malay peasants and workers might feel a greater sense of

---

3. Though the phrase *Malaysian Chinese* is still in common usage, it is a survival of past conceptual notions; today the adjective *Chinese* more appropriately modifies the noun *Malaysian*. Chinese-Malaysians I have questioned on this grammatical distinction agree wholeheartedly on the accuracy of this form. They suggest, however, that moving *Chinese* in front of *Malaysian* might be misconstrued as a shift emphasizing the priority of Chineseness, rather than being accepted as the simple grammatical rectification it in fact represents.

security and well being that could perhaps lead to a relaxation of communal antagonism. And if Chinese, both rich and poor, felt less vulnerable and less constrained in political terms, more enthusiastic and effective participation in all areas of national life might result. But the Malaysian mode of bureaucratic centralization as it is being developed at present can only produce an unbalanced integration of the various systems located on the political periphery. As attempts, however problematic, are made to bring some rural communities into the economic mainstream through planned development, others are pushed even further from the core of the political culture. Vincent suggests that "the immediate way ahead" for political anthropology lies in "the fleshing out of interdependencies between intraclass and interclass political action" (1978: 190). The Malaysian case demonstrates the continuing imperative to pursue more sophisticated understanding of interdependencies among political actions informed by ethnicity as well as by class. The common folk, in their daily lives, do not ignore or deny ethnicity; neither do the power structures that surround those lives. Where interclass political relations among different ethnic groups are virtually ruled out by the communal structuring of political groups, intraclass political action between representatives of these ethnic groups has crucial ramifications for both interclass and intraclass relations among fellow ethnics. Anthropological and sociological investigation must persist in seeking explanations and understanding of the complex interactions of power, ethnicity, and politics.

Appendix A. Chinese Character List

Cantonese terms are identified (C) and romanized in the Yale system; all others are given in Mandarin (Pinyin).

banzhang 班長

boqiquan 駁氣拳

Chaozhou fu 朝州府

Chen 陳

Chiqi xian 赤溪縣

cunzhang 村長

dabei 打杯

Dabu xian 大埔縣

fenjia 分家

ganxunban 幹訓班

ganbu 幹部

ganqing 感情

Gaozhou fu 高州府

guanxi 關係

Guangzhou fu 廣州府

Gugangzhou 古岡州

gungsi (C) (Malay: kongsi) 公司

Hanjiang 韓江

Hepo 河婆

Heshan xian 鶴山縣

huaqiao 華僑

huiguan 會館

jia 家

jiebai xiongdi 結拜兄弟

jieshang 街上

Jieyang xian 揭陽縣

jiuhuangye 九皇爺

laobeiren 老輩人

luzhu 爐主

Ma Hua zuiren 馬華罪人

Nanyang 南洋

natogung (C) 哪督公

neihangren 內行人

rexin 熱心

sei yap (C) 四邑

sixiang geming 思想革命

taijiquan 太極拳

tongxiang 同鄉

tongxing 同姓

xiang 鄉

xian 縣

xinsixiang 新思想

xincun 新村

yidajia 一大家

zahuodian 雜貨店

zagong 雜公

zhuxi 主席

zijiren 自己人

APPENDIX B. Sanchun Local Leaders in 1972

Name	Age	Speech group	Occupation	Residence	Position(s) of note
Chin Ta Hing	46	Cantonese	merchant	street	chairman: council, MCA, Gugangzhou association; board member/officer: school board, temple, etc.
Chong Kit	52	Cantonese	vegetable seller	village	councillor; mutual-aid association head; member of most boards
Choong Hah	deceased	Hakka	merchant, logging and mining boss	street	former headman
Choong Kwan Foh	41	Hakka	contractor	street	MCA secretary
Kong Ah Wah	25	Cantonese	rubber dealer	street	contributor to funds for school, temple, etc.
Lee Koi	71	Hakka	retired logger, club manager	village	"village head"; councillor; member of most boards
Lee Wan Chun	35	Hakka	teacher	gov't housing	MCA mutual-aid association secretary; newly appointed councillor
Liew Kam Ming	41	Hakka	agricultural entrepreneur	village	councillor
Loh Kow	37	Hunanese	dentist	street	councillor
Lung Sooi	65	Cantonese	merchant	street	council treasurer; chairman: school board, club; member of most boards
Lung Teng Yu	41	Cantonese	merchant	street	MCA mutual-aid association treasurer
Tan Tien Yu	deceased	Hokkien	merchant	street	former headman
Tan Siew Hing	48	Hokkien	merchant, rubber dealer	street	chairman: temple, Hanjiang association; member of most boards
Woo Lee Sen	42	Teochiu	merchant	street	member of most boards
Yap Hoi Fatt	39	Hakka	teacher	school quarters	task force mutual-aid association chairman
Wong Ching Chee	45	Cantonese	club manager	street	councillor

Bibliography

Abdul Rahman, Tunku. 1969. *May 13: before and after*. Kuala Lumpur: Utusan Melayu.

Asad, Talal, ed. 1973. *Anthropology and the colonial encounter*. London: Ithaca Press; Atlantic Highlands, N.J.: Humanities Press.

Bailey, F. G. 1968. Parapolitical systems. In *Local-level politics*, ed. Marc J. Swartz, pp. 217-226. Chicago: Aldine.

————. 1969. *Stratagems and spoils: a social anthropology of politics*. Toronto: Copp Clark.

————. 1971. The peasant view of the bad life. In *Peasants and peasant societies*, ed. Teodor Shanin. London: Penguin.

Balandier, Georges. 1970. *Political anthropology*. (*Anthropologie politique*, first published 1967 in French.) London: Penguin.

Barth, Fredrik. 1959. *Political leadership among the Swat Pathans*. London: London School of Economics Monographs on Social Anthropology, no. 19.

Beaglehole, J. H. 1976. *The district: a study of decentralization in West Malaysia*. London: Oxford University Press.

Bujra, Janet M. 1973. The dynamics of political action: a new look at factionalism. *American Anthropologist* 75 (1): 132-152.

Burridge, Kenelm O. L. 1957. Racial relations in Johore. *Australian Journal of Politics and History* 2 (2): 151-168.

Chander, R. 1972. *Banchi Pendudok dan Perumahan Malaysia 1970, Gulongan Masharakat* (1970 population and housing census of Malaysia, community groups). Kuala Lumpur: Jabatan Perangkaan Malaysia.

————. n.d. *Banchi Pendudok dan Perumahan Malaysia 1970, Rengkasan Kiraan Luar* (1970 population and housing census of Malaysia, field count summary). Kuala Lumpur: Jabatan Perangkaan Malaysia.

Chin, Kee Onn. 1946. *Malaya upside down*. Singapore: Jitts.

Clutterbuck, Richard. 1966. *The long, long war: counterinsurgency in Malaya and Vietnam*. New York: Praeger.

Cohen, Myron L. 1976. *House united, house divided: the Chinese family in Taiwan*. New York and London: Columbia University Press.

Corry, W. C. S. 1954. *A general survey of New Villages*. (Report to Macgillivray, High Commissioner of the Federation of Malaya.) Kuala Lumpur: Government Press.

Crissman, Lawrence. 1967. The segmentary structure of urban overseas Chinese communities. *Man* 2 (2): 185-204.

Dobby, E. H. G. 1952. Resettlement transforms Malaya: a case-history of relocating the population of an Asian plural society. *Economic Development and Cultural Change* 1 (3): 163-198.

Enloe, Cynthia H. 1970. *Multi-ethnic politics: the case of Malaysia*. Berkeley: Center for South and Southeast Asia Studies, University of California, Research Monograph no. 2.

———. 1979. *Police, military and ethnicity: foundations of state power*. New Brunswick, N.J.: Transaction Books.

———. 1980. *Ethnic soldiers: state security in a divided society*. London: Penguin; Athens, Ga.: University of Georgia Press.

Etzioni, Amitai. 1961. *A comparative analysis of complex organizations: on power, involvement, and their correlates*. New York: Free Press.

Evans-Pritchard, E. E. 1951. *Social anthropology*. New York: Free Press.

Fortes, Meyer, and E. E. Evans-Pritchard. 1940. *African political systems*. London: Oxford University Press.

Freedman, Maurice. 1957. *Chinese family and marriage in Singapore*. London: HMSO. (Colonial research studies, no. 20.)

———. 1960. Immigrants and associations: Chinese in nineteenth century Singapore. *Comparative Studies in Society and History* 3 (1): 25-48.

Friedrich, Paul. 1968. The political middleman. In *Local-level politics*, ed. Marc J. Swartz, pp. 199-204. Chicago: Aldine.

Gagliano, Felix V. 1970. Communal violence in Malaysia 1969: the political aftermath. Athens, Ohio: Ohio University Center for International Studies, Southeast Asia Program. (Papers in international studies, Southeast Asia series, no. 13.)

Gallin, Bernard. 1966. *Hsin Hsing, Taiwan*. Berkeley and Los Angeles: University of California Press.

Ghazali bin Shafie, Tan Sri Dato Muhammad. 1971. *Democracy: the realities Malaysians must face*. Kuala Lumpur: Ministry of Information.

Goh, Cheng-taik. 1971. *The May thirteenth incident and democracy in Malaysia*. Kuala Lumpur: Oxford University Press.

Grace, Brewster. 1976. *The politics of income distribution in Malaysia*. American Universities Field Staff Reports 24 (9).

Groves, H. E. 1964. Constitutional problems. In *Malaysia: a survey*, ed. Wang Gungwu, pp. 356-364. New York: Praeger.

Gwee, Hock-aun. 1966. *The Emergency in Malaya*. Penang, Malaysia: Sinaran Bros.

Hamilton, Gary. 1978. Pariah capitalism: a paradox of power and dependence. *Ethnic Groups* 2: 1-15.

Han, Suyin. 1970. *. . . And the rain my drink*. London: Mayflower.

Heidhues, Mary F. Somers. 1974. *Southeast Asia's Chinese minorities*. Melbourne: Longman, Studies in contemporary Southeast Asia.

Hirschman, Charles. 1974. Economic progress in Malaysia: how widely has it been shared? *United Malayan Banking Corporation Economic Review* 10 (2): 35-44.

Husin Ali, S. 1975. *Malay peasant society and leadership*. Kuala Lumpur: Oxford University Press.

Jackson, R. N. 1961. *Immigrant labour and the development of Malaya, 1786-1920*. Kuala Lumpur: Government Press, Federation of Malaya.

Jomo, K. S. (Sundaram, Jomo Kwame.) 1978. Class formation in Malaya: capital, the state, and uneven development. Ph.D. dissertation, Harvard University.

Kessler, Clive S. 1978. *Islam and politics in a Malay state: Kelantan 1838-1969*. Ithaca: Cornell University Press.

Lee, Kam Hing. 1980. In *Malaysian politics and the 1978 elections*, ed. Harold Crouch, Lee Kam Hing, and Michael Ong. Kuala Lumpur: Oxford University Press.

Lim, Ma Hui. 1979. *Ownership and control of the one hundred largest corporations in Malaysia*. London: Oxford University Press.

Maeda, Kiyoshige. 1967. *Alor Janggus, A Chinese community in Malaya*. Kyoto: Center for Southeast Asian Studies. (Reports on research in Southeast Asia, Social science series, S-1.)

Malaya, Department of Information. 1959. *Malaya under the Emergency*. Kuala Lumpur: Government Printing Office.

Malaysia. 1970a. *Federal Constitution, incorporating all amendments up to 1st June, 1970*. Kuala Lumpur: Government Printing Office.

———. 1970b. *Report of the Royal Commission of Enquiry to investigate into the workings of local authorities in West Malaysia*. Kuala Lumpur: Government Printing Office.

———. 1971a. *Laws of Malaysia, Act A30, Constitution (Amendment) Act, 1971*. Kuala Lumpur: Government Printing Office.

———. 1971b. *Second Malaysia Plan, 1971-1975*. Kuala Lumpur: Government Printing Office.

———. 1976a. *Act 171. Local Government Act*. Kuala Lumpur: Government Printing Office.

———. 1976b. *Third Malaysia Plan, 1976-1980*. Kuala Lumpur: Government Printing Office.

Malaysia, Ministry of National Unity. n.d. *New villages*. Mimeo.

Malaysia, Ministry of Technology, Research, and Local Government. n.d. *Local government*. Mimeo.

Mann, Lewis. 1977. Some effects of foreign investments: the case of Malaysia. *Bulletin of Concerned Asian Scholars* 9 (4): 2-14.

Mayer, A. C. 1966. The significance of quasi-groups in the study of complex societies. In *The social anthropology of complex societies*, ed. M. Banton, pp. 97-122. London: Tavistock Publications.

Means, Gordon Paul. 1976. *Malaysian politics*. 2nd ed. London: Hodder and Stoughton. (1st ed., 1970.)

Miller, Harry. 1959. *Prince and premier: a biography of Tunku Abdul Rahman*

Al-haj, first prime minister of the Federation of Malaya. London: George G. Harrap.

Mullard, Chris, and Martin Brennan. 1978. The Malaysian predicament: towards a new theoretical frontier. *Journal of Contemporary Asia* 8 (3): 341-354.

Nagata, Judith. 1975. Perceptions of social inequality in Malaysia. *Contributions to Asian Studies* 7: 113-136.

————. 1980. *Malaysian mosaic: perspectives from a poly-ethnic society.* Vancouver: University of British Columbia Press.

National Operations Council. 1969. *The May 13th tragedy: a report.* Kuala Lumpur: National Operations Council.

Newell, William H. 1962. *Treacherous river: a study of rural Chinese in North Malaya.* Kuala Lumpur: University of Malaya Press.

Nicholas, Ralph. 1968. Rules, resources, and political activity. In *Local-level politics*, ed. Marc J. Swartz, pp. 295-322. Chicago: Aldine.

Niew, Shong Tong. 1969. The population geography of the Chinese communities in Malaysia, Singapore, and Brunei. Ph.D. dissertation, University of London.

Nyce, Ray. 1962. The New Villages of Malaya: a community study. Ann Arbor: University Microfilms (63-3614). (Ph.D. dissertation, Hartford Seminary Foundation.)

Peltzer, Karl J. 1952. Resettlement in Malaya. *Yale Review* 41: 391-404.

Purcell, Victor. 1965. *The Chinese in Southeast Asia.* 2nd ed. London: Oxford University Press.

————. 1967. *The Chinese in Malaya.* 2nd ed. Kuala Lumpur: Oxford University Press.

Robinson, J. B. Perry. 1956. *Transformation in Malaya.* London: Secker & Warburg.

Robinson, Marguerite S. 1975. *Political structure in a changing Sinhalese village.* London: Cambridge University Press.

Roff, William. 1967. *The origins of Malay nationalism.* Kuala Lumpur: University of Malaya Press.

Rogers, Marvin L. 1969. Politicization and political development in a rural Malay community. *Asian Survey* 9: 919-933.

————. 1975. The politicization of Malay villagers. *Comparative Politics* 7 (2): 205-225.

————. 1977. *Sungai Raya: a sociopolitical study of a rural Malay community.* Berkeley: Center for South and Southeast Asia Studies, University of California, Research Monograph no. 15.

Sandhu, Kernial Singh. 1964. Emergency resettlement in Malaya. *Journal of Tropical Geography* 18: 157-183.

Scott, James C. 1968. *Political ideology in Malaysia: reality and the beliefs of an elite.* New Haven: Yale University Press.

Sendhut, Hamzah. 1962. The resettlement villages in Malaya. *Geography* 47: 41-46.

Short, Anthony. 1975. *Communist insurrection in Malaya.* London: Muller.

Skinner, G. William. 1957. *Chinese society in Thailand: an analytical history.* Ithaca: Cornell University Press.

————. 1958. *Leadership and power in the Chinese community of Thailand.* Ithaca: Cornell University Press.

————. 1968. Overseas Chinese leadership: paradigm for a paradox. In *Leadership and authority*, ed. Gehan Wijeyewardene. Singapore: University of Malaya Press.

Skinner, G. William, and Edwin A. Winckler. 1969. Compliance succession in rural communist China: a cyclical theory. In *A sociological reader on complex organizations*, ed. Amitai Etzioni, 2nd ed., pp. 410-438. New York: Holt, Rinehart and Winston.

Smith, T. E. 1963. *The background to Malaysia.* London: Oxford University Press.

Snodgrass, Donald. n.d. *Inequality and economic development in Malaysia.* Forthcoming.

Stenson, Michael. 1976. Class and race in West Malaysia. *Bulletin of Concerned Asian Scholars* 8 (2): 45-54.

————. 1969. Repression and revolt: the origins of the 1948 Communist insurrection in Malaya and Singapore. Athens, Ohio: Ohio University Center for International Studies Southeast Asia Program. (Papers in international studies, Southeast Asia series, 10.)

Strauch, Judith. 1975. Sanchun, Malaysia: local-level politics in a rural Chinese town. Ann Arbor: University Microfilms (Publ. 75-21, 902). (Ph.D. dissertation, Stanford University.)

————. 1978. Tactical success and failure in grassroots politics: MCA and DAP in rural Malaysia, 1972. *Asian Survey* 18 (12): 1280-94.

————. 1980a. General elections at the grassroots: perspectives from a Chinese new village in Malaysia. In *Malaysian politics and the 1978 elections*, ed. Harold Crouch, Lee Kam Hing, and Michael Ong. Kuala Lumpur: Oxford University Press.

————. 1980b. The Chinese exodus from Vietnam: implications for the Southeast Asian Chinese. Cambridge, Mass.: Cultural Survival, Occasional Paper Series, no. 1.

————. Forthcoming, 1981. Multiple ethnicities in Malaysia: the shifting relevance of alternative Chinese categories. *Modern Asian Studies* 15 (2): 203-208.

Swartz, Marc J. 1968. Introduction. In *Local-level politics*, ed. Marc J. Swartz, pp. 1-46. Chicago: Aldine.

Swartz, Marc J., Victor Turner, and Arthur Tuden, eds., 1966. *Political anthropology.* Chicago: Aldine.

Tarrow, Sidney. 1978. *Between center and periphery.* New Haven: Yale University Press.

T'ien, Ju K'ang. 1953. *The Chinese of Sarawak: a study of social structure.* London: London School of Economics Monographs on Social Anthropology, no. 12.

Tilman, Robert O. 1964. *Bureaucratic transition in Malaya.* Durham, N.C.: Duke University Press.

Tinker, Hugh. 1968. Local government and politics, and political and social theory in India. In *Local-level politics*, ed. Marc J. Swartz, pp. 217-226. Chicago: Aldine.

Vasil, R. K. 1971. *Politics in a plural society: a study of noncommunal political parties in West Malaysia.* Singapore: Oxford University Press.

———. 1972. *The Malaysian general election of 1969.* Kuala Lumpur: Oxford University Press.

Vincent, Joan. 1978. Political anthropology: manipulative strategies. *Annual Review of Anthropology* 7: 175-194.

Von Vorys, Karl. 1975. *Democracy without consensus: communalism and political instability in Malaysia.* Princeton, N.J.: Princeton University Press.

Wang, Gungwu, ed. 1964. *Malaysia: a survey.* New York: Praeger.

———. 1970. Chinese politics in Malaya. *China Quarterly* 43: 1-30.

Willmott, W. E. 1967. *The Chinese in Cambodia.* Vancouver: University of British Columbia Press.

Wolf, Arthur P. 1966. Childhood association, sexual attraction, and the incest taboo: a Chinese case. *American Anthropologist* 68 (4): 883-898.

Worsley, Peter. 1974. The state of theory and the status of theory. *Sociology* 8: 1-17.

Index

HARVARD EAST ASIAN SERIES

Meiji Japan. Kozo Yamamura.

77. *Between Tradition and Modernity: Wang T'ao and Reform in Late Ch'ing China*. Paul A. Cohen.

78. *The Abortive Revolution: China under Nationalist Rule, 1927-1937*. Lloyd E. Eastman.

79. *Russia and the Roots of the Chinese Revolution, 1896-1911*. Don C. Price.

80. *Toward Industrial Democracy: Management and Workers in Modern Japan*. Kunio Odaka.

81. *China's Republican Revolution: The Case of Kwangtung, 1895-1913*. Edward J. M. Rhoads.

82. *Politics and Policy in Traditional Korea*. James B. Palais.

83. *Folk Buddhist Religion: Dissenting Sects in Late Traditional China*. Daniel L. Overmyer.

84. *The Limits of Change: Essays on Conservative Alternatives in Republican China*. Ed. Charlotte Furth.

85. *Yenching University and Sino-Western Relations, 1916-1952*. Philip West.

86. *Japanese Marxist: A Portrait of Kawakami Hajime, 1876-1946*. Gail Lee Bernstein.

87. *China's Forty Millions: Minority Nationalities and National Integration in the People's Republic of China*. June Teufel Dreyer.

88. *Japanese Colonial Education in Taiwan, 1895-1945*. E. Patricia Tsurumi.

89. *Modern Chinese Literature in the May Fourth Era*. Ed. Merle Goldman.

90. *The Broken Wave: The Chinese Communist Peasant Movement, 1922-1928*. Roy Hofheinz, Jr.

91. *Passage to Power: K'ang-hsi and His Heir Apparent, 1661-1722*. Silas H. L. Wu.

92. *Chinese Communism and the Rise of Mao*. Benjamin I. Schwartz.

93. *China's Development Experience in Comparative Perspective*. Ed. Robert F. Dernberger.

94. *The Chinese Vernacular Story*. Patrick Hanan.

95. *Chinese Village Politics in the Malaysian State*. Judith Strauch.

(Some of these titles may be out of print in a given year. Write to Harvard University Press for information and ordering.)